The Alps in Colour

Text by Hugh Merrick

Photographs by Robert Löbl

The Alps in Colour

Constable London

*First published in 1970 by
Constable & Company Ltd.
10 Orange Street London W C 2
Text © 1970 by Hugh Merrick
ISBN 0 09 457240 2*

Printed in Germany by Obpacher GmbH, Munich

Contents	Introduction	pp. 9–20
	List of Plates	Facing page
1	The Wienerwald: Vienna's garden on the eastern threshold of the Alps	22
2	The Ötscher, near Mariazell, in Lower Austria	25
3	The Grosse Ödstein, in the Gesäuse	26
4	The Enns, with the Gesäuse Peaks, Reichenstein and Sparafeld	29
5	Vorderstoder in the Totengebirge	30
6	The Eastern Julian Alps, seen from the Dobratsch	33
7	The Planica Valley, in the Julian Alps	34
8	The north face of Triglav (Julian Alps)	37
9	The Prisojnik Towers (Julian Alps)	38
10	Lago Fusine and the Mangart (Julian Alps)	41
11	The Wischberg Group (Western Julian Alps)	42
12	The glacier world of the Gross Venediger	45
13	In the Dolomites of Lienz	46
14	Autumn on the Grossglockner	49
15	On the Grossglockner: between cloud and sky	50
16	Torstein, Dachstein and Dirndl	53
17	The Gollinger Fall, at the eastern edge of the Berchtesgaden Alps	54
18	The Giant Ice Caves of Werfen	57
19	The Attersee and the Höllengebirge	58
20	Hallstatt in the Salzkammergut	61
21	The village of Alm, at the southern foot of the Steinerne Meer	62
22	The Bischofsmütze (›The Mitre‹) in the Gosau Comb	65
23	The Hochkönig, near Dienten, Province of Salzburg	66
24	The Königssee and the east face of the Watzmann	69
25	The Wilder Kaiser range seen from the Schwarzsee	70
26	The Bettelwurf, rising high above the Inn Valley	73
27	The Grosser Ahornboden in the Karwendel range	74
28	The Laliderer Walls in the Karwendel	77
29	The Grosse Löffler in the Zillertal Alps	78
30	The Europabrücke with the Serles and the Habicht	81
31	The view from the Patscherkofel towards the Stubai Alps	82
32	The main chain of the Ötztal Alps from the Geislachkogel	85
33	Ehrwald and the Zugspitze	86
34	The view from the Wetterstein, near Seefeld	89
35	On the Hohe Ifen, in the Allgäu Alps	90
36	Ludesch, in the Rätikon – Vorarlberg range	93
37	Cheesemaker at work in the Allgäu	94
38	Above the Saminatal, near Feldkirch in the Vorarlberg	97
39	The Karwendel range from the Wagenbruchsee	98
40	Looking south to the Zugspitze from the Brauneck	101
41	The view towards the Inn Valley from the Zugspitze	102
42	The Estergebirge range, Werdenfels, Upper Bavaria	105
43	In the Ahrntal, to the south of the Zillertal Alps	106
44	The Drei Zinnen, in the Sexten Dolomites	109

		Facing page
45	The Cadini Group, above Misurina	110
46	The Sass Songher, near Corvara, Ladin Dolomites	113
47	The Langkofel Group, above the Grödnertal	114
48	The Santnerspitze in the Schlern massif	117
49	Cima Sappada, with Monte Siera (Carinthian Alps)	118
50	The Campanile di Val Montanaia, Eastern Dolomites	121
51	The Tofana di Rozes, near Cortina d'Ampezzo	122
52	The Croda da Lago, near Cortina d'Ampezzo	125
53	The Cima Bois, on the Falzarego Road (Dolomites)	126
54	The Cimone della Pala, near the Rolle Pass	129
55	The Marmolada and Gran Vernel from the Sella Pass	130
56	Sta Magdalena and the Geislerspitzen (South Tyrol)	133
57	Spring on the Mendel above Bozen	134
58	Stenico, on the southern fringe of the Brenta Dolomites	137
59	The Guglia di Brenta	138
60	The Lake of Garda, on the southern fringe of the Dolomites	141
61	The glacier world of the Ortler Group	142
62	In the icefall of the Trafoier Eiswand (Ortler Group)	145
63	The Churfirsten, in Eastern Switzerland	146
64	The Lake of Lucerne, from Pilatus	149
65	The Wetterhorn, above Grindelwald	150
66	The Eiger and Mönch from the north	153
67	Monte Rosa and Gorner Glacier, above Zermatt	154
68	The Öschinensee and the Blumlisalp Group (Bernese Oberland)	157
69	The Matterhorn from the Grenz Glacier	158
70	The G'spaltenhorn range from Mürren (Bernese Oberland)	161
71	The Matterhorn	162
72	The Matterhorn from the south	165
73	The glacier world of the Bernina	166
74	On Piz Palü	169
75	On the Weisshorn (Valais)	170
76	The Mischabel Group (Valais)	173
77	The Grand Combin, the western corner-stone of the Valais Alps	174
78	Mont Collon, above Arolla (Valais)	177
79	Soglio in the Val Bregaglia	178
80	The Great Aletsch Glacier (Bernese Alps)	181
81	The Klausen Pass (Glarus)	182
82	The Lake of Sils (Upper Engadine, Grisons)	185
83	Steinbock in the Swiss National Park	186
84	The Adamello	189
85	The Presanella	190
86	The Lake of Como	193
87	The Lake of Lugano and Monte San Salvatore	194
88	Isola Bella, Lago Maggiore	197
89	The Castle of Chillon and the Dents du Midi	198

		Facing page
90	The Gastlosen, near the Jaun Pass (Fribourg Alps)	201
91	Mont Blanc, the giant between France and Italy	202
92	On the Brenva face of Mont Blanc	205
93	Satellites of Mont Blanc: Tour Ronde and Grand Capucin	206
94	The north face of the Grand Charmoz	209
95	The Drus and Aiguille Verte (Mont Blanc Group)	210
96	The Pic Gaspard and the Meije (Dauphiné)	213
97	The Meije	214
98	A hairpin problem in the Maurienne	217
99	The Barre des Écrins (Dauphiné)	218
100	Monte Viso and the source of the Po	221
101	The icy satellites of the Gran Paradiso	222
102	Mont Aiguille, in the Vercors	225
103	The Organ Pipes near Dié (Dauphiné)	226
104	A stony desert: the Col d'Iseran (Savoy Alps)	229
105	The Col de la Cayolle (Alpes Maritimes)	230
106	The Col de la Croix de Fer and the Aiguilles d'Arves	233
107	The Gorges du Verdon, Alpes Maritimes	234
108	The Côte d'Azur, the Mediterranean rim of the Alps	237

Introduction One September day in 1960 my wife and I boarded a BEA ›Viscount‹, Romeward-bound on a visit to friends. It was her first experience of air travel, and beginner's luck all the way.

As we took off from Heathrow and zoomed into a low cloud-base, it was raining heavily from gray London skies, long arrows and runnels whipping diagonally across the window at our side. Minutes later, we were being dazzled by the blaze of the sunlight off the engine nacelles, as the aircraft levelled out above a brilliant white jumble of cotton wool cloud-sea under a flawless blue sky. Just before Paris, we cleared the coast-like hem of the clouds; the city lay, a clear neat map, 21,000 feet below the trailing edge of the wings. On we flew over the sunlit green and brown patchwork of Central France and then, incredibly, only twenty minutes later, high above a wispy field of broken cloud, there they were, a hundred miles away, biting into the blue on the farthest horizon – the Alps.

From that time, till we lost sight of them behind us in the heat-haze of Northern Italy, they were with us, far and near, for a long amazing hour, during which we saw and were able to identify almost every peak, ridge and valley we had visited in more than thirty years of walking, climbing and motoring together in the Alps, during every peacetime summer holiday when family ties permitted and finance was available.

The pilot told us over the intercom. that, in years on the Alpine run, he had rarely experienced such a day. For me this was a kind of crystallization and consummation of all my Alpine years for, at over sixty, I knew I had climbed my last serious peak the previous summer, though we would, of course, come back and back to the ›Perpetual Hills‹ while life lasted. All this and Heaven too for my wife, the first time she had entrusted herself to the unknown element. There can hardly ever have been a quicker convert to flying.

This is how I later described that incomparable experience:

> And then, suddenly, on the rim of the world, above archipelagos of cloud which floated far below us and cast their wandering shadows on the outspread Earth, we saw lifting, a hundred miles away, the tiny, gleaming lance-heads of the Alps.
> As we veered steadily south towards Geneva, first of all the distant Oberland peaks filed past above the Viscount's red port wing; then, in middle distance ahead, with a surf of thin cloud breaking at their feet, the Valaisian giants wheeled into sight in tumbled magnificence, while the Lake unrolled its dark velvet beneath the trailing edge. It had all been so smooth and silent and leisurely; only then did events begin to happen rapidly and with a temporary sense of the great speed of flight. Suddenly Mont Blanc was sliding swiftly under the starboard wing, the Midi's rocks, where we had stood last year on just such a day of blue and gold, whirled astern past our feet; and, for a moment, the Jorasses were vignetted between the nacelles of the port engines as we burst out across the dazzling glacier world – seemingly close

enough to touch – into the wide Italian air above the Aosta Valley, dreaming nearly twenty thousand feet below.

Glacier, valley, ridge upon ridge – the Matterhorn, Monte Rosa, the far-off Bernina, the still more distant Austrian Alps, shading away into a haze, somewhere near Vienna.

Turin and the vast Piedmont plain defiled gently beneath us, Genoa and its shipping, alight in the sun. Out over the gorgeous blue of the Mediterranean we soared. Elba . . . as the teeth of Corsica were bared to starboard and we swung on our new course towards the mainland, we looked back for the last time.

Less than half an hour and all of a hundred and thirty miles had dropped smoothly away behind the tail fin since that dazzling surge across Mont Blanc. And there, in rapidly receding miniature, but still crystal-clear, on the confines of the world, the great arc of the Alps swung through three hundred miles, from Dauphiné to the Julians, into Yugoslavia and endlessly on, to the Dinarics far down towards Albania. A cleanly-ruled line of fresh snow had turned every modest rock summit into a gleaming tooth or pinnacle for the day; below lay the haze of remote plains and valleys under autumnal heat. And beneath us, like the tilted page of some coloured atlas, stretched the slender waist of slumbering Italy, cradled between contrasting robes of ultramarine that were the Tyrrhenian and the Adriatic, jewel-studded with islets, capes and bays . . .

During that marvellous airborne hour of light and clarity and rioting colour, we had, as I have said, been blessed with a single encyclopaedic vision of the whole great sweep of the Alps from end to end, a wide horseshoe-shaped diadem, jewel-studded, in all its vast immensity and variety. Yet such was the day, and such the eagle's view on such a day, that thanks to our intimate familiarity with so much of what lay spread like a magic carpet beneath us, we could at the same time, in those relatively few minutes, absorb detail upon detail of a lifetime's love and knowledge of the Alps, as valleys in which we had strolled, high passes over which we had trudged on foot when young, hairpin roads we had motored along when less so, rock ridges and snowy summits on which we had stood in the morning sun after the long slog through the dawn from the night-dark hut at their feet, turquoise lakes in which we had played and swum defiled beneath us.

Robert Löbl, the master-photographer whose camera has produced the hundred and eight gorgeous colour plates collected in this book, took a great deal longer than an aircraft-hour to record, through his receptive eye and intimate knowledge of every nook and cranny in the great chain of the Alps, their widely-spread and infinitely varied beauties.

These pictures are, in fact, the result of twenty years of roaming the valleys and ridges of more than four hundred miles of the great mountain complex sundering Northern from Mediterranean Europe, the temperate zones from the warm South, the Teutonic from the Latin temperament and civilizations. They are the work of a mountaineer as well as of a camera-artist, a man well acquainted with the difficulties and dangers of serious climbing on rock faces, in icefalls and on snow slopes, a man who has sojourned among the great peaks so admirably portrayed, till he knew every aspect and angle, every foreground and backcloth which would set off their individual splendours and beauties to the best advantage. They are the work of a man who not only loves deeply every amiable and every inimical manifestation of the mountain world, but has himself suffered at its hand a grievous loss, yet still loves the relentless peaks for all their cruelty.

There can be few who have climbed great mountains for a long period of their lives who have not at one time or another experienced the loss of mountain friends and partners on the rope of many years' standing, feeling the severance the more keenly for the very special relationship forged between those with whom difficulty and danger have been shared, and who have learned to trust each other implicitly with their lives.

Robert Löbl's son Roland, who grew up as a boy to accompany his father on his mountain wanderings, to share his great love for the high places, to help him with his photography, himself developed into one of the most promising young climbers in the wide world of Austro-German mountaineering talent, and no mean photographer of mountains in his own right. Indeed, some of the photographs in this book, particularly those taken on high and difficult climbs – plate 92 is a good example – are from his hand.

His father, observing the lad's enthusiasm and natural talent, asked his great mountaineering friend, Toni Hiebeler, the leader of the first winter ascent of the Eiger's north face and a mine of knowledge and information about the Alps and all forms of mountaineering activity, to initiate him into the joys and hazards of serious climbing. Soon the older man and the boy were forging a regular rope-partnership in the Dolomites and undertaking more and more difficult climbs among them, on the rock faces of the Eastern Alps and on the snow and ice of the giant Western Alpine peaks, till finally the pupil had grown as good as the master. Graduating then to sterner stuff in the company of other young ›extremists‹, Roland fell to his death one tragic day on the grim north face of the Aiguille des Grands Charmoz, the most easterly peak in the famous chain of granite teeth which dominate the Chamonix Valley. Hiebeler writes of his shocked unbelief when he heard of the tragedy which cost him his young friend, but how, after a time, the passing years left only the memory of the highlights of their climbing days and of a wonderful bond of friendship forged in the mountains.

I should like to record here that I am indebted to Toni Hiebeler, with some of whose journalistic work I have been earlier associated, for material in the captions to the plates in the original German edition, which I have in many cases used for my own descriptive pages facing the photographs.

Particularly is this the case with the pictures taken among the Eastern Alps, such familiar home ground to the inhabitant of Vienna and Munich, from which they can be reached by car as easily as can Wales or, since the advent of the M1 and M6, the Scottish ranges, from London. To the Central European mountaineer the limestone ranges of the Gesäuse, the Karwendel, the Wilder Kaiser, the snows of the Hohe Tauern range and of the lovely Zillertal, Ötztal and Stubai peaks are the stamping ground of early and formative days; while the British mountaineer has more usually enjoyed his first Alpine experiences among the glaciers and peaks of the Western Alps, to which the German or Austrian climber is inclined to graduate after a longish apprenticeship on innumerable locally available rock faces and, later, in the Dolomites. Certainly, my own knowledge of the eastern end of the chain is derived less from walking or climbing experience, for all our younger and more active years were spent in the Oberland, the Valais, the Bernina and around Mont Blanc, than from traversing it by the great Alpine motor roads in later life, and piecing together the geography and the great beauties of the region from the lower levels of pass, valley and gentle lakeside.

It may perhaps be thought that this difference is to some extent emphasized in Robert Löbl's collection. The magnificent photographs of the stark, rocky walls of the Northern Limestone Alps, of the Gesäuse valleys and peaks, of the beautiful wide vistas over the snowy chains to the south of the Inn Valley, from local eminences easily accessible to the dwellers in Innsbruck, Salzburg and Munich, bear witness to his wide wanderings among the homeland hills and to his unbounded affection for the valleys and ranges among which he grew up and has lived. This is not intended as a criticism; for the British reader, who does not know the Eastern Alps as well as those lying closer to our shores and more readily accessible, will certainly find so much beauty revealed in the pictures of unfamiliar scenes that his appetite to visit them, and at least walk to and among them, is bound to be whetted, and his Alpine horizon greatly extended by so splendid an introduction to them.

It may also be that Löbl intentionally adopted a proportion of two to one for the less familiar and relatively unpublicized Alpine areas in his selection from a store of many hundreds of colour photographs taken over the years. He may well have felt that the great commercial climbing centres in the Western Alps and the ranges dominating them have had more than their fair share of publicity on postcards, posters which, to some extent, govern the situation; for instance, my son, an expert colour photographer, who also normally prefers Kodachrome, switches to Agfa for his winter-skiing photographs and obtains greatly improved results in landscapes entirely covered by snow under a clear blue sky, at high altitudes, the detail and texture of the sunlit snow and the lovely blue shadows which fall across it being markedly better on Agfa.

This, I think, throws an interesting sidelight on Robert Löbl's results. As I have said, the colour in them is for the most part of a very high order of acceptability and beauty; it is generally at its very best in the pictures portraying snow and ice among the great mountain peaks. (As examples, one cannot imagine the colour and texture in plates 13, 15, 51, 62, 66, 68, 69, 74, 77, 82, 84, 85, 91, 92, 95, 96 and 100 being improved on.) If there is, in a few, a falling off from the very high standards of the rest, it is in a tendency for the blues and the mauve-to-purple values occasionally to go astray in pictures taken at medium heights and including both much higher and lower levels. Lest this should be thought to be carping criticism, I should add at once that in many cases an artist painting the same scenes in oils might easily have resorted to a use of similar ›unnatural‹ colour to achieve a similar beautiful result, even if the eye of the photographer or painter was not actually seeing it as he surveyed the scene he was portraying.

Where such deviations from the ›natural‹ occur, whatever film may have been used, there is generally one almost insuperable difficulty for the mountain colour photographer, as for the colour photographer in general, though for the former in an accentuated form, which can be held responsible.

It is common knowledge that the latitude of exposure-error available to the colour photographer is very small compared with that in black-and-white photography where it is often possible to get away with an error four times as great. Perhaps it would not be excessive to say that the colour photographer will not achieve a completely satisfactory result unless his meter-reading and its subsequent conversion to aperture and exposure are absolutely ›spot on‹. The slightest deviation will result, in the case of underexposure, in a too great density and strenght-distortion of the colour and a thick negative or transparency; overexposure to a thin picture, lacking in detail, and pale, pastel-like colouring – exactly the opposite, of course, to the equivalent effects in black-and-white photography.

All landscape photography in colour but, most markedly of all, photography of the Alpine scene, confronts the photographer with what is, as already said, an almost insoluble problem. The lighting value of the foreground scene, trees, lakes and buildings is invariably far lower how can we blame him? And perhaps it is not too much to hope that the gaps will one day be covered by a further collection of his lovely camera-work?

I think it will be generally agreed that the greater number of the pictures so magnificently reproduced in this volume by the most modern of printing techniques are not only wonderful examples of Alpine photography but more than usually acceptable for their colour values.

One could write a small tome on colour in photography, and indeed in the eye of the beholder, long before it ever comes to the appreciation of the colours in a photographic slide or print, or on a television screen. For it has been established that a very high proportion of people suffer from some degree of colour deviation or variation. It will, I think, be accepted as a truism that when a friend says: ›Isn't the sky a lovely blue this morning?‹ and you are entirely in agreement, you have no means whatever of knowing what he means by ›blue‹ in the first place, or whether you are both enjoying the same colour or a completely different one. It is only when you reach the point where he says there is a lovely greenish tint in the blue, and to you it is pure blue without the slightest suggestion of green in it, that you realize there is a divergence in the colour consciousness of your two separate pairs of eyes.

This is, of course, the reason why there is so great a divergence of opinion about the colours used by painters in their pictures, and the success or failure of your own colour slides or prints to impress those to whom you show them, or a given television set to satisfy two of the five people looking at it, while the other three find it so satisfyingly true to nature. It is also the reason for the large variety of colour films available on the market, each with a different colour base and values, to cater for the differing colour susceptibilities and preferences of those who swear by one brand and cannot abide the results produced by another.

I was, therefore, mildly surprised to see that the pictures in this book were all taken on Agfa C7 18 film, for usually I find Agfa (red base) unacceptably strong, especially in its reds, greens and browns, and have never myself taken a colour photograph with it that satisfies my own scale of colour values for normal purposes. (In self-defence, I should perhaps state that I underwent one of the stiffest colour tests ever devised, the Japanese Kamikaze pilot book during the last war, and came out of it with a better than average rating.) And my own experience in colour photography (transparencies) has been that I only take a picture which really satisfies me as producing the colour I actually saw, when using the Kodachrome (blue base) range of films. Though, here again, there are differentiations in the subject being photographed some magnificent aspects of its sharp spire to be taken from the fine high glacier crossing by the Lauteraarsattel, on over the Finsteraarjoch and down the Unteraar glacier to the Grimsel. Once arrived there, the cauldron of stony wastes, whose boulders offer an incredible beauty of colour, about the Hospice and the last windings of the pass to its summit and the lonely Totensee, a few minutes' walk from it, offer subject after subject for colour photography.

One is also left with a sense of deprivation that the six pictures reproducing the scenery of the greatest gathering of high peaks in the Western Alps, the Pennine ranges in the Valais, are limited to Monte Rosa, the Matterhorn, the western side of the Mischabel and Mont Collon.

One can only imagine what Robert Löbl might have done with the classic view of the Weisshorn from near the Weisshorn Hut above Randa, taken shortly after dawn, when the full eastern light strikes low and level on its snowy face, across the lightless blue depths of the Nikolaital, where the great white pyramid goes streaking, narrow-shouldered, to the sky.

Undeniably, too, the Gornergrat commands the greatest circular panorama in the Alps and the little lakes below it at Roten Boden on the Riffel provide wonderful foregrounds not only for Monte Rosa and the Matterhorn but for half a dozen other giant peaks. Here again one is almost physically hurt by the omission of a picture of the Dent Blanche, the Obergabelhorn, the Rothorn and the Weisshorn; though, perhaps, the most beautiful and pictorially satisfying aspects of all three lie on their reverse (western) side and are best captured from the lovely Val d'Anniviers, the fine road up which, to Vissoye, St Luc, Ayer and Zinal, leaves the Rhône Valley highway a mile or two to the east of the busy industrial centre of Sierre. The omission of any pictures of these beautiful mountains cannot but leave one with a sense of deprivation: Saas Fée and the magnificent eastern aspect of the Mischabel are also notable absentees. However, here again, our photographer may well have considered that the scenes enumerated have been over-photographed by millions of photographers, holiday amateurs and professionals alike, and have become altogether too hackneyed for inclusion – though in all humility I suggest that no great view in the Alps can ever become so, the Matterhorn not excepted, when rendered in a well-composed picture by a master-photographer who knows and loves his Alps. Again, it may have been that, hard up against the eternal problem of space available and costs of production, faced ultimately with the heart-rending dilemma of ruthless selectivity, he decided to concentrate, for the greater informational benefit to the viewer, on the less popularized and less overcrowded areas of his homeland ranges. Confronted with the wealth of lovely and unusual pictures he has given us, and in pamphlets, and in the multitude of photographs published time and again as illustrations to mountaineering books and mountaineering journals.

This would be a perfectly fair and tenable argument. There will, however, be many who, like myself, will undoubtedly regret that in a book of this superb standard of photographic skill and excellence there are, almost inevitably, a number of gaps which leave one hungry for the faces of loved ones among the great mountains of the Western Alps, which some might claim could scarcely be ignored in a comprehensive colour-photographic survey of the Alpine scene.

The Bernese Oberland, for instance, is represented by only four plates. The most notable absentees in this great area of wonderful peaks, glaciers and valleys are the Jungfrau – to many eyes, as seen from the neighbourhood of Wengen, the most beautiful mountain in the Alps; that shy monarch of the Oberland ranges, the Finsteraarhorn; and the marvellous mauve chaos of rock surrounding the summit of the Grimsel Pass.

Plate 64 shows the northern faces of the Eiger and the Mönch above Scheidegg; somehow it feels as if one had been subjected to a drastic surgical operation when the next picture does not go on to the right to show the lovely ice draperies of the Jungfrau, the flawless snow pyramid of the Silberhorn and the incomparable cliff-sided rift of the Lauterbrunnen Valley's level, green-carpeted floor, as seen from the shelf on which Wengen nestles or from the marvellous view-point of the Männlichen, so easily reached in a few minutes by ropeway above it.

Löbl has given us a lovely picture (plate 70) of a comb of relatively minor peaks from the Mürren side of that most beautiful of valleys. It simply leaves one hungry for the one he has not provided of the matchless view of the valley itself, 5,000 feet below, and the great 13,666-foot peak, so beautiful in the proportions of her snowy shoulders and breast, as seen from that green and well-pathed *belvedère*. For it can surely not be disputed that the views over peak and valley from the Wengen side and from the sunny, smiling Wengen terrace itself are even more beautiful than those from Mürren's narrow, more shadowed and too closely dominated ledge? And if the peace and quiet of that rare relic of bygone days, a traffic-less locality, is one of the latter's great attractions, Wengen is equally road- and car-free, and the most serious peril menacing the stroller in its main street is a bump from one of the little electric trolleys on which the hotel porters ferry luggage up from the station. It has not yet happened to me.

The Finsteraarhorn, lying some miles back from the main northern wall of the Oberland, is a difficult mountain to photograph, but there are than that of the sky and the great brightly-lit peaks blazing into it thousands of feet above. Even worse is the problem at half-way levels, where a deeply-shadowed valley falls away at one's feet with hardly any light values; if correctly exposed for this the upper planes of the picture will appear vague, pale and excessively blue. If the exposure is correct for the high and distant mountains and the sky, the foreground greens and browns are liable to be exaggeratedly strong and dark in tone.

Opinions differ widely as to the best way to deal with this ever-present problem but, on the whole, experienced photographers prefer to accept the foreground risk which can, after all, be less disturbing to the eye, and try to obtain a correct meter-reading for the higher light values of the upper areas of the composition. The peaks will then be strongly rendered in their natural colours and in good detail, avoiding the disappointments of a pale, thin and over-blue background, and the lesser distortion of the foreground values is very often so slight as to be quite acceptable.

If, in a few cases, the dilemma has defeated even Löbl's camera, his almost invariable success in overcoming it in one technically-difficult picture after another assures us that, in the circumstances obtaining, the problem was insoluble and that the particular view has been included in his selection mainly for its scenic and geographically informational value and not for its excellence as a colour photograph. As for the best examples, and one does not know where to start or stop counting those of the highest level of excellence (though nothing in the book enchants me more than plate 20), I for one do not know where one can hope to find so many masterpieces of mountain photography – or even of Alpine photography without emphasizing the colour aspect – as are collected between the covers of this lovely book.

For me, at least, some of the pictures have so marvellously caught the scene portrayed that a mountain lover can feel the ›kick‹ in the air, smell the scent of the pines, hear the song of the translucent torrent rippling over its stony bed and foaming against its boulders.

The book is, moreover, so much more than a mere collection of colour plates such as one might find in a Continental Christmas calendar. By his wide-ranging coverage of the great chain of the Alps and of every aspect of the Alpine scene, of every activity carried on in the valleys, on the high green alps and among the soaring peaks, he has somehow contrived to write in photographs a comprehensive guide to the Alps, of infinite value alike to those who are already devotees and those who have yet to make their first acquaintance with the joys and beauties of the high and enduring hills. For there is so much in each of these pictures that they have contrived effortlessly to translate their message into facts and figures of interest and importance to every type of visitor, who may already have visited the scenes illustrated, or will be irresistibly lured by what he sees in them to go and look for himself at the first possible opportunity. There is no aspect of the delights the Alps have to offer which is not covered, portrayed and highlighted in their message and in their pressing invitation.

In them there is something for everyone. There are ›portraits‹ of great individual peaks and rock faces which will appeal equally to the mountaineer, to whom they offer an instant challenge or who has already climbed them and for whom they will reawaken memories of the place and the day; and, for their sheer beauty, to the traveller who never gets much farther than the door of his hotel in the valley, but has looked up, or will yet look up, at that particular mountain in awe and delight. There are sweeping panoramas of whole mountain ranges seen from easily-accessible half-way heights, to which even the old and infirm can nowadays be comfortably and safely spirited by cable-car or chair-lift. There are idyllic scenes in deep, wooded valleys where the rambler can walk all day in the shade of the scented pines, by the rim of crystal-clear waters roaring suddenly into cataracts, past waterfalls which droop like curtains of glittering lace down from the cliffs above; places where he can stretch his tired limbs in mossy glades or flower-starred meadows, glades or slopes and, as he rests, has only to make a lazy turn of the head to focus on some tower, spire or snow dome, fabulously high above him in the remote blue sky. For the less energetic there are shining vistas of the peaceful shores of wide lakes, whose waters mirror the hills that girdle them, the picturesque villages and gay bathing beaches which fringe their steeply-wooded shores.

Perhaps the category of Alpine addict who comes off a shade least well, though even he is not forgotten – several of the finest pictures being scenes, viewable without leaving a car, along the great Alpine pass-roads – is the mountain motorist, on whose behalf I should like to put in a fervent word. For the motorcar has become indispensable in these days of haste and hectic living, even to the man whose main objective is the climbing of difficult routes and the attainment of high summits, enabling him to combine the time-saving pleasures of the Alpine road with his more strenuous ambition. He can stop at high villages, summit hospices or mountain refuges on the way, and from their high springboard climb his chosen peak, returning exalted from the heights to continue his armchair voyage to the valley beyond. He can thus use his car to link days of climbing in the Valais with others in the Ortler, the Dolomites or the Julian Alps, enjoying the rest and enchantment of the mountain roads uncoiling their ribbons between the far-flung groups. While the mere lover of an uphill walk can always find somewhere to improve upon the roadside view by idling up the mountain slopes for an hour or two before returning to his parked car and continuing his pursuit of new prospects, ever unfolding around the next corner.

There is, however, another aspect of motoring these great roads which traverse high, remote and otherwise less accessible tracts of the great mountain masses of the Alps, continually unfold changing vistas of peak and glacier, forest and lake, gorge and valley, and panoramas extending far out over the distant carpet of the multi-coloured plains. This is their appeal not only to those who in the full prime of their powers are fain to climb but fear to fall, but to those who have in the heyday of their youth climbed many a high peak and have reached a stage in their life where such strenuous delights are, for one reason or another, or solely on account of ageing limbs and muscles, no longer possible.

For these it is not excessive to claim that this mechanized form of mountain travel can become a complement to and an extension of their active mountaineering days; for the older but not yet infirm ex-climber, the ›bagging‹ of passes can prove as delightful an obsession as that of a certain peculiar brand of mountaineer who cannot rest till he has set foot on all the ›Four-thousanders‹ – the peaks of over 4,000 metres, or roughly 13,000 feet – in the Alps. I have walked and climbed in the Alps since I was a boy, and nobody could have enjoyed more keenly the delights of reaching a high summit or the saddle of a glacier pass on his own feet and by his own exertions; but I cannot remember the time when the passage of one of the great Alpine passes by car or Postal Motor did not give me a different but hardly less satisfying kind of mountain thrill. And now, at threescore years and ten, the delight of driving over them and climbing, car-borne, to sudden dazzling vistas of familiar snowfields, creaming glaciers and stark rock spires, is as sharp as once was the thrill and joy of stepping through the cornice rim of some icy summit cap at the end of a long and arduous climb. The motorist, whether he be an established mountain lover or still to fall in love at first sight and for a lifetime with the peaks and valleys of the Alps; whether he be already a mountaineer in the true sense or never likely to attempt a serious climb, who takes up this exciting and rewarding form of mechanized sport, will find among other things that he is wafted again and again with comparative ease into the very heart of the kind of scenery for which Robert Löbl's photographic record must surely have inspired a great hunger.

In the descriptive pages facing each photograph, an attempt has been made, as it was in the brief captions to the original edition, to give some idea of the possibilities open to every kind of mountain lover who visits the neighbourhood of the scenes depicted, whether he be a climber, a mountain rambler, an elderly path-walker, a motorist or a ›mere‹ tourist in search of peace and rest on the sunny shores and blue waters of a lake.

Many books dealing with the Alps tend to concentrate mainly on the serious climbing angle, as if only the climber in search of ridges, faces, traverses and summits could find anything worthwhile among high valleys and the peaks which dominate them with their fortresses of rock and snow.

The true mountain lover knows that a man need never have set foot on the rock, snow or ice of a recognized climb to succumb to the spell of the mountain world and learn that time cannot wither nor custom stale its infinite variety.

For every devotee who has moved on glacier ice and the brand of snow which never melts, or attempted a rock-pitch demanding the use of hands as well as feet to preserve his vertical balance, there are thousands who have strolled on valley paths, rambled on woodland ways to above the tree line or humped a pack over the tracks which cross high saddles between the great peaks from one valley to another. There are millions, too, who have gazed in wonder at the great peaks winging overhead, to them remote, mysterious, inhospitable, from the many famous view-points accessible by a day-long slog up a zig-zag path – their nearest and unforgettable approach to a genuine mountaineering feat – or by rack-and-pinion railway, aerial ropeway or the tortured hairpins of incredibly-engineered motor roads.

There are indeed a myriad facets to this passion for the Hills. Few are they who can give a rational account of their own brand of it. But then, how many are able to explain what it is they see in the face, form and character of the Beloved?

It is precisely this many-sidedness of the Alpine world which Löbl has so successfully captured in the varied scope and textures of his beautiful and affectionate pictures.

Hugh Merrick

*The Wienerwald: Vienna's garden on the
eastern threshold of the Alps*

The pleasant undulating hills of the Wienerwald ring the western and southern fringes of Vienna's great conurbation. They are the extreme outliers of the great arc of the Alps, which curves away westwards for more than 400 miles to the Dauphiné and through the Alpes Maritimes to the Mediterranean. These wooded hills and dales are much frequented, for they not only afford the Viennese the nearest area in which they can indulge their fancy for scenic beauty, but here, after a journey of only a half to three-quarters of an hour, they can enjoy comparative peace and quiet in a number of places still little visited by crowds. Here they will find a comprehensive network of well-maintained footpaths, which can be combined to provide attractive walking tours covering several days.
The Wienerwald, however, is not only visited by family parties on excursions, or by swarms of at times somewhat rowdy trippers, but by serious rock climbers who come to the various craggy outcrops either as novices, there to learn their craft and win their first spurs, or as experienced mountaineers, to devote every minute of their spare time to keeping themselves in top condition for the bigger climbs farther afield, which they will be attempting when their holidays come round again.
One of the best-known of these practice grounds is the famous Peilstein, only twelve miles to the south-west of Vienna, on which the climber can find a variety of routes ranging from ›moderates‹, suitable for a novice, to those involving the expert in ›severe‹ difficulties. On one of these, an extremely airy traverse has been appropriately decorated with a notice lifted from a Vienna tramcar: its laconic message reads ›*Nicht hinauslehnen*‹ – ›don't lean out!‹ Many of the great Austrian climbers, later active in all the world's highest ranges, have made their first acquaintance with the joys of rock in early youth on the Peilstein.
There are more than forty huts and refuges scattered the length and breadth of the Wienerwald, catering especially for the hiker and the climber who wants to spend his weekend in open-air delights.
The adjoining photograph shows only a small sector of the Wienerwald, in the neighbourhood of Mödling, to the south of Vienna. In the background, on the highest wooded ridge, at 1,656 feet, stands the Husarentempel, with the castle of Mödling on a hilltop below it, in the centre of the picture.

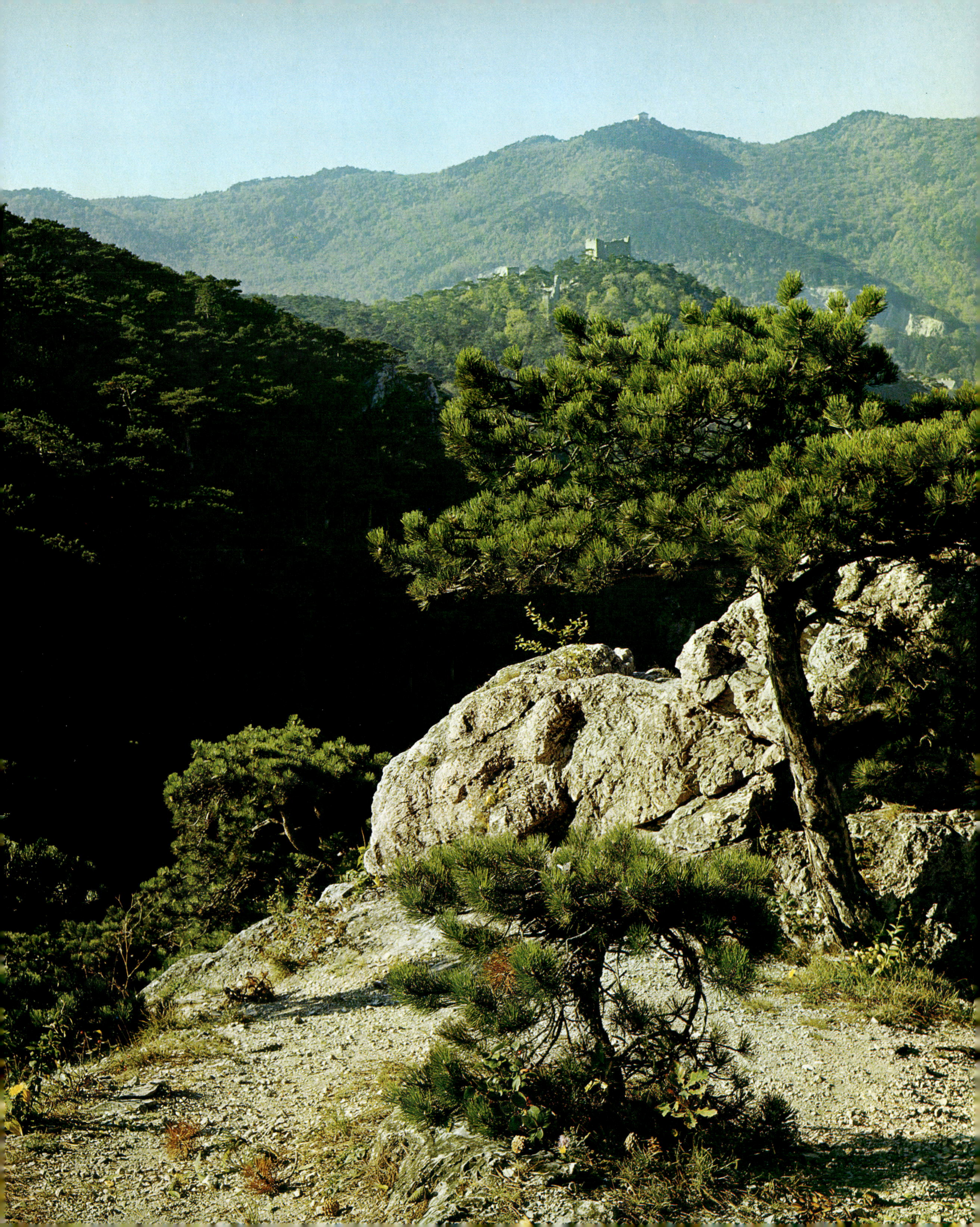

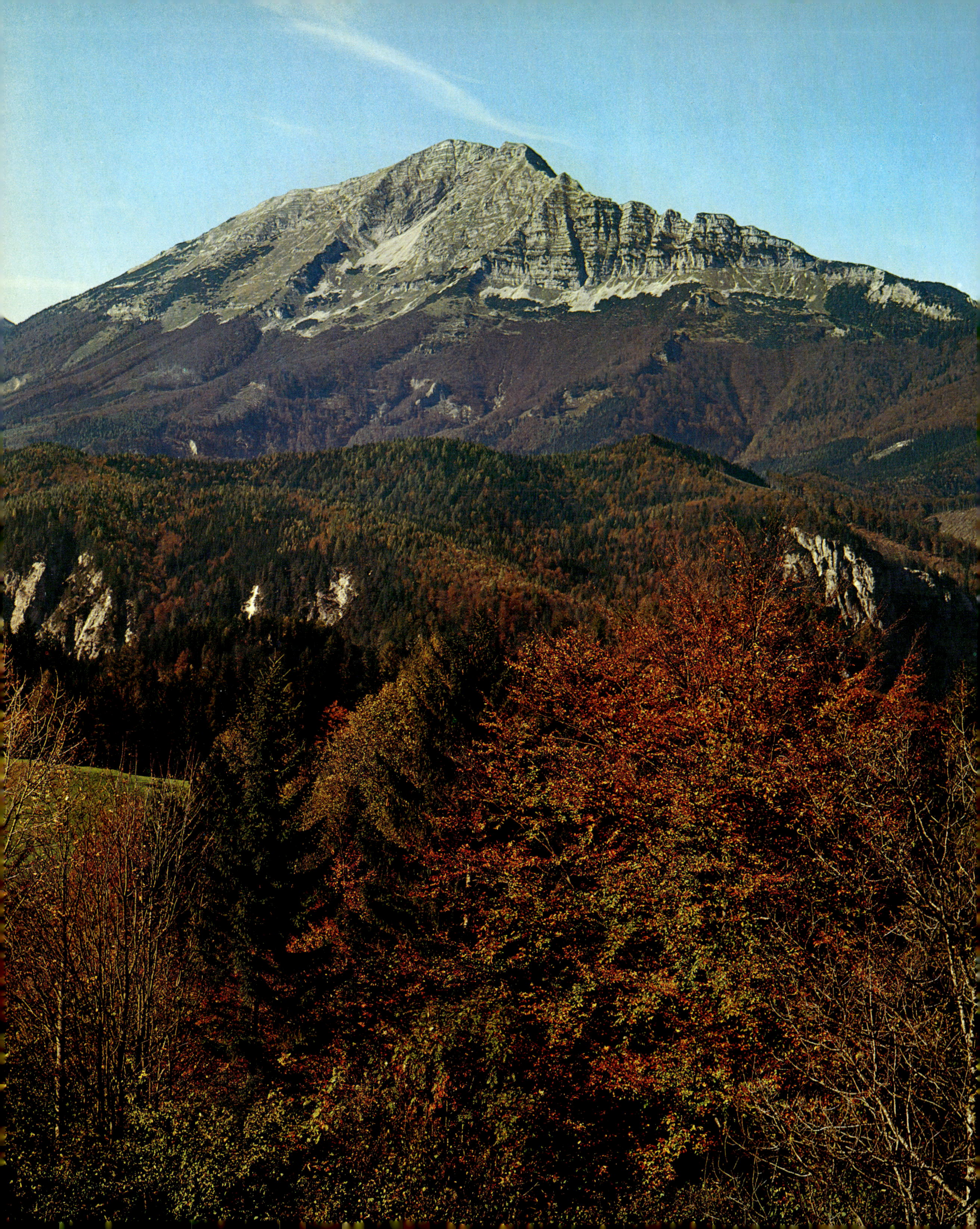

The Ötscher, near Mariazell, in Lower Austria

The Ötscher, only 6,210 feet high, is a mere dwarf when compared with the giant peaks in the main chain of the Alps, but it is the second highest mountain in Lower Austria, and its long ridges give it a most impressive appearance.

The mountain has always enjoyed mythical associations, and was ascended as long ago as the sixteenth century. One of the earliest of Alpine guides, Andreas Schöggl of Lackenhof, climbed it 800 times. His first ascent was on the eve of the solstice in 1820, in order to establish whether or no the time-honoured local legend, to the effect that night did not fall on the Ötscher on such occasions, was true. (It is to be hoped that he was not too disappointed when darkness insisted on its natural rights.)

The photograph shows the Ötscher with its extended north-east ridge – the ›*Rauhe Kamm*‹ or ›Rugged Ridge‹ – an indented comb of rock, which provides the favourite ascent route for those who are sure of foot and have ›a head for heights‹. The route is well marked and there are even protective handrails at the more vertiginous points. It is a lovely ascent, slung high between the dark forests below and the blue sky above, and can be completed in about two hours.

There are, however, other more comfortable routes by which the ordinary tourist, who does not care for quite so much exposure, can reach the summit.

The Grosse Ödstein, in the Gesäuse

A few miles to the east of Admont, the river Enns flows through the wildest and most beautiful mountain tract in its whole course – the Gesäuse, a sector of outstandingly lovely scenery in Styria's rocky Ennstaler Alps. There is no gainsaying that the Gesäuse is one of the most impressive and varied ranges in the Eastern Alps.

In the background of the photograph looms the massif of the Grosse Ödstein, 7,660 feet high, whose famous north-west arête is seen clearly defined between sunlight and shadow. This steep ridge, whose renown has penetrated far beyond the frontiers of Austria, was first climbed in 1910 by the celebrated Dolomite guides, Angelo Dibona and Luigi Rizzi, with two amateurs from Vienna, G. and M. Mayer; it is now considered one of the classical Grade IV (›Very Difficult‹) climbs in the Eastern Alps.

To the left of the summit rises the great wall of the Ödsteinkar[1], offering several climbing routes. The wall is bounded on its left by the Ödsteinkarturm[2], a pinnacle also much favoured by climbers. The summit ridge of the group continues over the Festkogel, Festkogelturm and Haindlkarturm to the Hochtor (not visible in the picture).

One of the favourite Gesäuse climbing tours is the traverse of the whole series of crests from the Hochtor to the Grosse Ödstein, involving nothing more exacting than Grade II (›Moderate‹) climbing, and requiring anything from three to five hours.

The picture shows the Ödstein dominating the lower and middle Johnsbachtal valley, a favourite beauty spot beloved by walkers.

---

[1] *Kar*, which appears repeatedly in the nomenclature of the Eastern Alps, is the term for any deep re-entrant, coombe or ›cwm‹.

[2] *Turm:* tower.

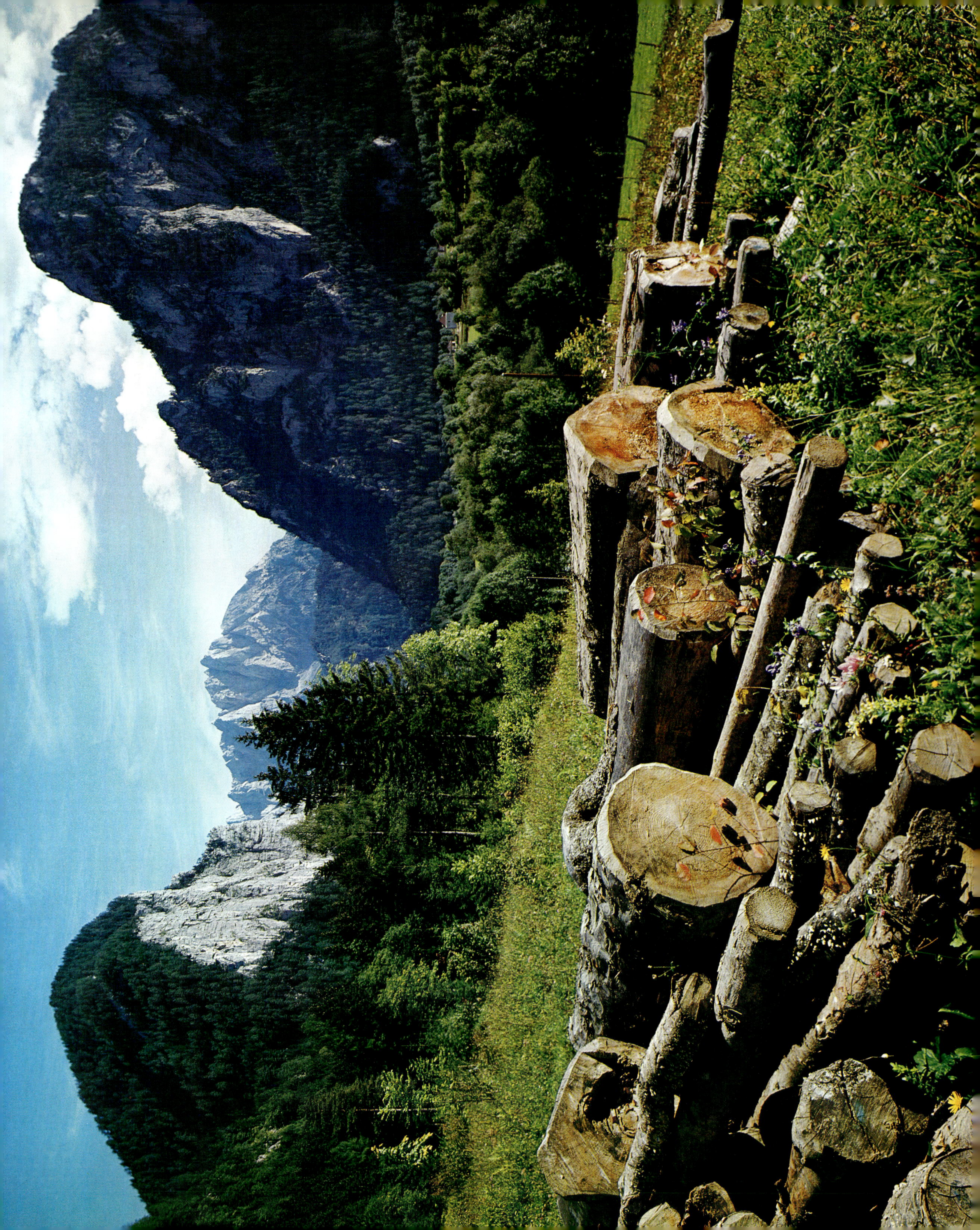

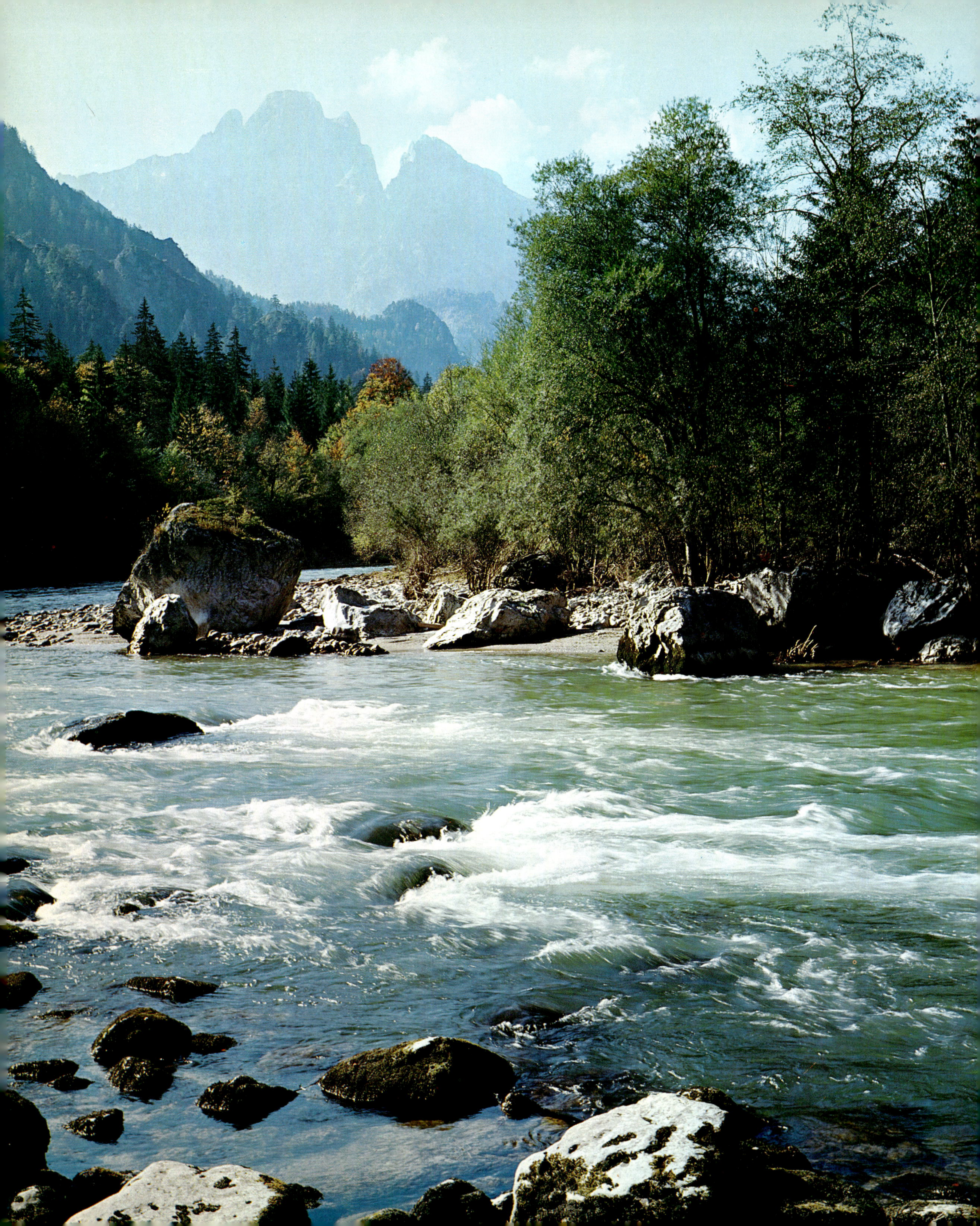

*The Enns, with the Gesäuse Peaks,
Reichenstein and Sparafeld*

The Enns is not the largest mountain stream in Styria, but it is certainly one of the wildest and most beautiful. It rises in the Nieder Tauern range and flows through the rocky region of the Gesäuse peaks between Admont and Hieflau; at Enns it falls into the Danube, which is by this time not so blue. It boasts an Enns Valley, an Enns Gorge, which confronts mountain-canoeists with the most formidable problems, a small eponymous town and a whole mountain area, the Ennstaler Alps, embracing the Gesäuse peaks, which include the 7,370-foot Admonter Reichenstein, one of the most shapely of them all.

In the photograph, to the left of the main summit stands the prominent head of the Totenköpfl (›The Death's Head‹, 7,120 feet), a name which has a somewhat sinister ring in a mountaineer's ears. To the right of the highest point rises the sharp spike of the Admonter Spitze and, beyond the next savagely-deep indentation in the group, looms the massif form of the Sparafeld (7,365 feet). The north-eastern or northern walls of both peaks fall some 1,400 feet to the point where the Enns bursts through the gateway of the Gesäuse Gorge.

The beautiful side valleys provide rewarding digressions from the main trench of the Enns. Particularly lovely is the Johnsbachtal (see previous plate) to the east of the Reichenstein, appearing to the left of the mountain in this picture. It is a typical example, and offers a lovely excursion all the way to Johnsbach where the famous climbers' cemetery, dreaming peacefully at the heart of the forests, overshadowed by the gaunt rock faces, is in itself worth a visit.

Vorderstoder in the Totengebirge

The Totengebirge, the ›Dead Mountains‹, whose northern slopes belong to Upper Austria, the southern to Styria, is very much like the Dachstein range (see plate 16) but, rising to only 8,250 feet, is a little lower. It takes its name from the deathly-bleak wastes of its considerable summit plateau. The range attains its loftiest altitude at the eastern end, where it breaks away in fearsomely-steep precipices into the Stodertal.

Vorderstoder, the village shown in the picture, is dominated by the fine massif of the Warscheneck and nestles in a lovely landscape, through which runs the picturesque motor road linking it with Windischgarsten.

Huge limestone peaks ring this beautiful valley on all sides. One of the finest, the Grosse Priel (8,250 feet) can be climbed in six hours without any great difficulty from the Priel Refuge. Rock climbers are specially attracted by the beautifully-shaped Spitzmauer (8,025 feet), which offers routes more suitable for the expert.

The Stodertal is still relatively quiet – one of those charming and unspoiled corners occasionally to be found in the Alps even now. One of the main reasons for its not yet having been overrun by tourists is that there has been no guidebook to the Totengebirge in print for many years past.

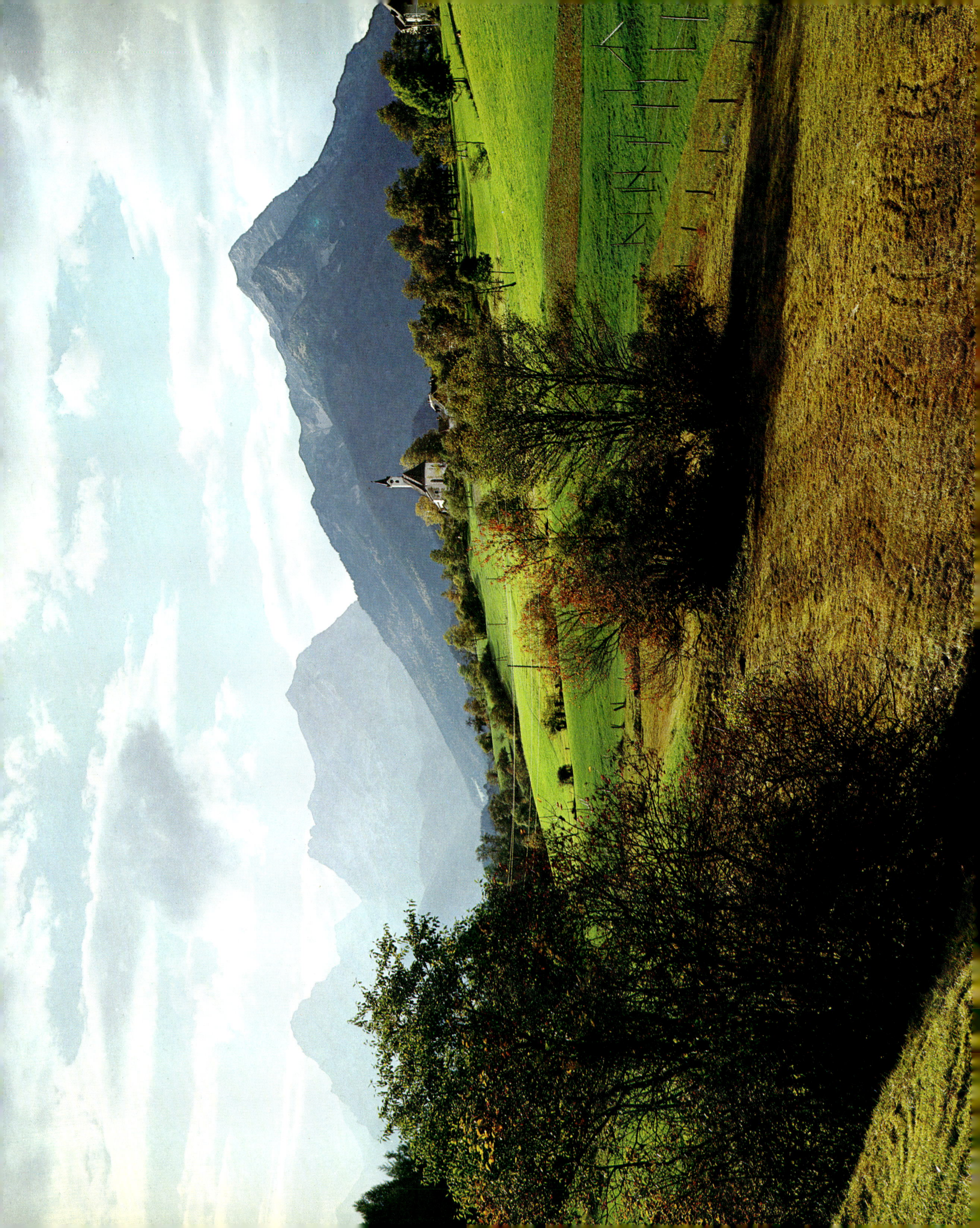

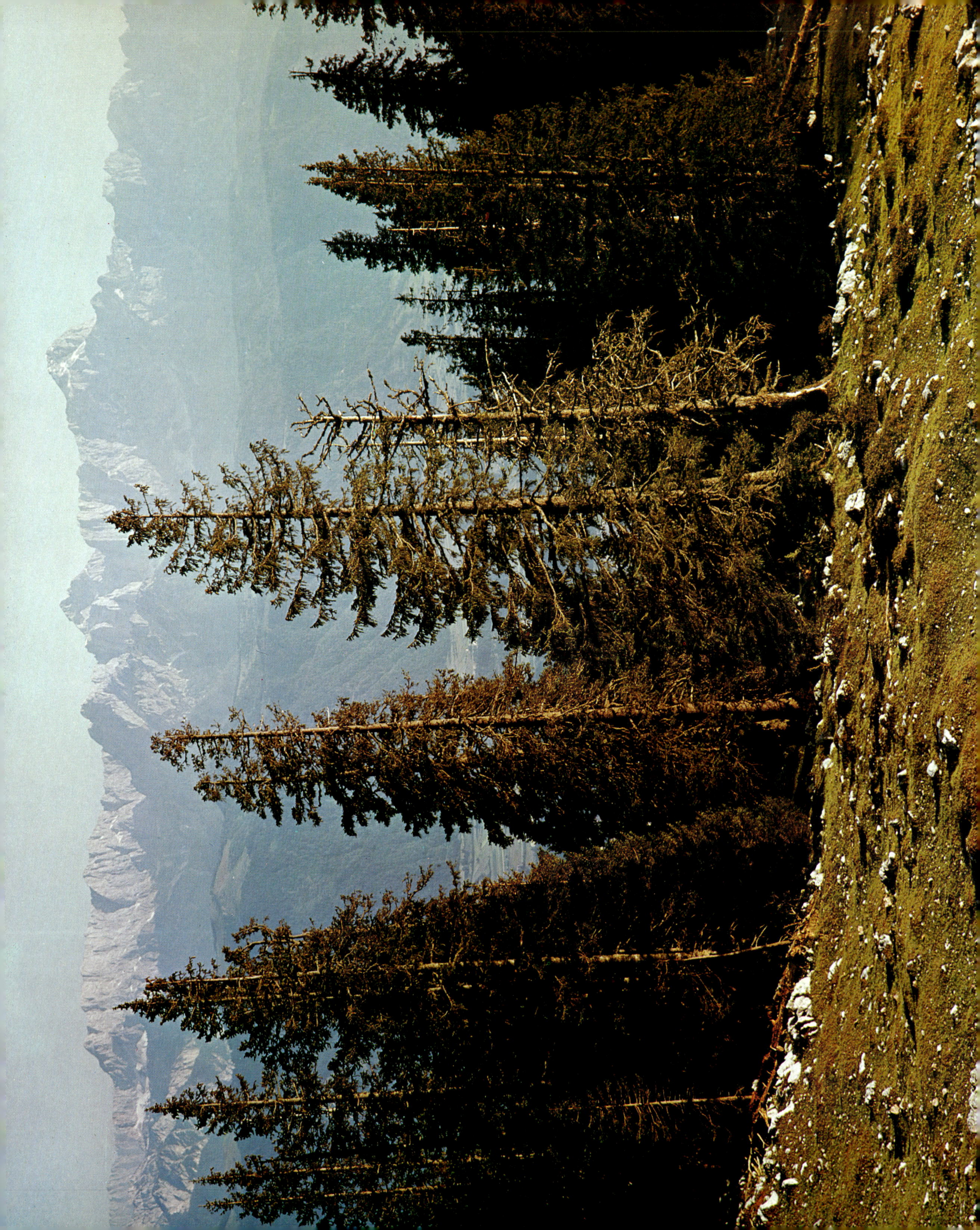

The Eastern Julian Alps, seen from the Dobratsch

The Dobratsch is an upland ridge, ten miles long from east to west and three miles wide from north to south, rising to the west of the Styrian town of Villach. It culminates in the Dobratschgipfel, a summit 7,110 feet high, and the whole feature is sometimes referred to as the Alps of Villach.

Parts of the eastern end of this little mountain range are accessible by a road. There are several huts at the disposal of ramblers and skiers, for whom the Dobratsch is a favourite playground. The Dobratsch is, in short, a mountain tract regarded by the people of Villach as their home ground.

Deeply embedded to the south of the range lies the Gailtal. In our picture, the eye travels away over that valley and the wooded heights which form the outliers of the Karawanken range, to the towering peaks of the Eastern Julian Alps with their magnificent north faces.

Rising above the third and fourth pine trees on the left, soars the northwest face of the Grosse Mojstrovka (7,765 feet, see following plate); to its right, between the fifth and sixth, the north wall of Travnik, with next to it the pyramid of Jalovec and then the huge trapeze of Monte Mangart (8,785 feet). The chain of peaks rises some ten to twelve miles distant from the Dobratsch, and the photograph shows about ten miles of its commanding length.

The Planica Valley, in the Julian Alps

The head of the Planicatal in the Eastern Julian Alps of Slovenia (Yugoslavia) is without doubt one of the most impressive in the whole of the Eastern Alps.

The valley is four miles long. It runs due south from Ratece, close to the triangular meeting-point of Yugoslavia, Italy and Austria, to where the broad, wonderfully-stratified north-west face of the Grosse Mojstrovka, 1,700 feet high in places, flanked by its huge neighbours, Travnik and Jalovec, bars its upper end. Only the Mojstrovka is shown in this photograph (see also previous plate).

At its feet, on lovely green upland meadows, in a woodland setting, stands the Tamar Hut (3,635 feet), which is the starting-point for every walk or climb in the upper reaches of the valley. Here there is room for fifty to sleep, and the hut is serviced all the year round.

There are several climbs from Grade IV to VI (›Extremely Severe‹) on the north-west face. Taking into account the great height differential between the hut and the summit of the mountain – something like 4,000 feet – it is easy to realize how great an undertaking is involved in any attempt to climb the face.

One of the peculiar characteristics of this region is that the tree-level and the conifer-zone (larches) have found it possible to invade the very steep belt of slabs to a considerable altitude.

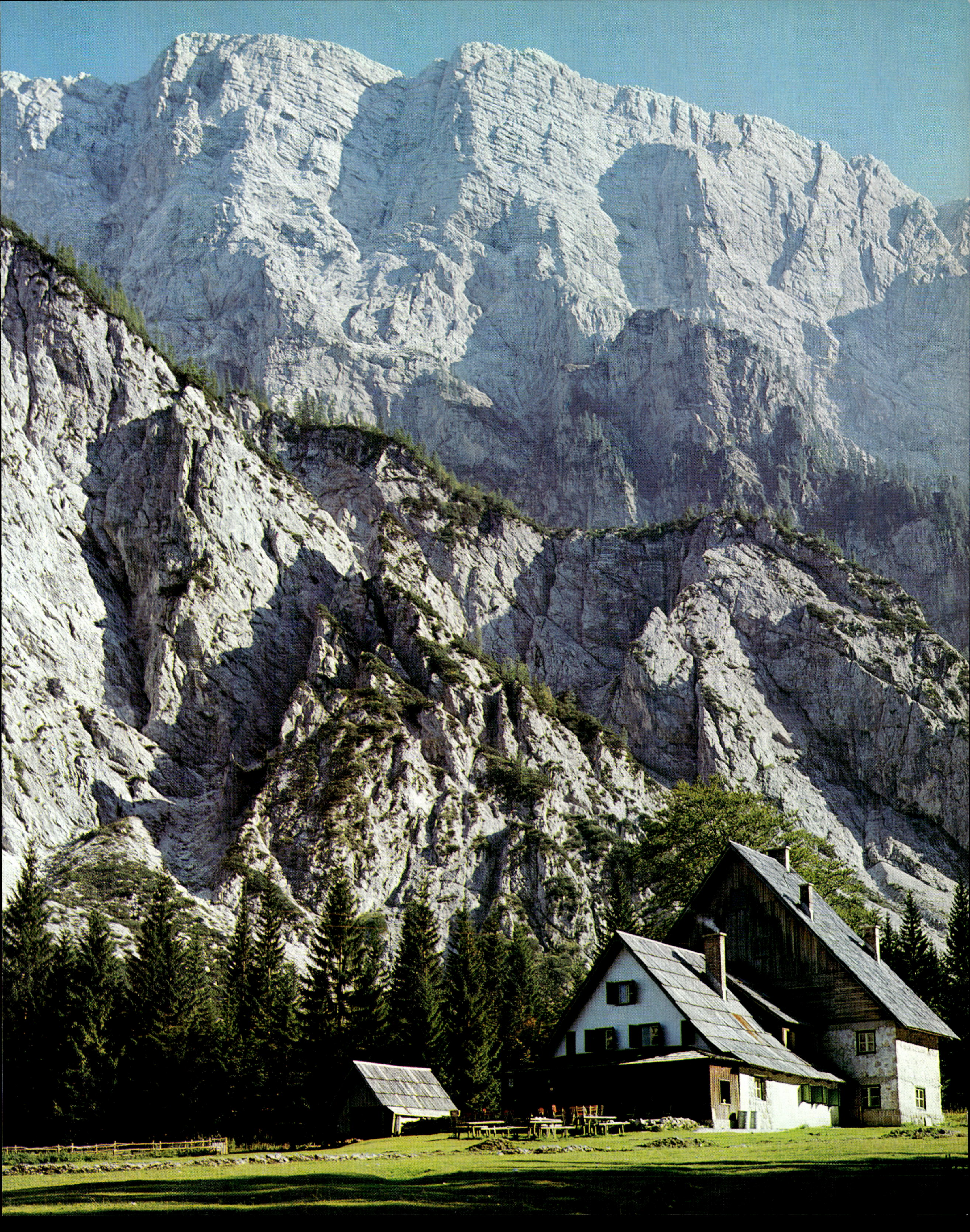

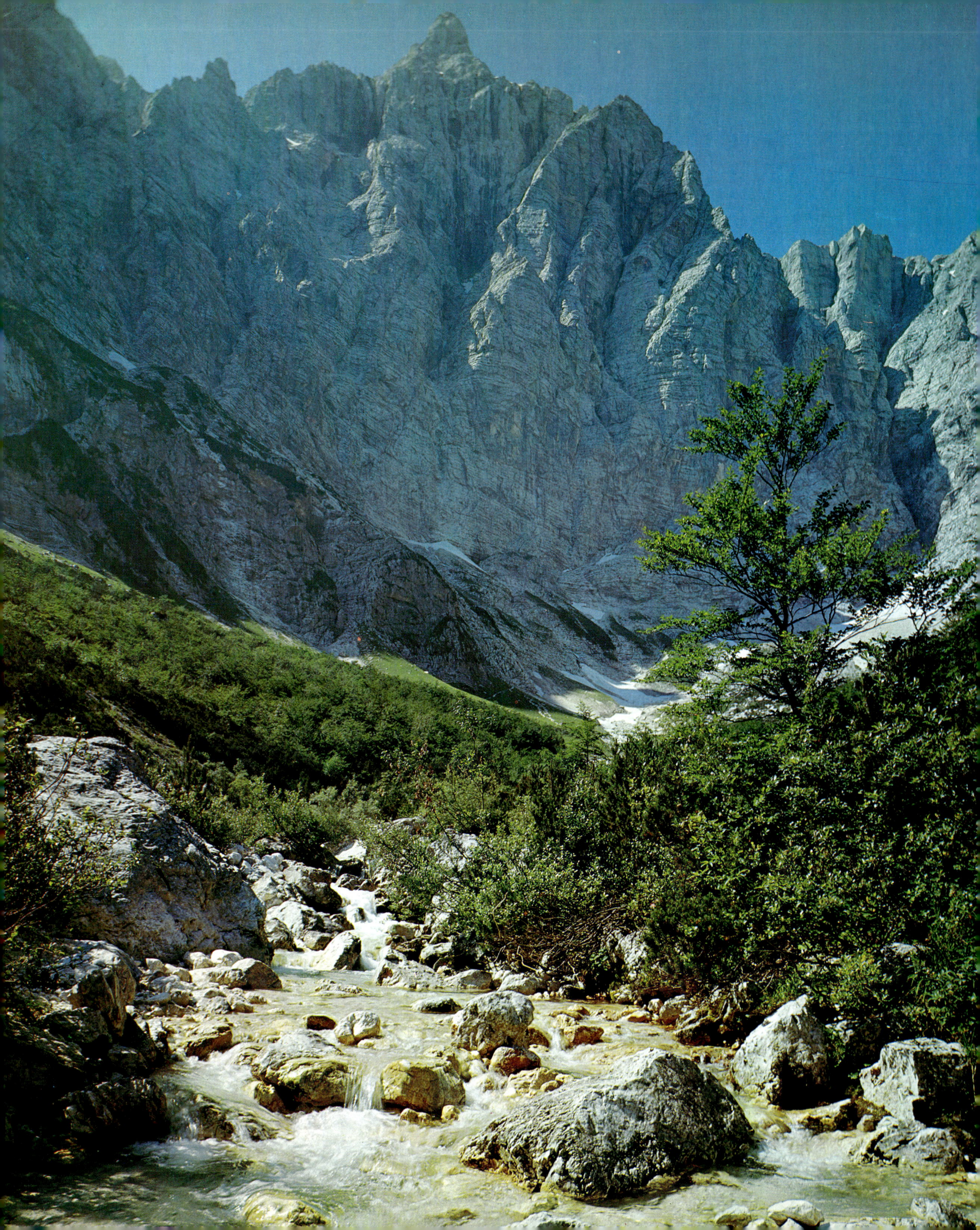

The north face of Triglav (Julian Alps)

Triglav (or Terglou, 9,400 feet) in the Eastern Julian Alps, is a truly magnificent mountain. It is not only the highest peak in the whole range, but one of the most famous and certainly one of the most awe-inspiring. Its 5,000-foot north face, rising from the romantically-savage Vrata Valley, is one of the loftiest in the Eastern Alps.

During the last six decades, the efforts of tough, pioneering rock climbers have mastered more than twenty routes up this mighty wall of rock. Had we attempted to sketch them all in on the accompanying photograph, the result would have looked like a kind of spider's web. Every gulley, every arête and every buttress carries the name of a climbing route. Their difficulties range from those of a ›Moderate‹ Grade II to an ›Extreme‹ VI. There is even a horizontal route, running across the two-mile wide wall about half-way up – the Zlatorog Ledges, on which a continuous ›Girdle-traverse‹ was opened up in 1931.

However, the startingly beautiful Vratatal is visited not only by those who enjoy grappling with precipitous walls of rock but by more moderate mountain lovers, who find a rich reward in its haven of delight.

Little more than a mile from the foot of the face, at 3,330 feet, stands the Aljaz-Haus with its 150 beds and room for another sixty on mattresses. It is worth while devoting at least a whole long day to the surroundings of the hut.

And even mighty Triglav can be safely climbed from the south and west on clearly-marked and well-protected ›club paths‹.

The Prisojnik Towers (Julian Alps)

Prisojnik (or Prisank, 8,380 feet) is distinguished from all other peaks in the Eastern Julian Alps by its peculiar structure; for it alone does not consist of a solid mass of rock but, with its considerable fragmentation and prominent projections, presents a varied aspect of towers, gulleys and arêtes, some of which start quite close to the larch forests at its feet.

A road runs along the western base of the group, giving access to several refuges and providing a link from north to south across the main ridge of the Julian Alps, thus enabling the least adventurous of ramblers to enjoy the region's lovely scenery.

Mountain walkers who are at home on protected ›club paths‹ can reach the summit of Prisojnik, for there are five such routes to the top. Only the Prisojnik Towers themselves, with their precipices of sheer light-grey limestone, remain the exclusive province of the trained rock climber.

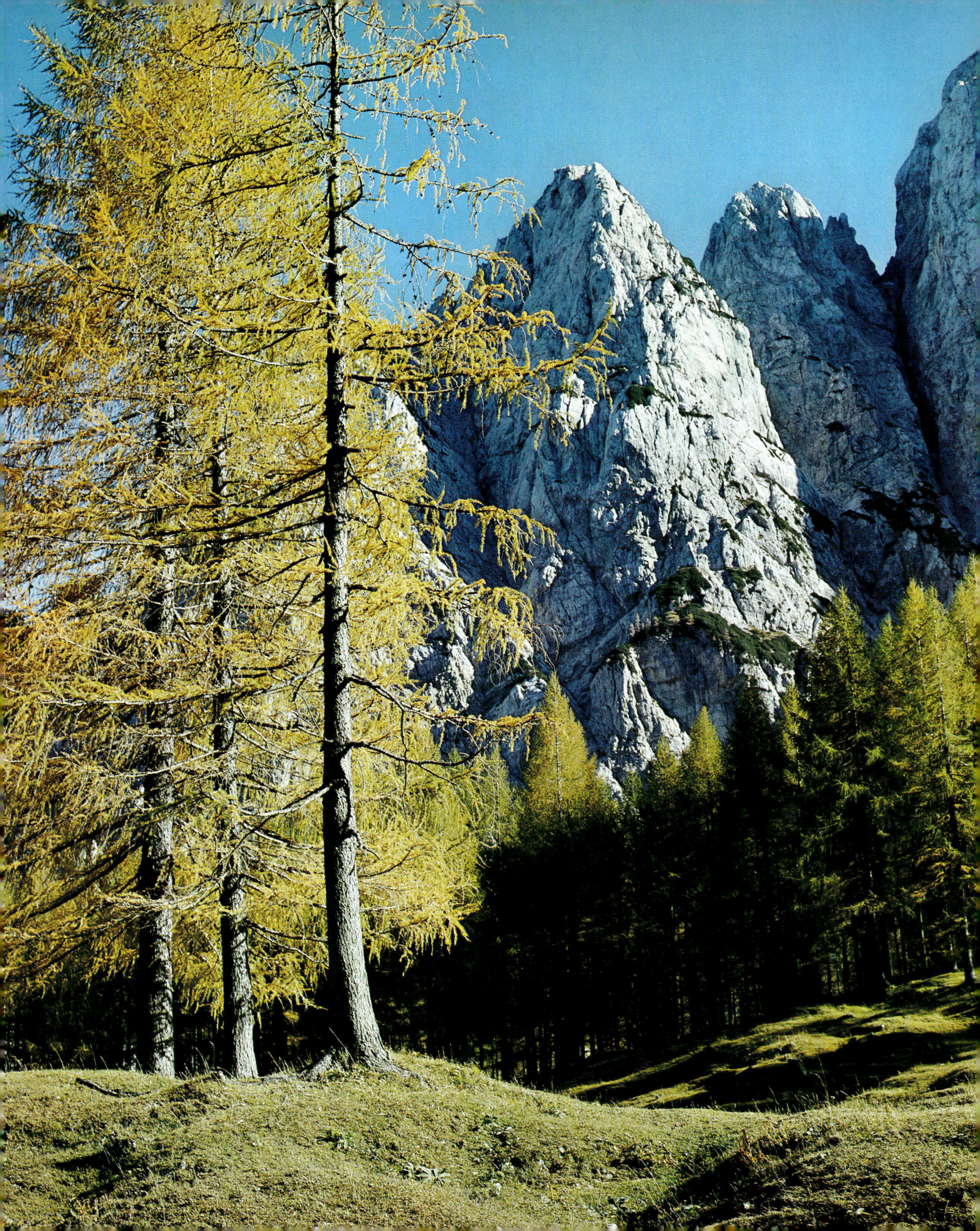

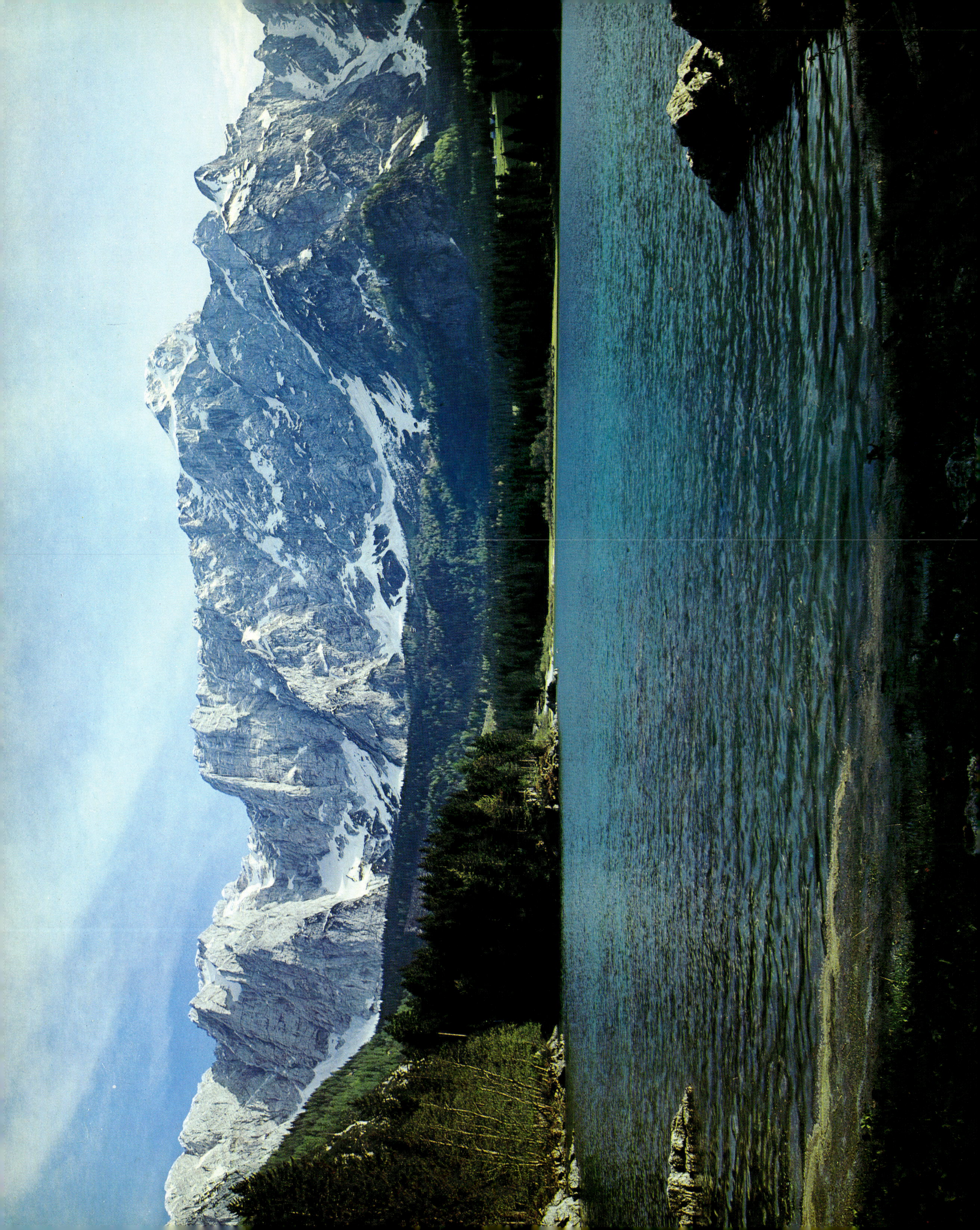

Lago Fusine and the Mangart (Julian Alps)

The broad and immensely impressive Monte Mangart (Mangrt in Slovak, 8,785 feet) is one of the highest summits in the Julian Alps and dominates their central sector. The southern slopes of this great mountain mass belong to Slovenia, the northern to Italy.

Italians mostly see this huge peak from the angle shown in the photograph, for the pretty lake of Fusine, set deep in the mountain scene at only 3,060 feet, lies on Italian ground. From here there is an impressive ›club path‹ leading all the way to the summit, though it is of the kind where it is essential to have some experience of climbing and to be absolutely free from vertigo. Those who are lacking in these qualifications would be well advised to content themselves with the lovely walks along the woodland paths and across the grassy uplands at the foot of this gigantic rock peak, which can at times assume a somewhat grim aspect.

The Wischberg Group (Western Julian Alps)

The mighty northern precipices of the Wischberg chain, in the Western Julian Alps to the south of Tarvisio, constitute an awe-inspiring corner of the mountain world, which might cause even the hardiest of Alpine climbers to shudder, for the light of the sun only touches them – and then in summer – for a few hours a day.

Nevertheless, there is a climber's hut at the heart of this vast semicircle of rock walls, affording a wonderful close-up view of their mighty surge. This is the Luigi Pellarini Hut, standing at an altitude of 4,920 feet, and erected in 1924; there is sleeping-room here for forty people, and it takes about three hours to reach the hut from the valley, the path starting to the north of Valbruna.

In the photograph, the Kaltwasser Gamsmutter, with its 1,850-foot north face, rises above the tallest of the pines. To the right, in succession, follow the Kleinspitze or Innominata, the Gamsmutterturm and the 8,755-foot Wischberg itself. All the climbs on this side of the group are long and very difficult enterprises.

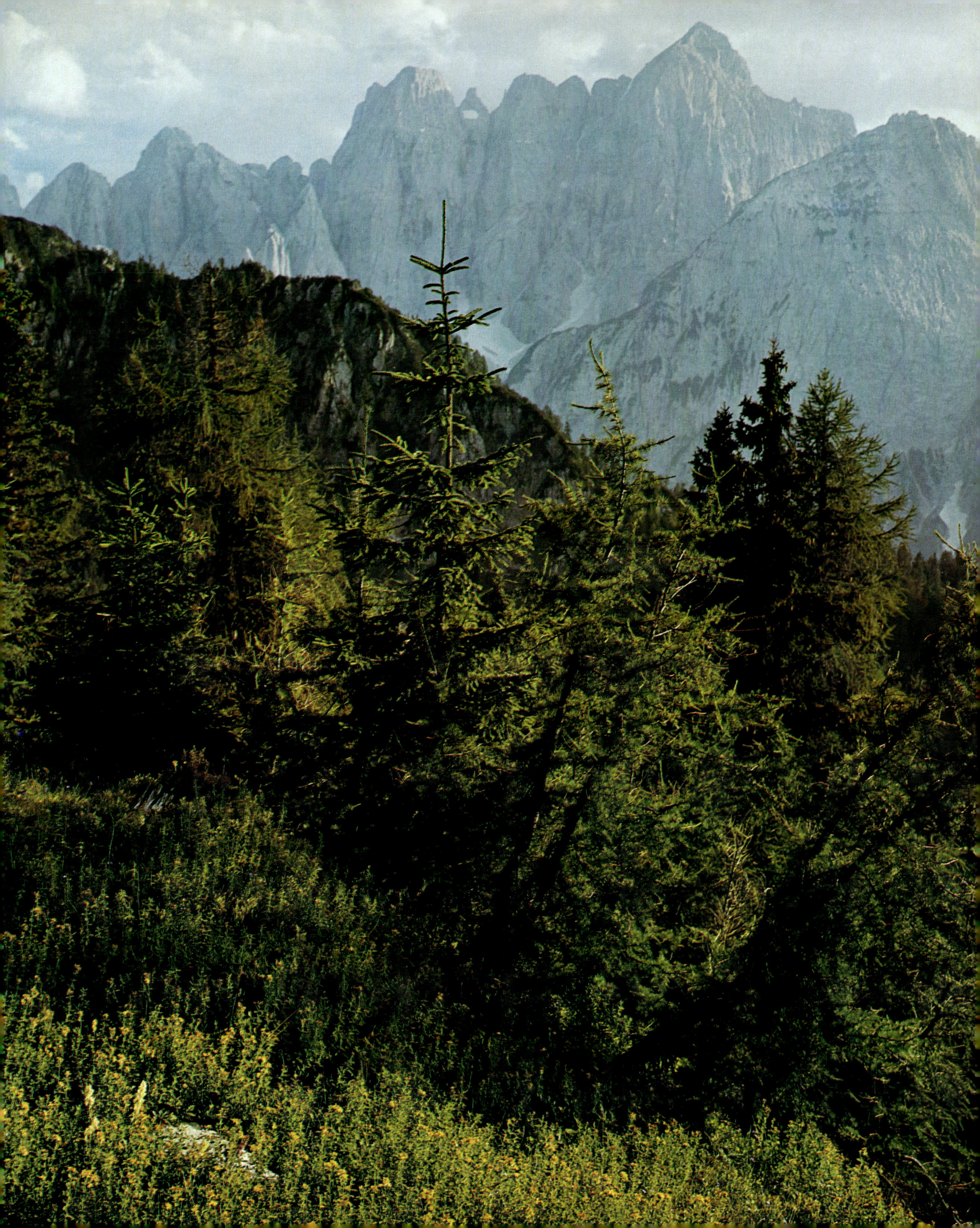

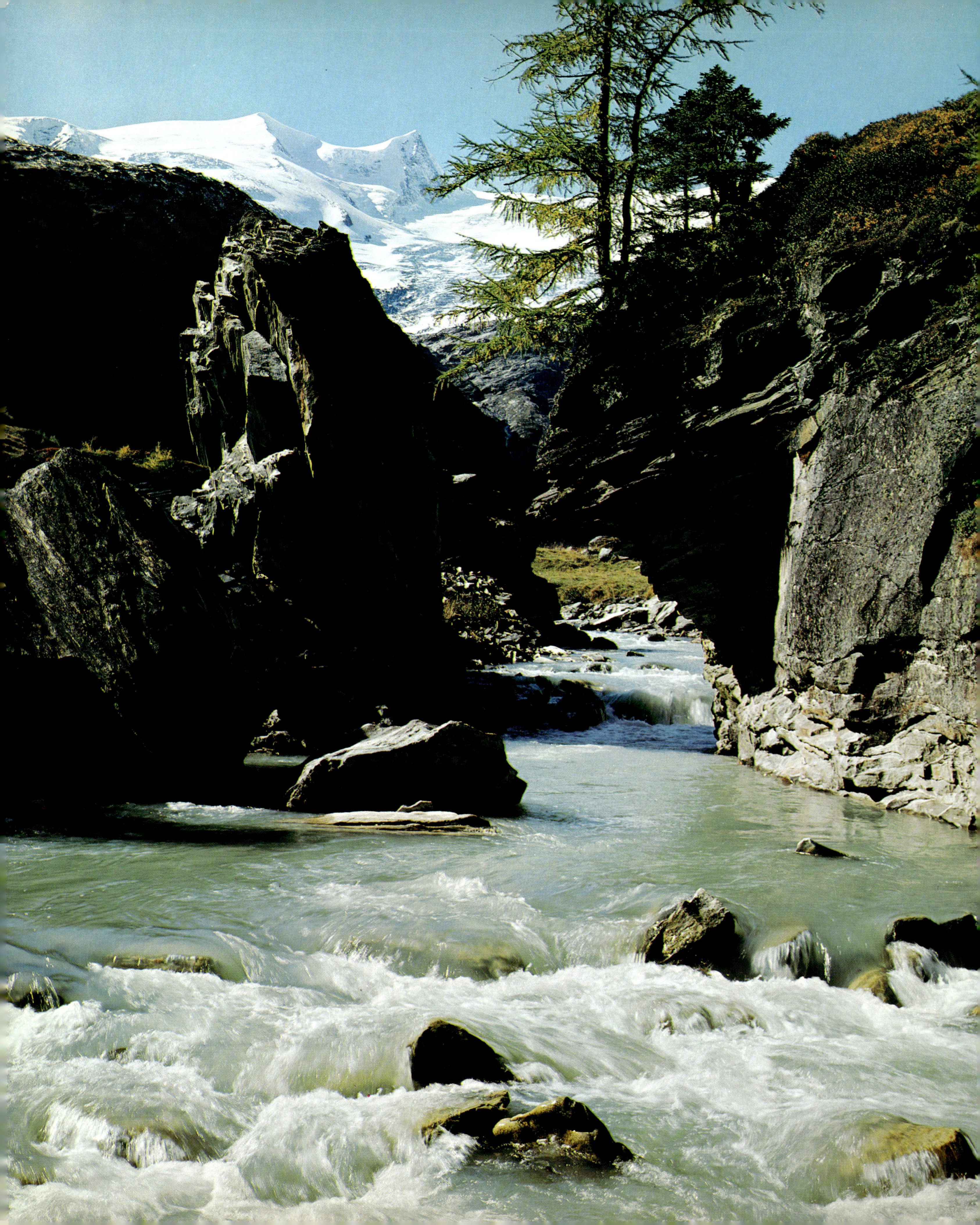

The glacier world of the Gross Venediger

The Venediger Group, topped by its 12,010-foot monarch, the Gross Venediger, is first and foremost a typical glacier area; of all the groups in the Eastern Alps it is the most heavily glaciated, its glacier surfaces covering 22.2 per cent of the whole massif.

The group is bounded on the north by the Salzach Valley, to the east by the Felber Tauern and Matrei Tauern Valleys; through the former runs the new motorway piercing the main Alpine chain below the Venediger in a tunnel three and a quarter miles long, at an altitude of more than 5,000 feet. To the south lie the Virgental, the Dabertal and the Defereggental; to the west, the Ahrntal, the Birnlücke and the valley of the Krimmler Ache. The Gross Venediger is among the easiest to climb of the high summits in the Eastern Alps.

The photograph shows the eastern aspect of the mountain, from which it is seen to best advantage. There is no call for any Alpine experience to enjoy this view of the Venediger's snowy pyramid, for it is only an hour and a half's comfortable walk from the Matreier Tauernhaus, which is accessible by Postal Motor from Matrei to the Innergschlöss Guest House.

Here the infant Tauernbach ripples and roars through gulleys and gorges of dark gneiss, still surrounded at this point by meadow cushions of soft grass. These grow sparser and sparser as you go up the valley, to be replaced ultimately by bare rock and later still by the region of eternal snow and ice.

In the centre of the picture, directly below the sharp peak of the Gross Venediger, can be seen the partly-crevassed icefall of the Schlattenkees[1], while the flattened triangle of the Hohes Aderl (11,493 feet) sweeps, white and gentle, away to the left.

---

[1] *Kees* is the Austrian for glacier.

In the Dolomites of Lienz

The Lienzer Dolomites, in Eastern Tyrol, cover an area to the south of Lienz more than twenty miles long from east to west and up to six miles deep from north to south. The outlines of its peaks are very reminiscent of the Dolomites of South Tyrol.

The group is a subsidiary of the Gailtaler Alps, being bounded to the south by the Gailtal and to the north by the Valley of the Drau (Drave). A hundred and fifty years ago it was known as the Blaiberg Chain, later as the ›Dolomitenkofel‹ of Lienz, the ›Kreuzkofel‹ group, the Lienzer Gebirge and finally as the Lienzer Dolomiten. Whatever it was called, it was not thoroughly explored till the turn of the century.

The picture shows the Karlsbader Hut (7,390 feet), close to the rim of the Laserz See. To the right rises the vast head of the Laserzkopf (9,150 feet), and to the north in the background, beyond the blue depths of the Drau Valley, the Schober Group, so prominent a feature from the southern side of the Grossglockner road. Lienz lies deep in the valley; from the city it takes six hours to reach the hut, which was built as long ago as 1888.

Owing to the length of time taken by this laborious ascent, there is no fear of running into a crowd of ›mere trippers‹ hereabouts, and every lover of the silent summits and solitary walks among them will be enchanted by this unspoiled mountain tract from his first acquaintance with it.

Here again, it is significant that the last edition of a walking and climbing guide to the Dolomites of Lienz saw the light in 1922.

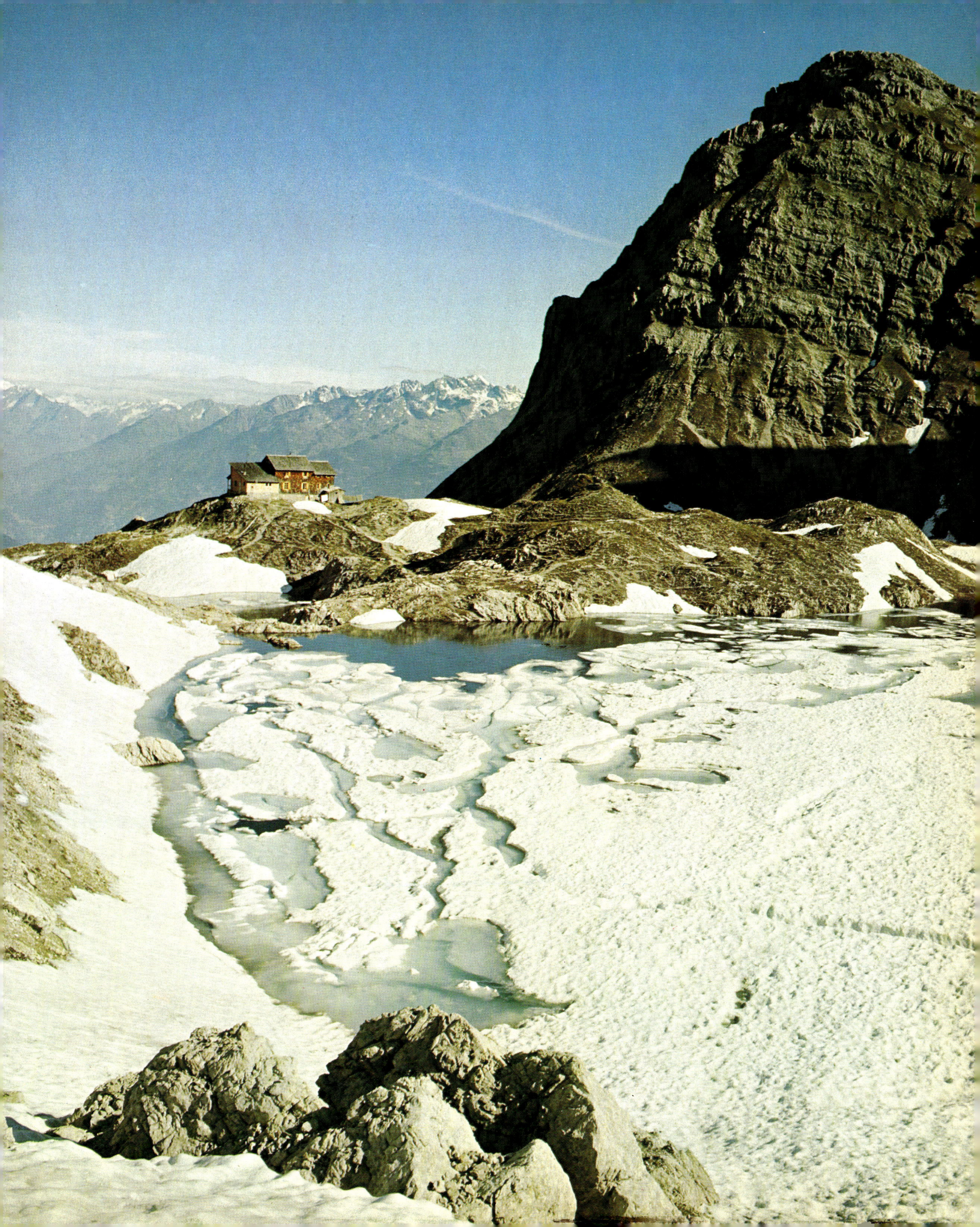

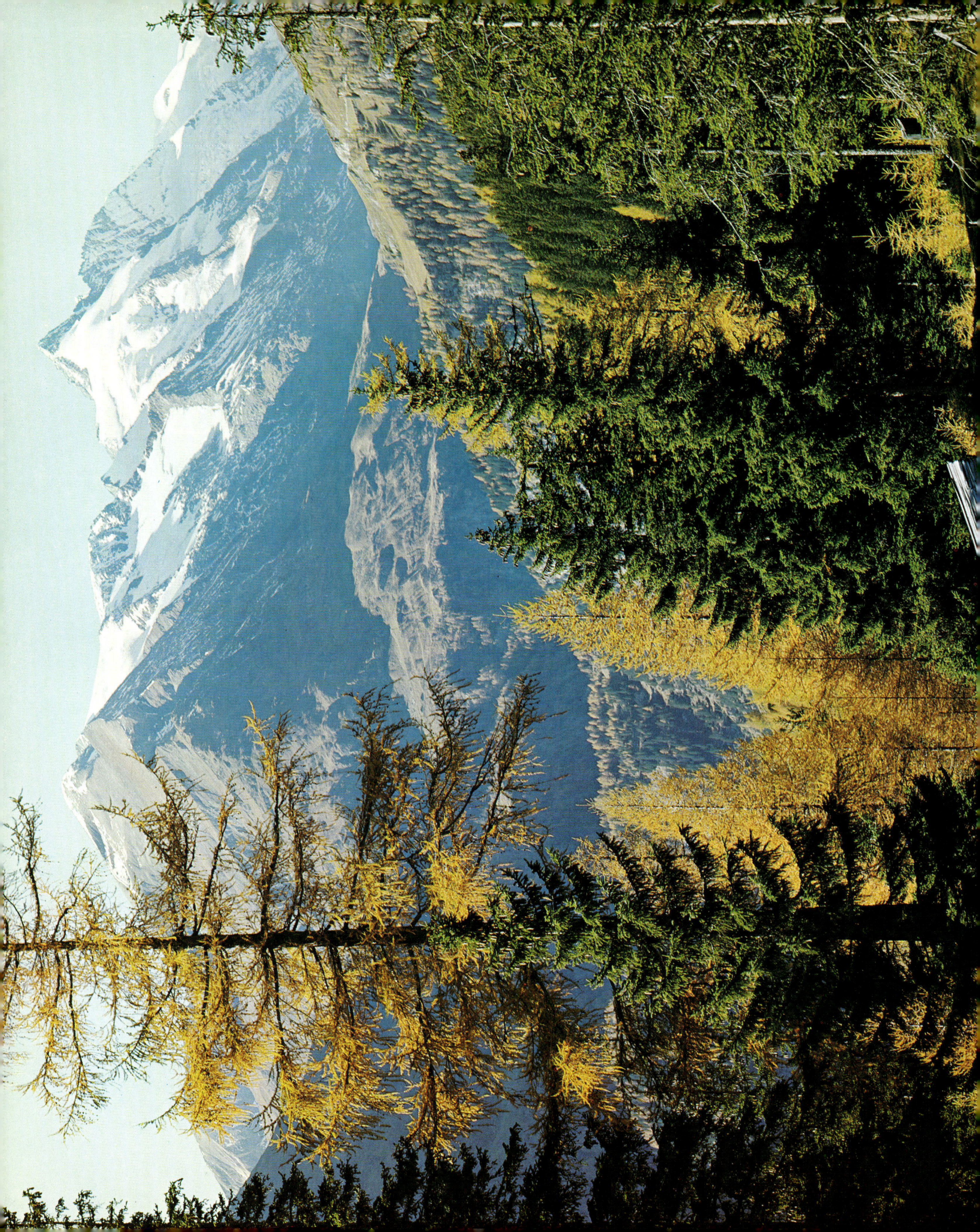

Autumn on the Grossglockner

The 12,460-foot Grossglockner is the highest peak in Austria, including the Eastern Tyrol and Styria, and is in fact the monarch of the Eastern Alps. The northern foot of this soaring giant in the Hohe Tauern range is based on the Pasterzen Glacier, the biggest in the Eastern Alps – with an area of twenty square miles and a length of six; it is surpassed in size only by the Aletsch, the Gorner and the Mer de Glace ice-streams in the Western Alps. The peak was marked on a map as early as 1561. The first ascent, in 1799, was an outstanding Alpine achievement.

The picture shows the mountain as seen from the south-east. To the right of the sharp summit rises the rock face of the Glocknerwand, heavily covered in snow. To its left, the snow and ice slopes of the Hoffmankees, over which numerous climbs keep the local guides fully occupied during the summer season, are seen falling towards the viewer. Although the ascents by these normal routes are strenuous, they present few technical difficulties; more adventurous climbers find rewarding routes on the mountain's northern precipices.

Even the motorist, who prefers the (relative) safety of an asphalt road to the occasional perils of the glacier world, can obtain fine near views of the Glockner. In 1935, the wonderful Grossglockner Hochalpenstrasse, among the highest and finest passes in the Alps, was at last opened, after a bitter twelve years' struggle with wind and weather. This, the highest motor road in Austria, starts from the picturesque village of Heiligenblut, with the Glockner already rising supreme above its slender and celebrated church spire. To obtain the best close-up view of the mountain and the great glacier at its feet, the main road to the pass is left at Guttal (6,310 feet), whence a spur road leads to the Franz Josef's Höhe (7,935 feet), high above the glacier basin, and affording an unforgettable view of the great peak, its satellites and the broad, frozen river of the Pasterze.

This is a dead-end, and it is necessary to return to Guttal if you are crossing the 8,212-foot pass, through the Hochtor tunnel at its summit, to the north side of the Alpine chain and down to Ferleiten and Bruck in the broad, smiling Pinzgau Valley.

On the Grossglockner: between cloud and sky

Dark rock, glittering snow, a seething sea of cloud, a deep blue sky – this is a picture to stir the heart of all lovers of the high mountain scene; though one can see at a glance that the ascent of the Grossglockner is no life-and-death affair. In a good summer more than a thousand enthusiasts reach the summit, most of them guideless.

The photograph shows five climbers on the 12,400-foot Kleinglockner, over whose ridge the normal route runs. In spite of the iron stakes, care is essential here, for the cornices – snow-shields blown by the wind and hanging unsupported above the abyss, as seen in the picture – are always a tricky feature; even experienced climbers can never be sure how firm they are. (Hermann Buhl, the great Austrian climber, who made the first ascent of 26,660-foot Nanga Parbat in the Himalaya solo, later lost his life when a cornice broke under him during the descent of Chogolisa, in the Karakorum, his companion, that other great Austrian climber Kurt Diemberger, escaping with his life.)

Even if the technical difficulties of the normal route up the Grossglockner are relatively slight, careful belaying with the rope and the availability of ice-crampons are essential.

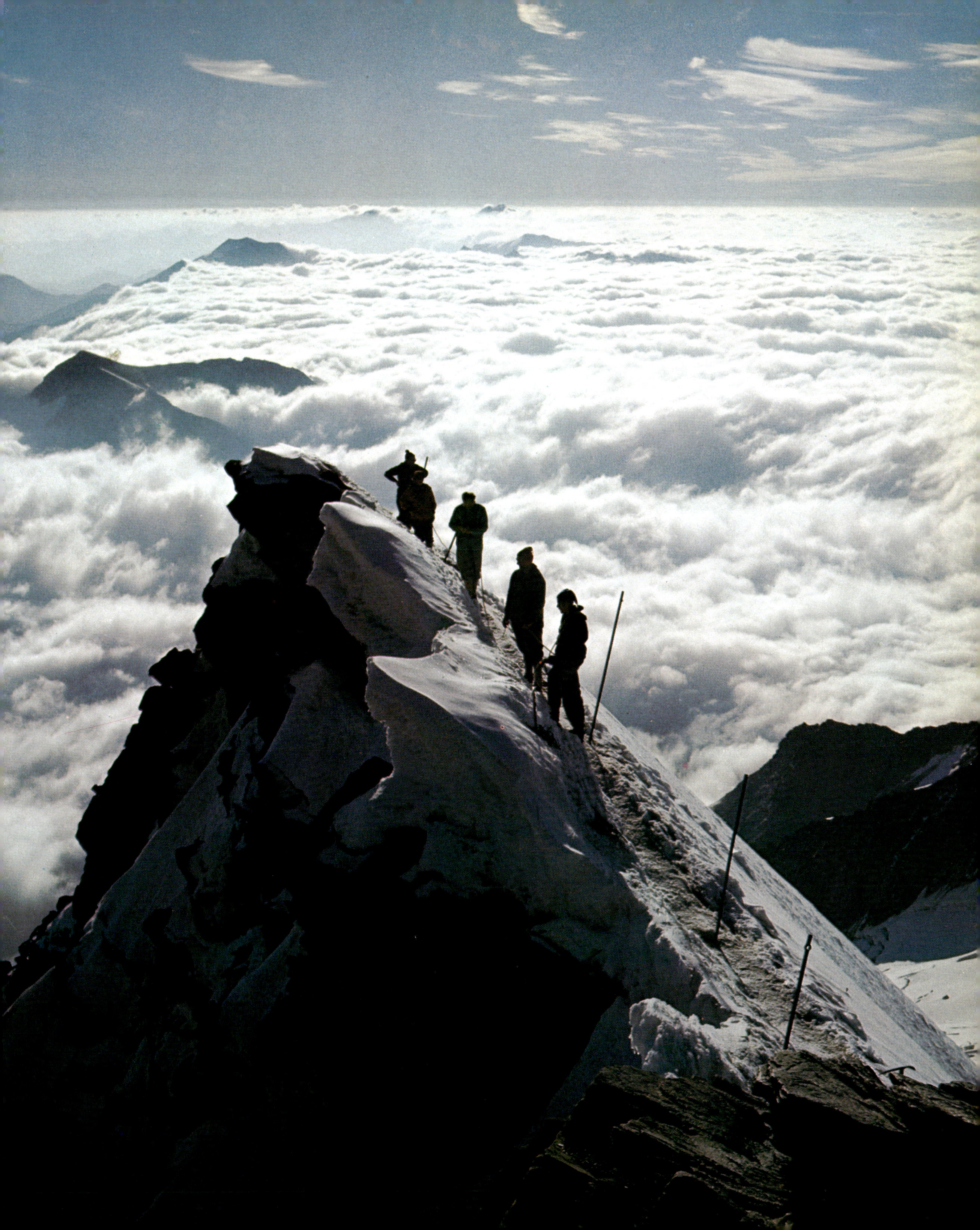

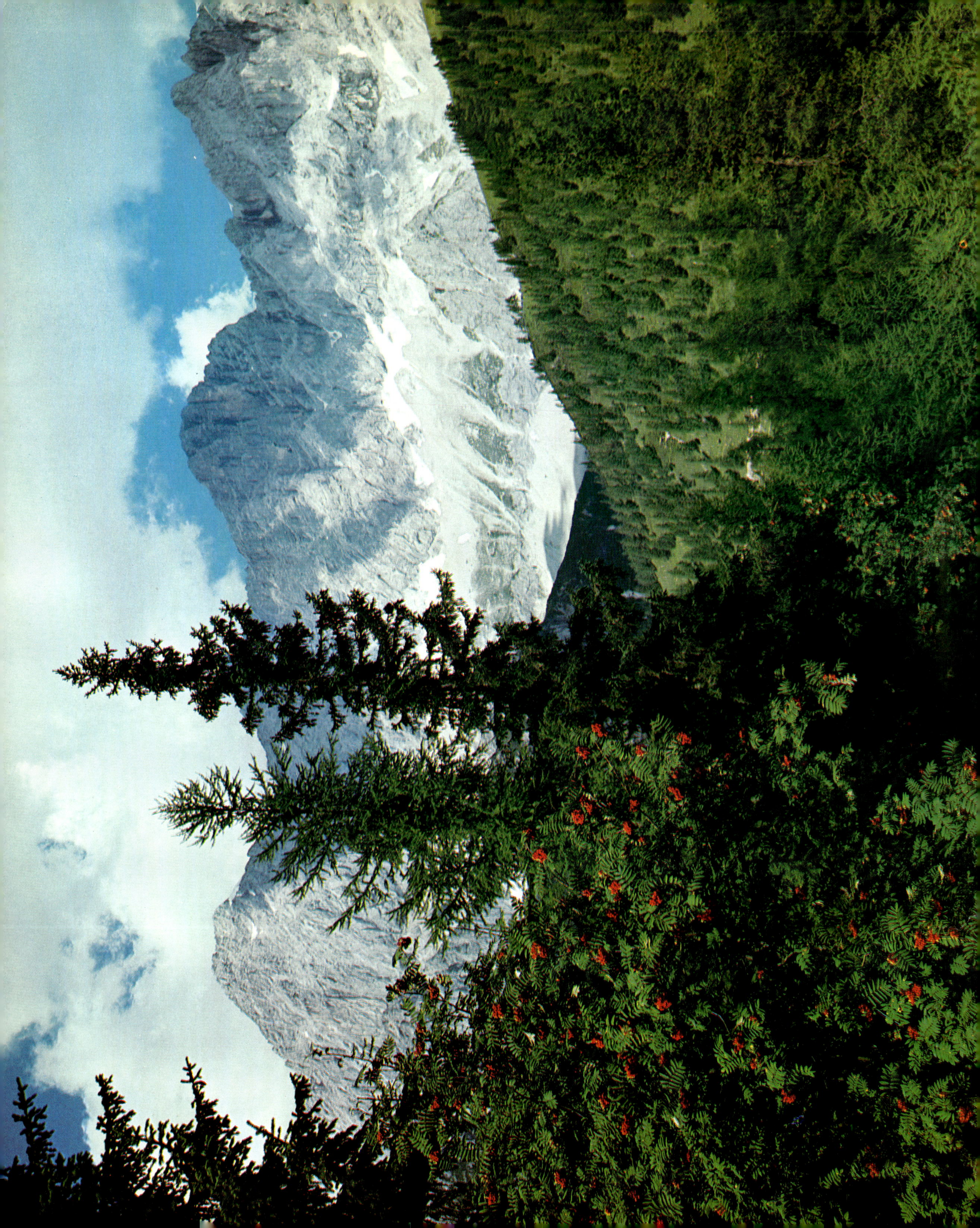

Torstein, Dachstein and Dirndl

The Hohe Dachstein (9,815 feet) is the highest summit in the Dachstein range and the second highest in the Northern Limestone Alps. The frontier between Upper Austria and Styria runs over its summit ridge. It is a ›versatile‹ mountain, for the walker can find in its domain as many delights as the ski-runner and the Grade VI rock expert.

True, solitude is not often to be found here and then only in a few places, but the region has never yet been faulted for its scenic beauties. The assiduous builders of ropeways have even planted their steel trees on the stony slopes of these high places, and the huge southern precipices to the right of the main summit can now be ›climbed‹ in a swaying ropeway-cabin. In spite of all this, the south face of the Dachstein remains one of the favourite Grade IV (›Very Difficult‹) climbs in the Northern Limestone Alps.

The photograph shows, from left to right, the Torstein (9,665 feet), the Mitterspitz, only sixty-six feet lower, hidden behind the tall tree; then the Dachstein itself; the little prominence of the 8,977-foot Dachsteinwarte (the ›Watchtower‹) and the Hohe and Niedere Dirndl, both over 9,000 feet high.

There is a lovely and absolutely safe footpath running the whole length of this three-mile-long southern wall of the Dachstein group.

*The Gollinger Fall, at the eastern edge
of the Berchtesgaden Alps*

Some twenty miles to the south of Salzburg lies the pretty village of Golling, in a widening of the Salzach Valley, ringed by the mountains of the Tennengebirge, the Hagengebirge and the Berchtesgaden Alps. To the east, the Castle of Rabenstein looks down on the village from high above. Numerous wild mountain torrents rush swiftly and noisily down from all sides into the Salzach, already a sizeable river at this point. One of them is the Weissenbach, which has its source in the valley of the same name, to the west of Golling, rising close to the Purtscheller Haus on the Hohe Göll.

About an hour's delightful walking along the Alpenverein's marked path, which leads from Golling to the Purtscheller Haus, brings one to the Gollinger Waterfall, a feature of such rare natural beauty that it is an excellent place to choose for a rest. There can be no finer example of primeval nature, especially when the headlong rush of the waters is seen in the lovely light caught by the camera in this picture.

If the three-hours' grind up the Weissental all the way to the hut, by way of the Eckersattel, is too much to contemplate, the walk as far as the waterfall offers a pleasant diversion for the traveller passing through the Salzach Valley on his way to or from the south.

The fall is, of course, at its best in the early summer, up to mid-July, when the torrent comes roaring down at its wildest and loudest, fed by the melting snows.

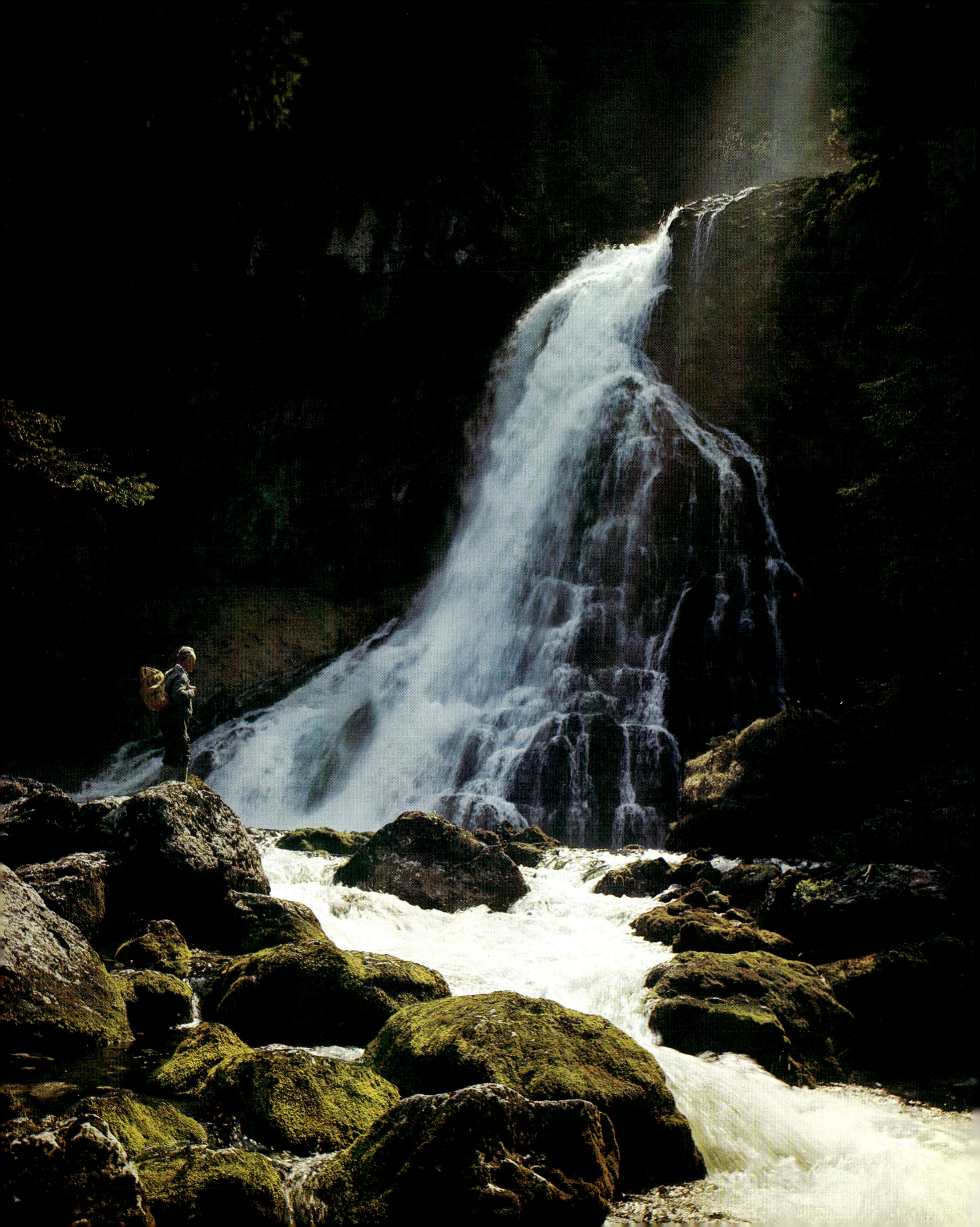

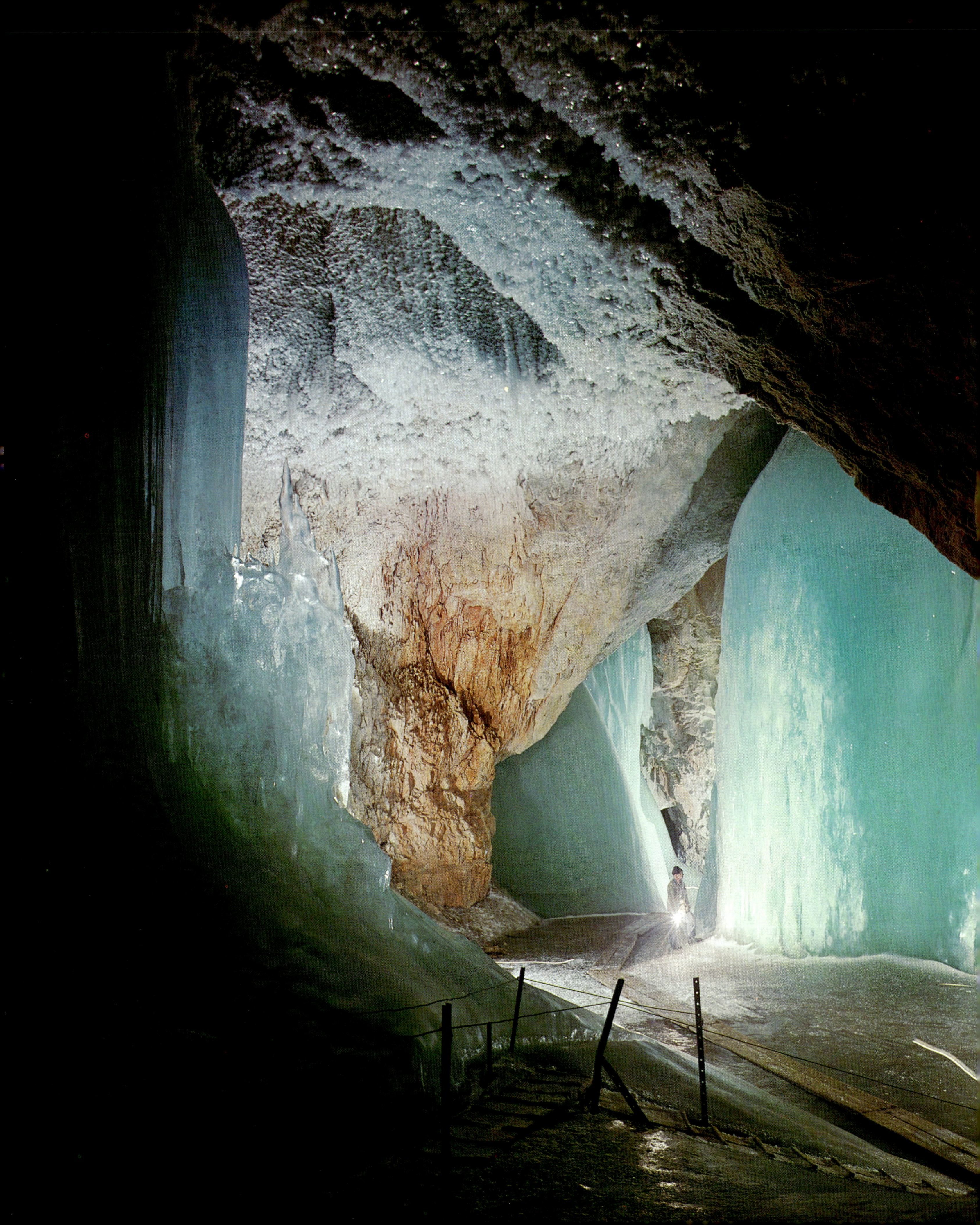

The Giant Ice Caves of Werfen

On the journey southwards from Salzburg along the Salzach, you come, after about twenty miles, to the little town of Werfen, lying between the Hagengebirge, part of the Berchtesgaden Alps to its west, and the Tennengebirge to its east. This historic town was already well-known for its market as long ago as 1242 AD.

Lying above Werfen, at 5,350 feet, there is to be found, on the south-west fringe of the Tennengebirge, one of nature's masterpieces – ›The Giant Ice World‹, Europe's largest-known system of ice caves. Their full extent measures thirty miles, which have been opened up and provided with gangways for the large number of foreign tourists who visit them.

The quickest means of approach is by the regular bus service from Werfen to the Parkplatz at Fallstein, followed by a walk of about forty minutes, then an ascent by cable-railway and another fifteen minutes' walk.

This gigantic world of caves is open from May 1st to September 30th. You can take your choice of two conducted tours: the first takes two hours and is confined to the initial glaciated sector. The second, designed for the visitor who really wants to know what the bowels of the Tennengebirge look like, lasts eight to twelve hours and, embracing the ice-free sectors as well, is known as the ›Grosse Führung‹ (the ›Grand Tour‹). Whichever you choose, it is a wise precaution to have warm clothing with you.

The Attersee and the Höllengebirge

The Salzkammergut's Höllengebirge, to the east of the Attersee, is a mountain tract which appeals first and foremost to the walker, who can cross the broad massif, eight miles long from east to west and at places nearly three miles wide, on a well-marked footpath in a matter of seven to nine hours, without any difficulty or danger.

Moreover, the Hochfläche – the whole range is a kind of elevated plateau – can be reached in comfort by the Feuerkogel railway from Ebensee. The upper station stands at 5,228 feet, which is already fairly high up the mountains, whose highest eminence, the Grosse Höllkogel, rises to no more than 6,107 feet. This point can also be attained by a marked ascent route offering no difficulties. Even in the photograph, one can see that there are no great differences in height to hinder progress over the plateau. This comparatively small range offers a choice of four refuges, three huts and a hotel on its upper levels.

Mountain lovers of no great accomplishment can find much to delight them about the shores of the beautiful Attersee itself. There are numerous charming walks and excursions on the western and eastern banks of this lake, which is twelve miles long, three miles wide and 575 feet deep.

A finely-engineered motor road runs round the whole lake, so that even those lazy people, the motor tourists, never had it better.

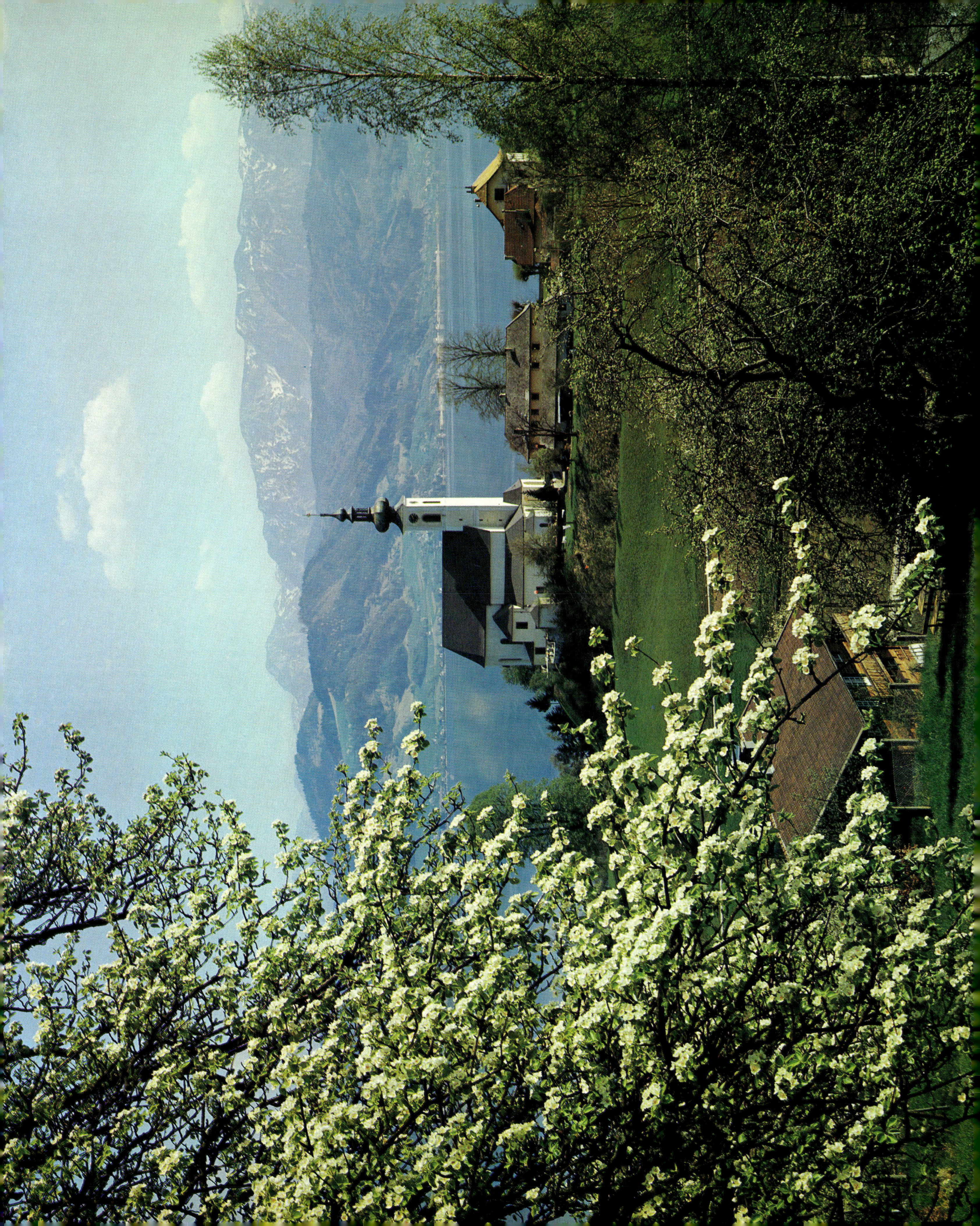

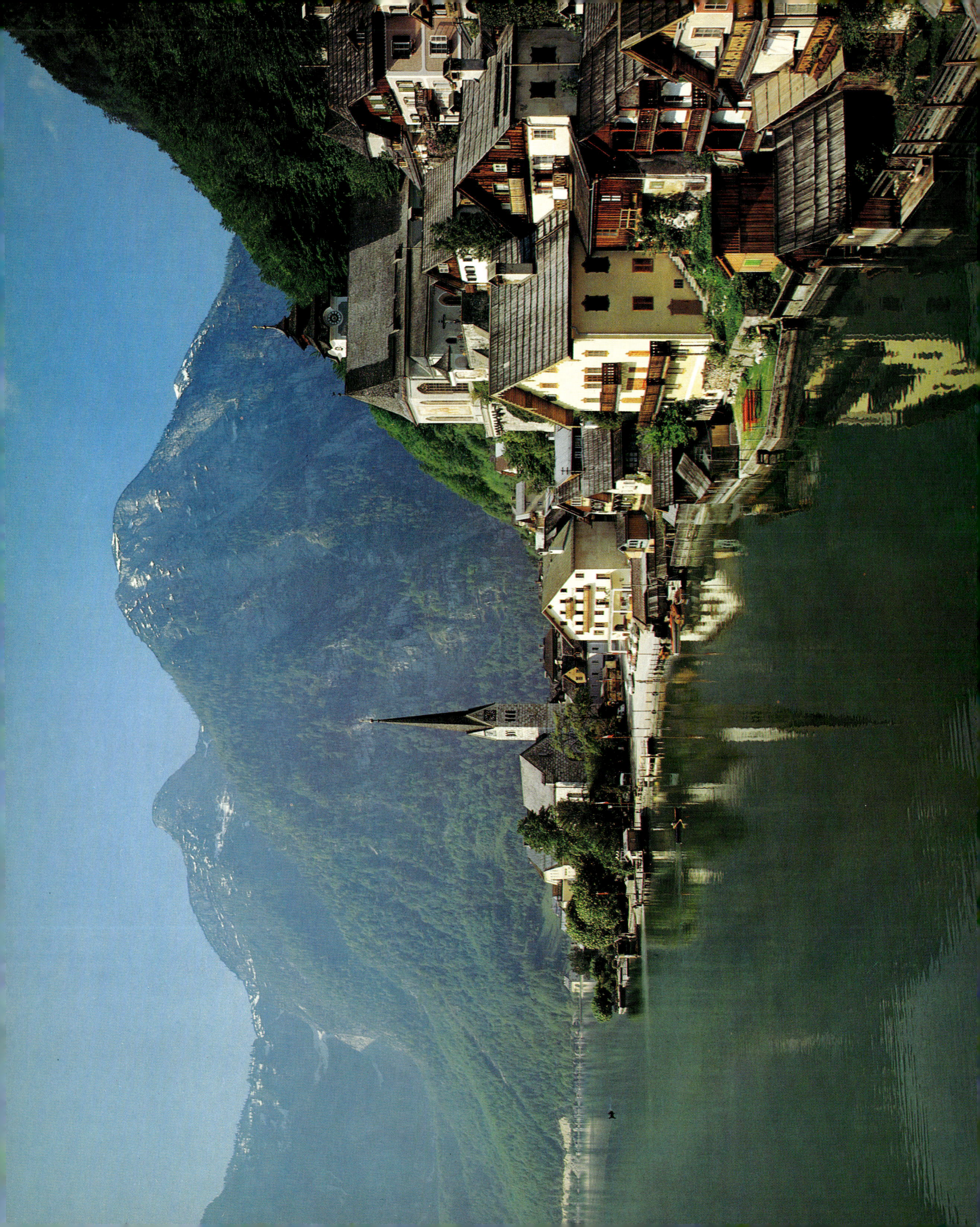

Hallstatt in the Salzkammergut

The Hallstatter See, surrounded by the northern outliers of the Dachstein range, is one of Austria's finest beauty spots. Five miles long, when viewed from above, it looks like a Norwegian Fjord. Picturesque Hallstatt is the most important place on this romantically-beautiful lake, not only for its attractions to the foreign tourist but on account of its cultural history.

It was not till 1846 that excavations, carried on with interruptions till 1939, revealed the relics of the Hallstatt civilization, which reached its peak when the Bronze Age passed over into that of Iron. Between 1846, when a miner sinking a shaft came upon a skeleton, and 1864, digging revealed 993 graves and over 6,000 exhibits – weapons of bronze and iron, helmets, precious ornaments and household utensils. The site of these discoveries lies in the sleepy Salzbergtal, a narrow valley named after the local salt-mines, almost a trench which one only recognizes when one has arrived in it. The men of the Hallstatt Age (900–390 BC) even seem to have climbed the Salzstock in the upper part of the valley.

The mountains around the Lake of Hallstatt offer every lover of nature's peace and solitude countless opportunities, from walks in the forests high on their slopes to good, stiff climbs in the Dachstein group itself (plate 16).

*The village of Alm, at the southern foot
of the Steinerne Meer*

The Steinerne Meer, ›The Sea of Stone‹, is a huge rock plateau, eight miles by three in dimension, on the southern fringe of the Berchtesgaden Alps, of which it forms part.

To the south of this big mountain tract, four miles to the east of Saalfelden, at a height of 2,600 feet, lies the pretty mountain hamlet of Alm. The place was once a well-known pilgrim centre; today it is much frequented, in summer, by happy holiday makers, in winter by winter-sports addicts.

In the photograph, the church spire is seen against the Mandlköpfe, to the left of which bulks the wedge-shaped mass of the Schönfeldspitze, 8,700 feet, one of the most imposing peaks in the Berchtesgaden Alps. The long main ridge continues to the left, falling to its lowest point at the Ramseider Saddle (6,895 feet), on which stands the Riemann Haus, which can be reached from Alm in three and a half hours by a well-marked path. The hut is a favourite objective for practised mountain walkers who do not suffer from giddiness. To the left of the saddle, the ridge rises again to the 8,190-foot Breithorn (extreme left).

Once on the plateau, with its characteristic barrow-like formations, the hardest part of the work is over. For the experienced mountain rambler, the traverse of the Steinerne Meer from south to north, coming down on the lovely Königsee, near Berchtesgaden (see plate 24), is a most attractive and repaying undertaking. It should, however, only be embarked on during a spell of settled weather, for in conditions of cloud and fog there may be considerable difficulty in finding the way.

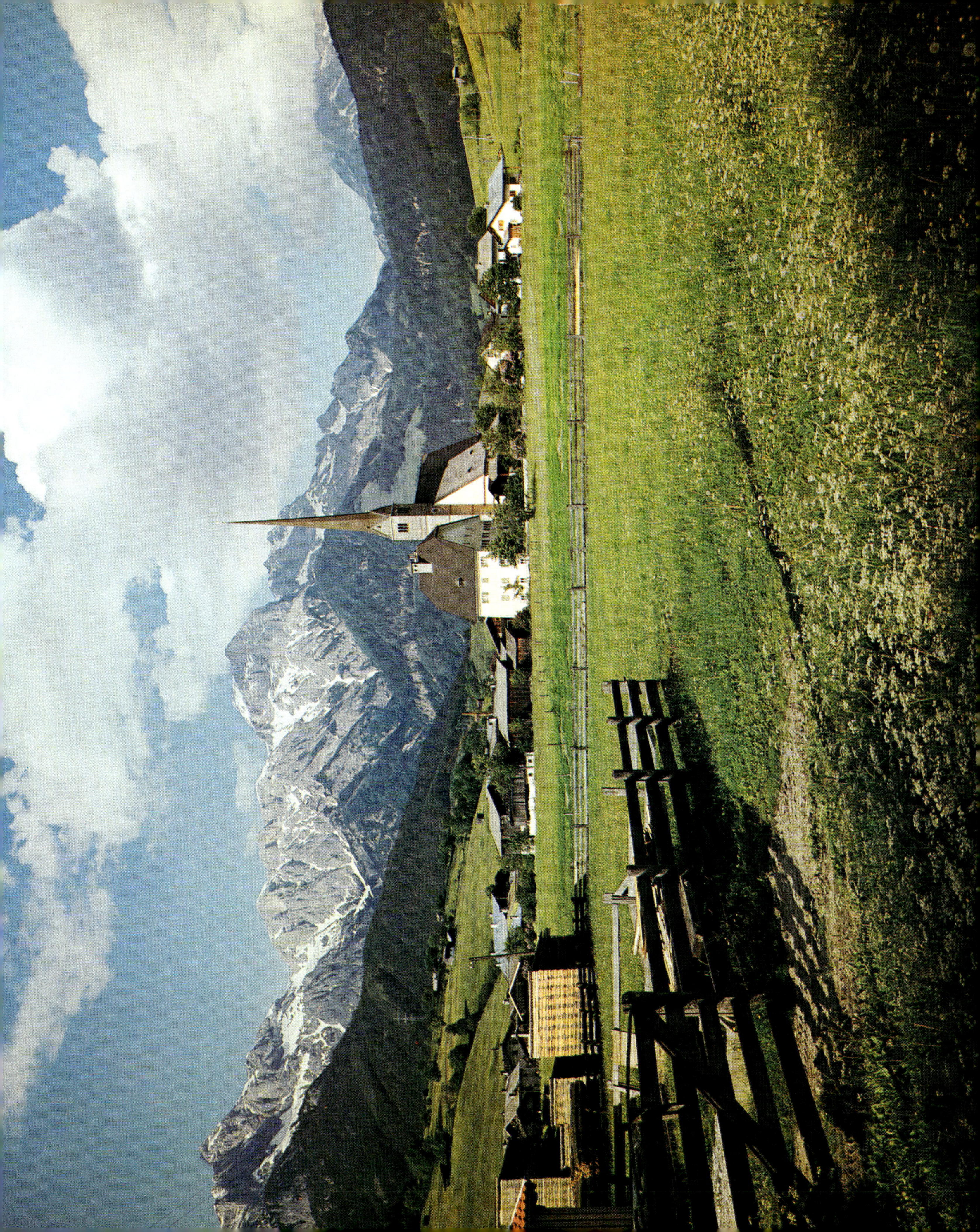

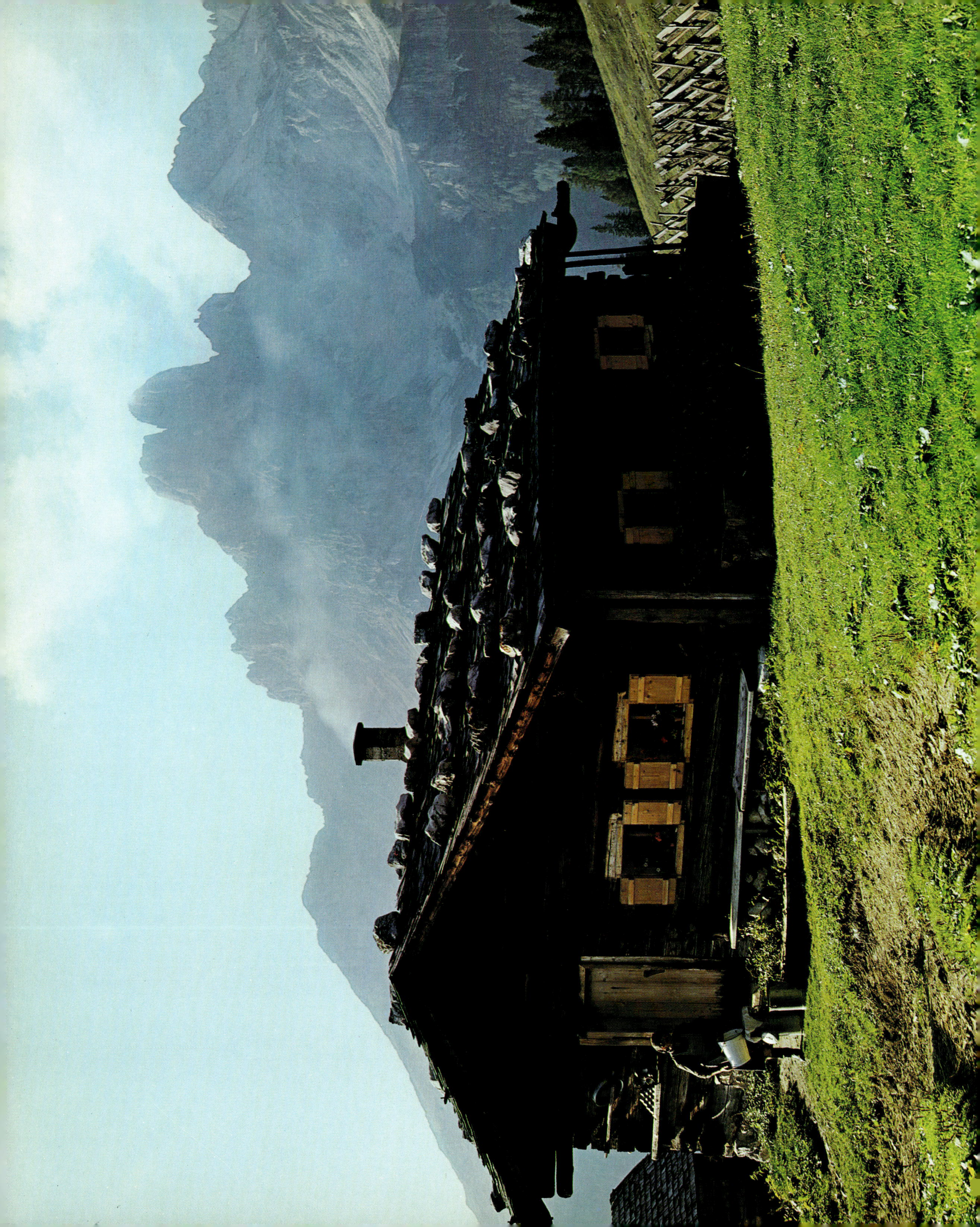

The Bischofsmütze (›The Mitre‹) in the Gosau Comb

Our picture of the Gosaukamm (›Comb‹) is dominated by the splendid outlines of the twin Bischofsmütze summits, the Grosse (8,050 feet) and the Kleine.

The Gosaukamm is the name given to the western sector, five miles long and two wide, of the Dachsteingebirge's main range, a favourite haunt for rock climbers. On the Grosse Bischofsmütze alone there are nearly two dozen routes and numerous variants, but easiest, which goes up the gulley between the twin peaks, is a ›Moderately Difficult‹.

Needless to say, the region is also visited by numbers of walkers and tourists. For their delectation there is a perfectly safe path, on which they can do the complete round of the Gosaukamm, and there are five climbers' huts at their disposal.

The photograph shows the southern aspect of the Bischofsmützen massif, as seen from Filzmoos (3,380 feet), at a distance of about four miles. To the north, behind the mountain group lie the unusually charming Gosau lakes, which are seen to great advantage from high up on the circuit by the above-mentioned path.

The Hochkönig, near Dienten, Province of Salzburg

The great massif of the Hochkönig (9,640 feet, 2,941 metres), whose summit so nearly qualifies as a ›Three-thousand-metre-peak‹, is a rock mass measuring about four miles each way, and is extremely impressive when seen from Dienten, to its south, as in the picture. To the left the broad Rosskar soars into the clouds, to the right of the photograph the precipitous teeth of the Weisskar. In between, directly above the cluster of châlets in the foreground, rises the summit, almost obscured by cloud.

Although the Hochkönig, dominating the extreme south of the Berchtesgaden Alps, looks such a giant, the ascent of its summit is surprisingly easy; there are, in fact, four separate well-maintained Alpine Association paths to facilitate the ›climb‹, which presents no difficulties and takes from four to five hours from the valley level.

Once on the summit, not only are the visitor's exertions rewarded by a magnificent panorama in all directions, but he can eat his meal and slake his thirst with any kind of beverage to his taste; for, up there, on the top of this high mountain, he will find a comfortable mountain hut, the Hochkönig- or Matras-Haus, equipped with thirty-two beds and sleeping-space for another fifty. One cannot ask for much more than that on the summit of one of the highest and grandest of the peaks in the Northern Limestone Alps.

Moreover, if you are making the ascent from the south, on the Dienten side, you will be astonished, on reaching the summit ridge, to find yourself suddenly faced by a genuine glacier, covering an area of more than three square miles, and graced with the extraordinary name of ›The Flooded Meadow‹ (Die Übergossene Alm).

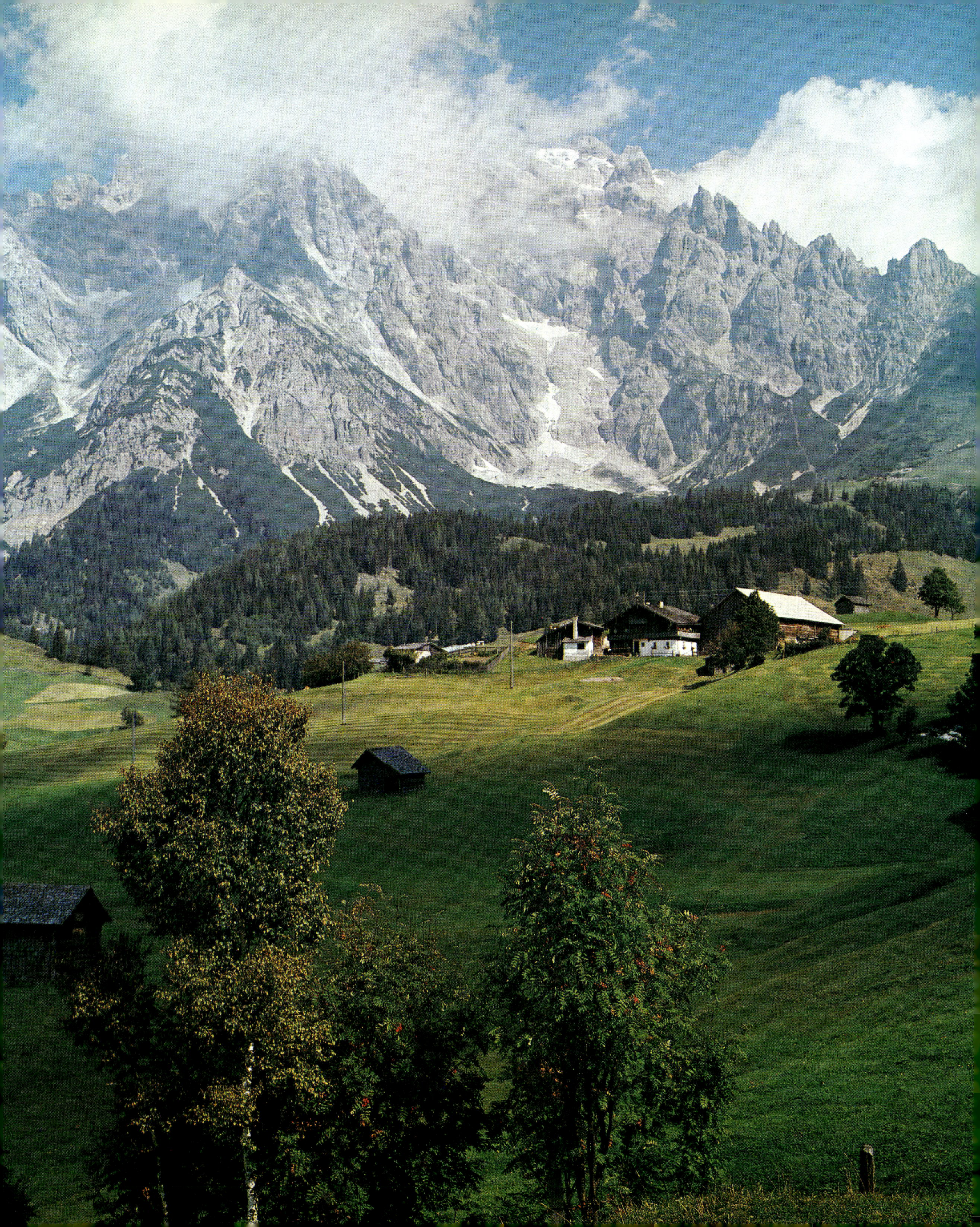

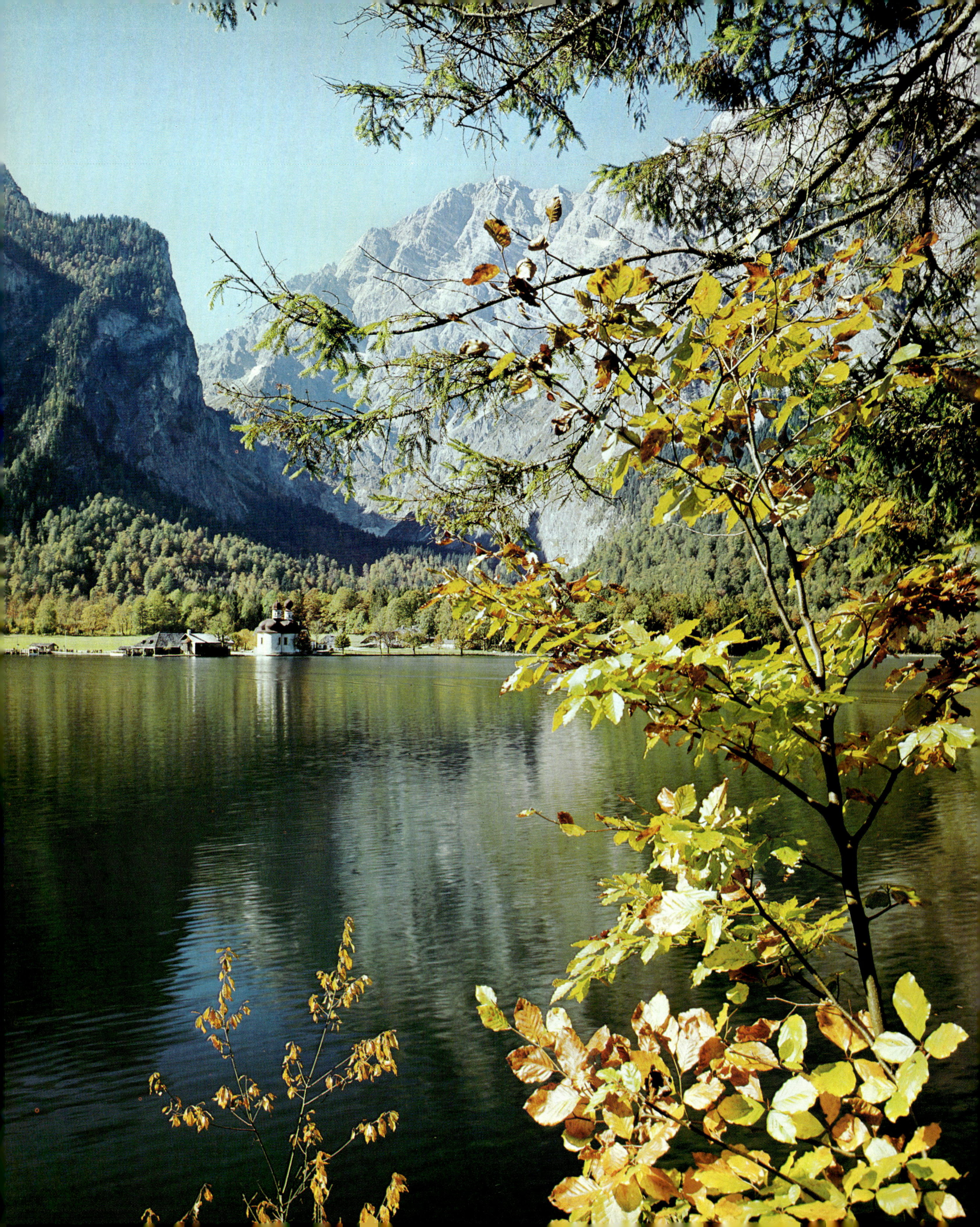

The Königssee and the east face of the Watzmann

Immediately to the south of Berchtesgaden, the Königssee lies at a quite unusual depth between the mountain walls which contain it. It is generally held to be one of the most beautiful of all Alpine lakes, and is certainly one of the most frequented beauty spots in the Bavarian Alps.

The lake is five miles long and a mile wide, with a maximum depth of 609 feet. During the summer months motorboats ply on it, calling at numerous fine view-points, and finally at St. Bartholomae on the west shore of the lake's southern arm. (The famous chapel with its twin towers is seen in the picture nestling at the foot of the great grey limestone curtain of the Watzmann in the background.) The ordinary tourist can unfortunately find no overnight accommodation here, though there is a small hut, equipped with mattresses, for climbers intending to grapple with the difficulties of the east face. There is enough to be seen and done at lovely St. Bartholomae to warrant spending a whole afternoon there and thereabouts, though there is no access to it by lakeside path; the only way to get there is by motorboat, unless you are strong and fit enough to hire a rowing boat for the three-hour stint.

From the hamlet it is about fifty minutes' walk to where the east face of the Watzmann, 5,900 feet high, goes winging up to the 8,710-foot summit. This is one of the loftiest faces in the Alps, and its first ascent was made as long ago as 1881 by Otto Schück from Vienna and Johann Grill-Kederbacher, a Ramsau guide; but even today the climb is a dangerous one, the face being notorious for its volleys of falling stones.

The Wilder Kaiser range seen from the Schwarzsee

The Wilder Kaiser is an appropriate name for this small but extraordinarily savage range, whose main crest runs for ten miles from Kufstein in the Tyrol to the neighbourhood of St. Johann.

Its cliffs and gulleys are famous as a rock climbers' paradise, offering a variety of routes from the difficult to the extreme of severity. Its description as ›the great Munich climbing-ground‹ is in no way an exaggeration, for on any fine Sunday from June to September it seems as though all the climbers in Munich have arranged a rendezvous here – an assignment made all the easier by the fact that the foot of the Fleischbank's tremendous eastern face can be reached from the centre of the city in two and a half hours.

It was the Munich school of young German climbers which, after the First World War, pioneered the ›new‹ climbing on faces and ridges previously considered impossible, using the non-U artificial aids and completely new rope techniques. They were accused at the time, not without some justice, of introducing a cult of almost suicidal nationalism into what had been regarded as an international sport, and casualties were all too numerous. Hitler certainly bestowed honours for outstanding performances. From their early efforts stem all the fantastic ›artificial‹ achievements of the last three decades by climbers of all nationalities on all the world's great peaks.

The range holds equal attraction for the walkers. The path through the Kaisertal, for instance, is one of the most enjoyable walks in the Northern Limestone Alps. It is also possible to cross the main ridge at a number of places, partly by means of artificially-protected ›club paths‹.

The Ellmauer Tor, the deep gateway in the centre of the photograph, and the Steinerne Rinne (›The Rocky Gulley‹), falling northwards from it towards the viewer, form the true heart of the range. In early summer, when the remains of the winter snow are still lying in the huge corridor, its passage is not unattended by danger.

The little Schwarzsee, lying only a few hundred yards to the west of the famous summer and winter resort of Kitzbühel, is beautifully situated, and the whole extent of the Wilder Kaiser's main crest is visible from its shore.

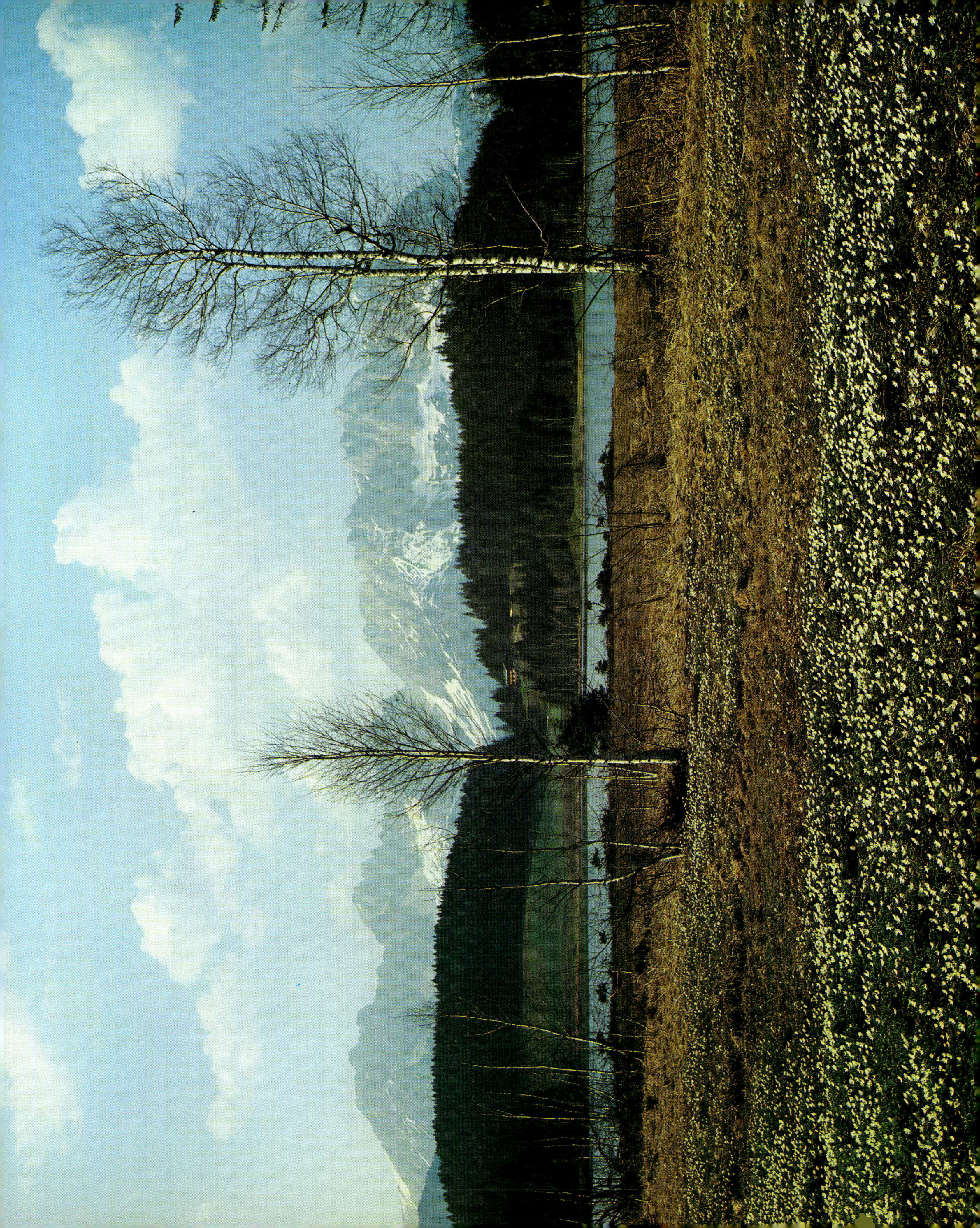

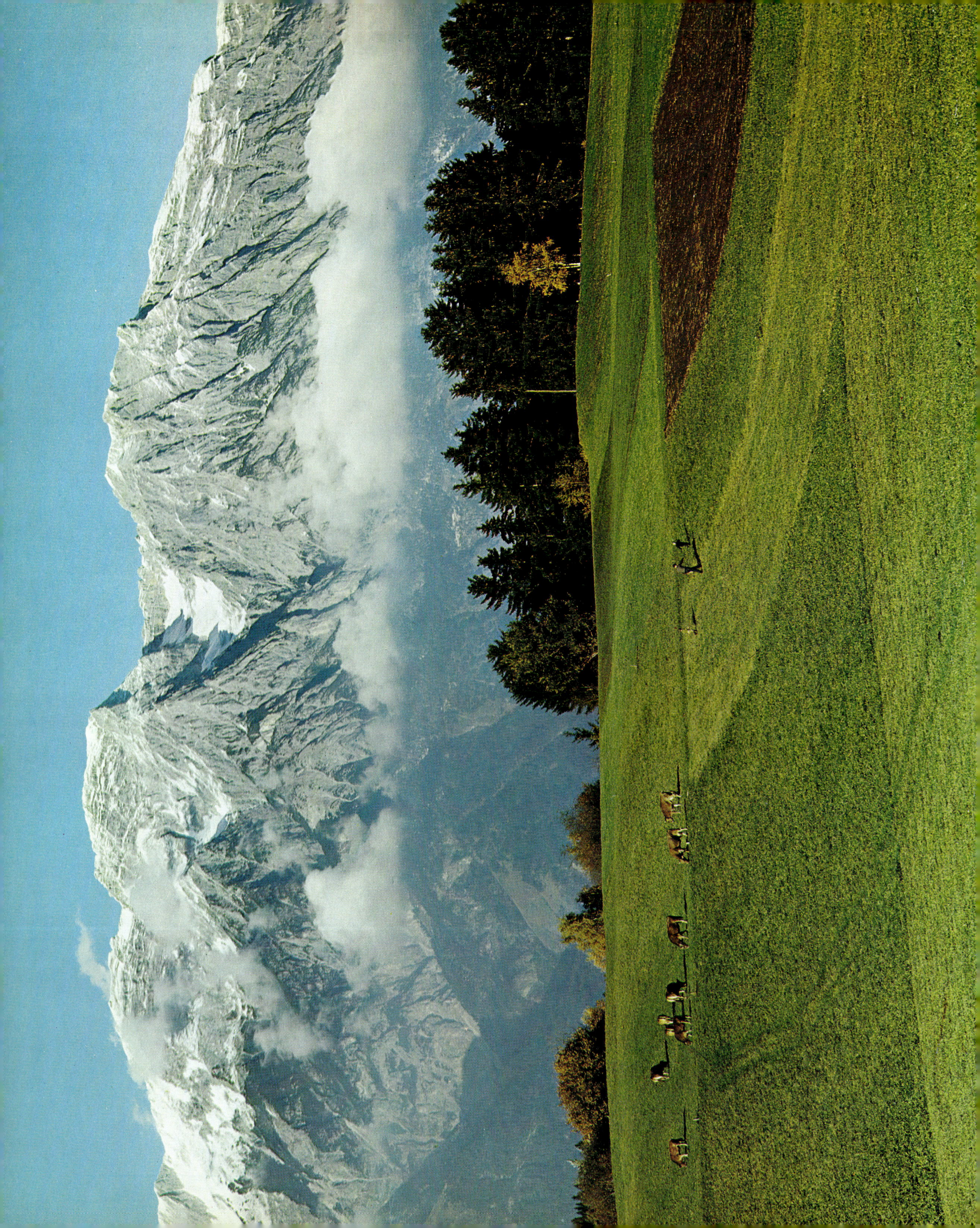

The Bettelwurf, rising high above the Inn Valley

The Bettelwurf (8,940 feet) is a massive clump of rock, riven by hollows, grooves and gulleys, whose summit dominates the valley of the Inn only six miles to the north of Innsbruck.

The vertical difference between that summit and the valley-level is nearly 7,000 feet. The ordinary tourist, with no acquaintance at all of the mysteries of mountaineering, can make the ascent by one of the Alpine Association's marked paths, so long as he is sure-footed and commands a steady head. From Solbad Hall in the Valley of the Inn this entails a climb of six to seven hours, but after not much more than four one arrives at the Bettelwurfhütte (7,380 feet), a convenient point for breaking the journey into two bites of a day each.

In the left of the picture the snow-capped summit of the Kleine Bettelwurf (8,692 feet) is seen with clouds drifting about it; immediately to its right comes the great wedge of the Grosse Bettelwurf and on the extreme right the broad massif of the Fallbachkarspitze (8,445 feet).

These mountains form the north-eastern extension of Innsbruck's northern range, but they belong more properly to the Gleiersch-Halltal chain of the southern Karwendel range.

The Grosser Ahornboden in the Karwendel range

Anyone who has not seen the Grosser Ahornboden, the famous ›Maple Grove‹ in the Karwendel, cannot be said to know the Northern Limestone Alps, or indeed the Eastern Alps, at all well, for it is undeniably one of the loveliest beauty spots in the whole of the Alps.

The grove is at 4,585 feet in the Hinter Engtal, which can be reached by bus from Bad Tölz by way of Fall and Vorderriss, and adjoins the Engalm, on whose green meadows stands the mountain inn of Eng. Some of the maple trees are 800 years old, and the contrast between them and the limestone faces soaring some 3,000 feet to the sky behind them is overwhelming.

To the left of the picture rises the sharp summit of the Spritzkarspitze (8,560 feet), on the extreme right the 8,730-foot Grubenkarspitze.

The Eng area is not only a magnet for motorists in search of nature's beauties, but the perfect springboard for walks and longer rambles; but none of the peaks here can be climbed by anybody who is not an experienced mountaineer.

The best time of all to see the Maple Grove is in the autumn, when the colouring of their foliage is at its most gorgeous. The two-mile-long valley floor of the Eng is an absolute oasis of loveliness. On its level meadowland of 200 hectares grow more than a thousand mountain maples, the relics of a mixed forest, which hundreds of years ago completely filled the bowl at the foot of those mighty rock walls.

A few years ago, more than 400 saplings were planted here; they will have to remain protected by a fence for fifteen years, to guard against damage from pasturing cattle and less domestic creatures.

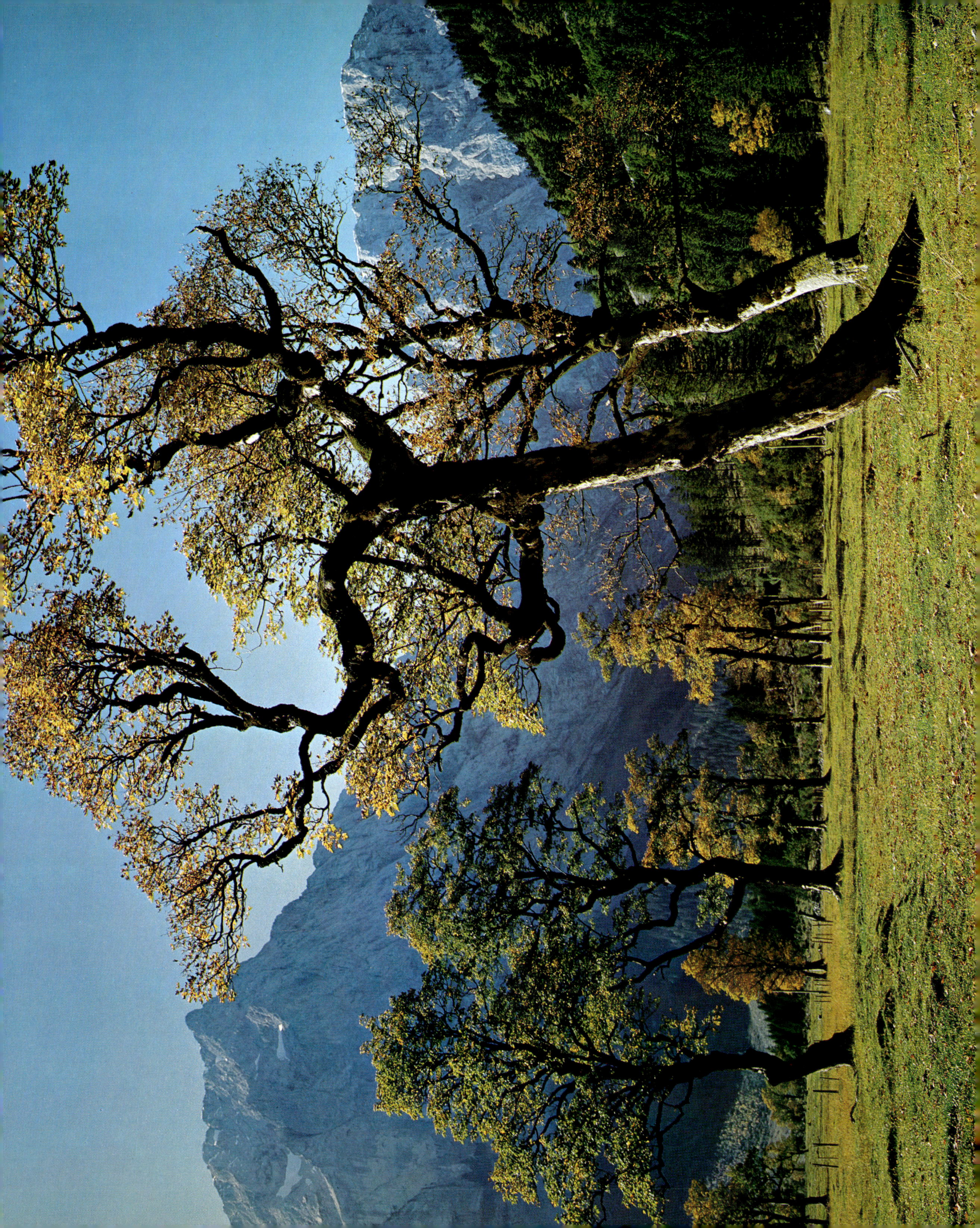

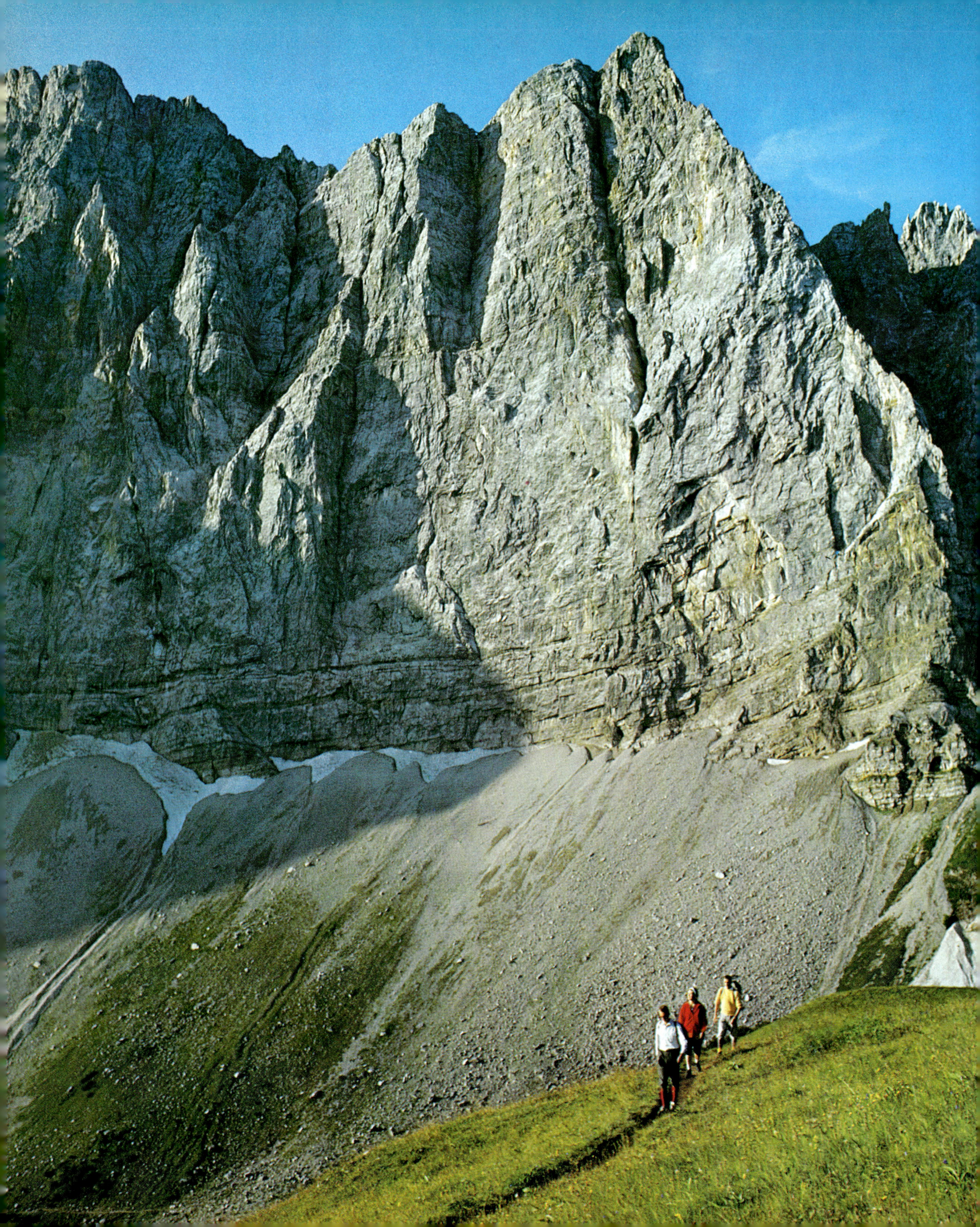

The Laliderer Walls in the Karwendel

Only four hours from the city of Munich, with its million inhabitants – an hour and a half by car and two and a half on foot – the most magnificent and impressive of all the spectacles to be found in the Northern Limestone Alps unfolds its wonders: the 3,000-foot high Laliderer Walls, with their great gulleys, arêtes and beetling overhangs of rock.

The photograph was taken close to the Falken Hut, the starting-point for the exciting crossing of the Karwendel range, which can be completed, without entailing the slightest danger, if needs be in three or four days; though it is much better to take a week over it, for so manifold are the beauties of nature in the Karwendel, which lies between Mittenwald, famous for its violins, and the Achensee, Innsbruck and Bad Tölz, that one could not tire of them in seven or, for that matter, fourteen days.

To the left of the picture soars the Laliderwand (8,577 feet), to the right of the centre the Laliderspitze (8,472 feet) and at the extreme right the towers of the Laditztürme. The north ridge of the Spitze is seen winging up in a single unbroken sweep to its summit.

The mountaineer who has the skill to master this sky-raking ladder (Grade VI: ›Extremely Severe‹) can rate himself a first-class climber. For that matter, anyone who includes any of the five great routes, slashing up these tremendous rock faces, in his repertoire is a true expert in his craft.

The contrary is true for the rambler who is fit enough; any lover of the mountains who is prepared to walk for several hours a day can enjoy the glorious scenery of the Karwendel to his heart's content.

The Grosse Löffler in the Zillertal Alps

The Grosse Löffler (11,095 feet) rises from the main comb of the Zillertal Alps, a sector of the central Eastern Alps. The frontier between Austria and Italy (South Tyrol) runs over its summit. Seen from the west, the mountain is a lovely pyramid of snow; from the north-east, the aspect shown in the picture, it is a massive rocky triangle. The peak's north-east face, impressively scored by steep gulleys between prominent ribs, rises some 1,400 feet from the heavily-crevassed Löfflerkees glacier at the far head of the Stillupptal. This offers a Grade III (›Difficult‹) climb, requiring four to five hours from the foot of the face to the summit.

The mountain is, however, normally climbed by its western slopes, starting from the Greizer Hut in the upper reaches of the Floitental; this is a very rewarding glacier tour, demanding three or four hours from the hut.

The summit is a magnificent observatory, with exciting views deep down into the valleys to the north, while to the south it commands the pleasant Pustertal (Val Pusteria) and the savage Dolomite spires beyond it. Close by, to the south-east, rises the fine Rieserferner group.

The Grosse Löffler can also be ascended from the Ahrntal to its south, where the Schwarzenstein Hut, standing on Italian soil, provides a springboard for the climb; but the ascent over the much-crevassed Pripbachkees glacier requires greater technical experience than the route from the Greizer Hut.

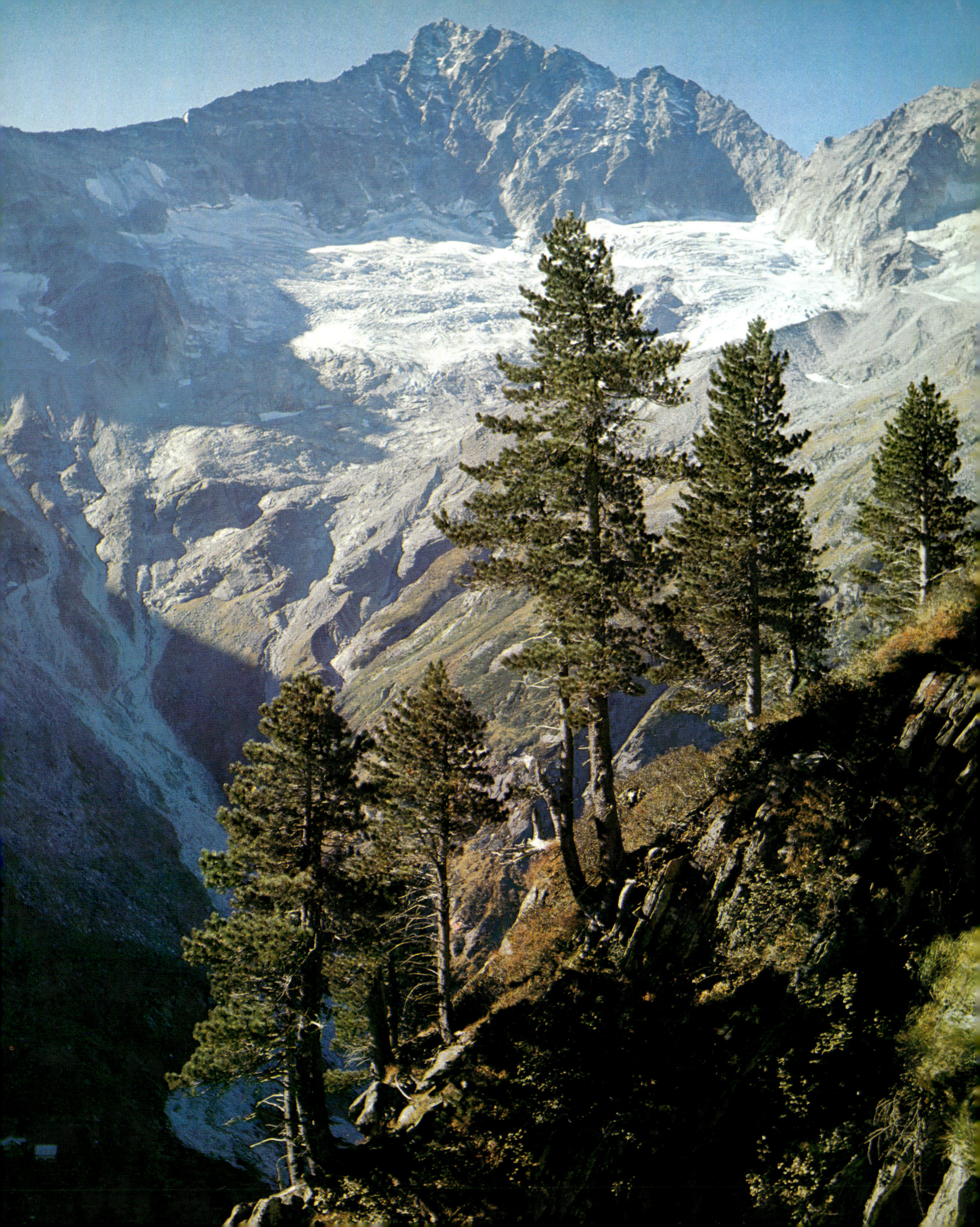

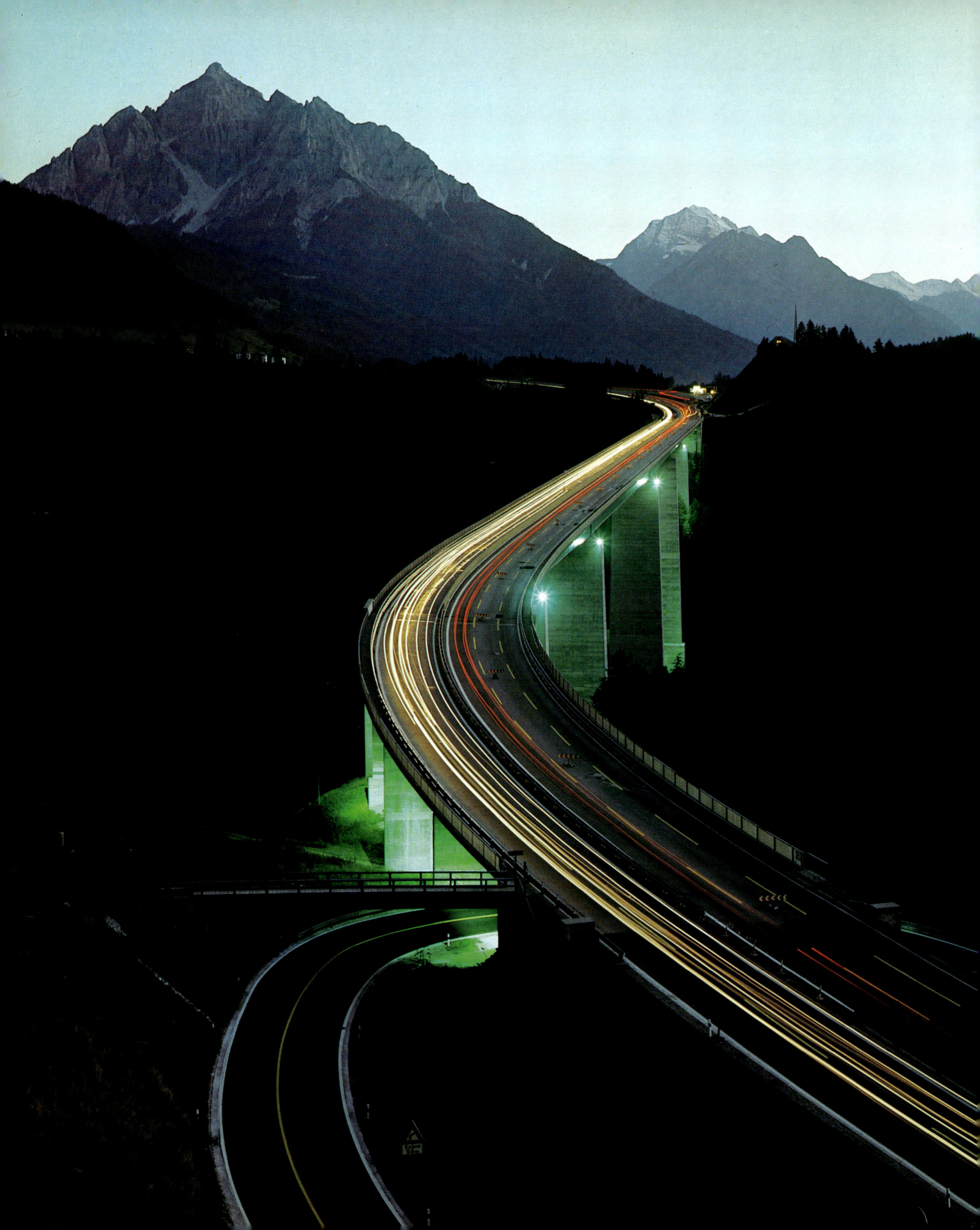

The Europabrücke with the Serles and the Habicht

Every motorist who has recently crossed the Brenner Pass into Italy will be familiar with this lovely view, harmonizing the beauties of superb engineering skill with those of nature, only a few minutes to the south of Innsbruck.

The Europa Bridge forms part of the great new *Autobahn* which, since 1963, has replaced the old historic northern approach to the 4,495-foot Pass, where Austria and Italy meet. When in due course the corresponding work on the steeper southern (Italian) side is complete, it will provide the essential mountain link in an unbroken motorway from the Channel coast to the network of *Autostrade* and so to Rome, Naples, Venice and Trieste.

As the lowest and gentlest of carriageways across the main backbone of the Alps, the Brenner, first mentioned in 13 BC, when Augustus crossed it from Roman Oenopontum (Innsbruck) to subdue the tribes of the Tyrol, has ever since been the traditional route for the invasion of the fertile Italian plain by northern ravagers – the Allemani and the Goths in the third century, Attila and his Huns, Odoacer and the Rugii, Theodoric and later the Ostrogoths and the Franks. It played a major part in the wars of Charlemagne and the Lombards, and in continual strife over the centuries, till in 1914, during the First World War, it was again submerged in bitter fighting.

In this brilliant photograph, on which the unbroken streamers of head- and tail-lights indicate the usual heavy traffic moving in both directions through the dusk of a clear evening, the sharp peak of the Serles (8,920 feet), one of Innsbruck's famous local landmarks, rises to the left of the bridge's graceful curve. The motorway continues to the left through the Wipptal to reach the summit of the pass in a few more miles. Directly behind the end of the bridge is seen the 10,760-foot snowy crown of the Habicht, which rises above the Stubaital, a lovely valley continuing beyond the right-hand edge of the picture and ending in the Stubai peaks of the great frontier-range, among which there is to be found much delectable snow and glacier climbing of no great technical difficulty, from a number of comfortable and well-serviced huts.

The summit of the Habicht itself can be reached by a marked path through the Pinnstal from Neustift in the Stubai Valley.

The view from the Patscherkofel towards the Stubai Alps

This glorious view to the south from the Patscherkofel (7,265 feet) can be enjoyed by every rambler, for the mountain, which rises steeply from the southern outskirts of Innsbruck, is accessible by cable-railway up to 6,420 feet and thence it is less than 1,000 feet more to the summit by path.

The wooded spurs of the Serles with its sharp, dark summit (just to the right of the tall pine), divide the main valley rising from Innsbruck (bottom right) into the Wipptal, through which the Brenner road runs up to the left, and the deep trench of the Stubaital, stretching away in the right centre for fifteen lovely miles to lose itself in the snowy, glaciated regions of the high Stubai peaks (Zuckerhütl 11,520 feet, Wilde Freiger, Wilde Pfaff and others of about 11,000 feet, all ascended from the Dresdener and Nürnberger Huts) at its distant end. This sector of the main Alpine chain forms the frontier ridge between Austria and Italy. One of the most attractive and relatively easy climbs in the district is that of the Zuckerhütl; from its summit there are superb views away across the upper valley of the Adige, far below in Italy, to the distant towers and spires of the Dolomites and the huge Ortler (12,800 feet) with its snowy satellites.

The dark limestone group of the Kalkkögel (highest peak 9,210 feet) on the extreme right of the picture, though composed entirely of rock peaks, offering rock climbing of great severity, actually forms part of the otherwise higher and glaciated Stubai Alps.

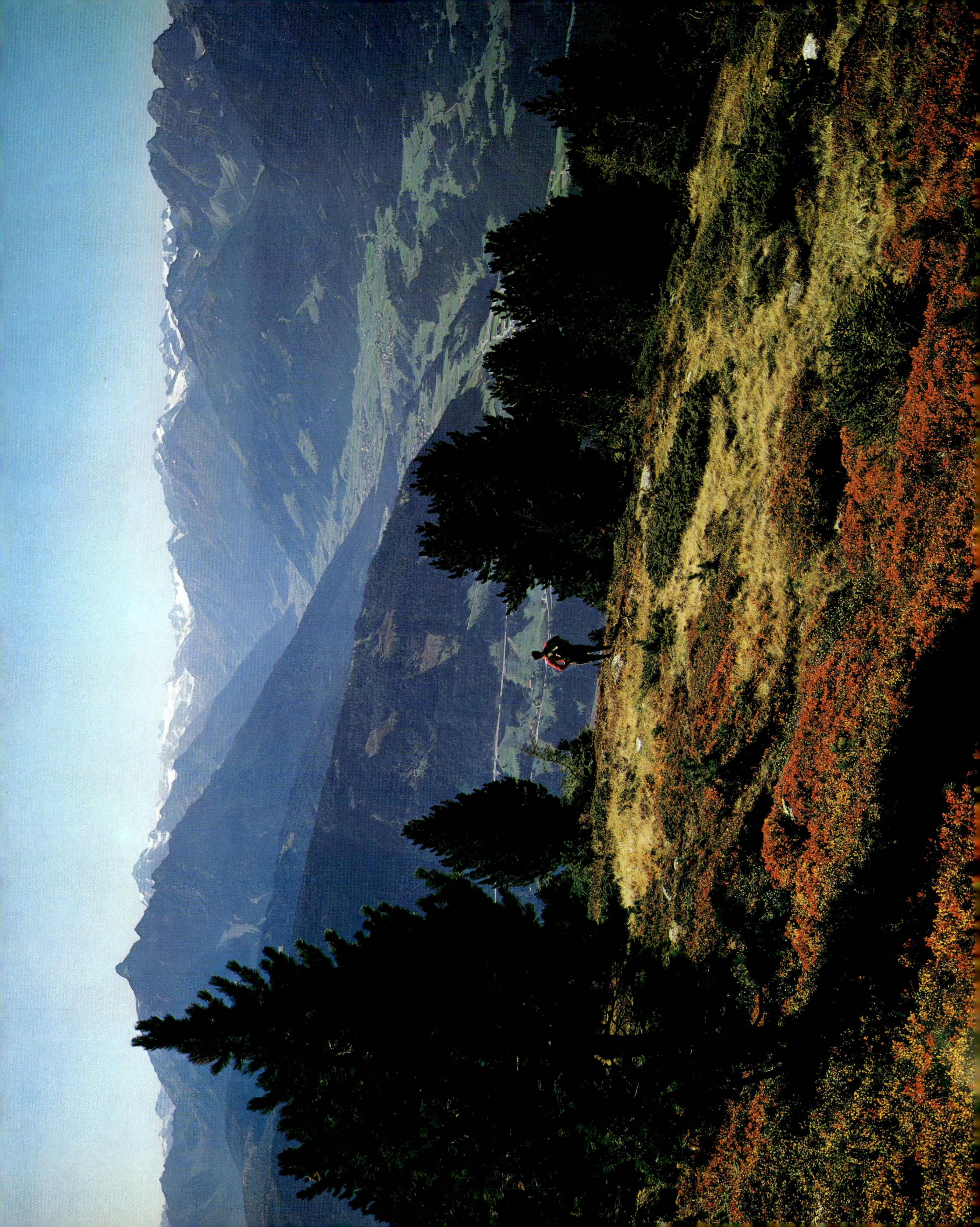

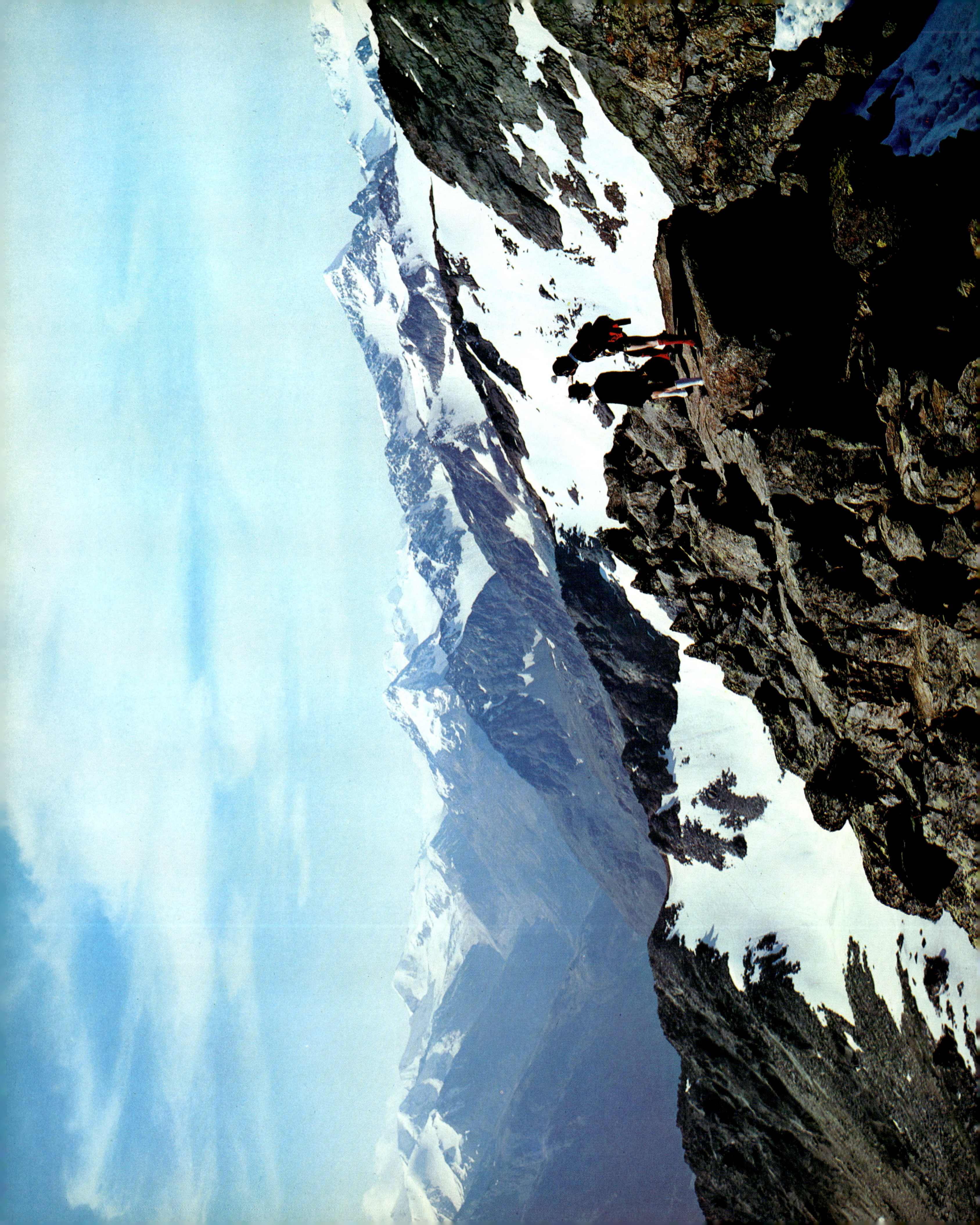

The main chain of the Ötztal Alps from the Geislachkogel

The Geislachkogel (10,015 feet), to the south-west of Sölden in the Ötztal, was not much visited until recent years, which is an illuminating thought, for its ropeway happens to be of recent construction. Now that it has become possible to climb this three-thousand-metre peak in the comfort of a ropeway-cabin, young and old alike can be seen disporting themselves on and about its summit.

In summer it is a most rewarding view-point, from which the wide prospect towards the main Ötztal chain opens up in all its splendour; in winter, a ski-mountain, with headlong downhill runs on it and also offering a starting-point for one or two high-level skiing tours.

At the right hand edge of the picture can be seen the snowy eastern spurs falling from the unseen Wildspitze (12,380 feet), the highest peak in the Ötztaler Alps, which can, in early spring, be ascended almost to the very top on ski. To their left rises the graceful white pyramid of the 11,190-foot Weisserkogel, whose long east ridge falls away to the left into the Ventertal. Remote, beyond the far head of the valley, stands the snowy triangle of the Similaun (11,835 feet), across whose summit runs the frontier between Austria and the (Italian) South Tyrol. At the extreme left, in shadow, rises the snow pyramid of the Hintere Schwärze (11,020 feet).

Ehrwald and the Zugspitze

Bavaria, famous for more breweries than (even) moderately high mountains of about 8,200 feet, is forced to share the 9,720-foot Zugspitze, Germany's highest peak, with its neighbour, the Austrian Tyrol.

During the last few decades, the Zugspitze has definitely become a railway and ropeway summit, for the Bavarians have two aerial ropeways, a railway and three ski-lifts (as far as the Platt); while the Austrians also command a ropeway, which overleaps a 5,200-foot differential between Ehrwald, at the foot of the mountain, and its summit, and covers the cable's actual length of 3,413 yards in seventeen minutes. When the area of the mountain mass was partitioned, the Tyrolese came off rather badly, for they were only given possession of the peak's north-western third.

In the photograph, the actual summit can be seen clearly on the extreme left. Immediately to its right are the Schneefernerkopf, the Wetterspitzen and, on the extreme right, the Plattspitze.

Hardy walkers who scorn ropeways can reach the summit on Shanks's pony in seven hours from Ehrwald; those who do so report that the beer at the Münchner Haus on the summit tastes exceptionally good.

The shoulder of the Ehrwalderkopf (about 7,500 feet) appears near the left-hand edge of the picture. At this point it is possible to leave the ropeway in order to ski down to the valley; but only in the late winter and even then the descent is for expert ski-runners only.

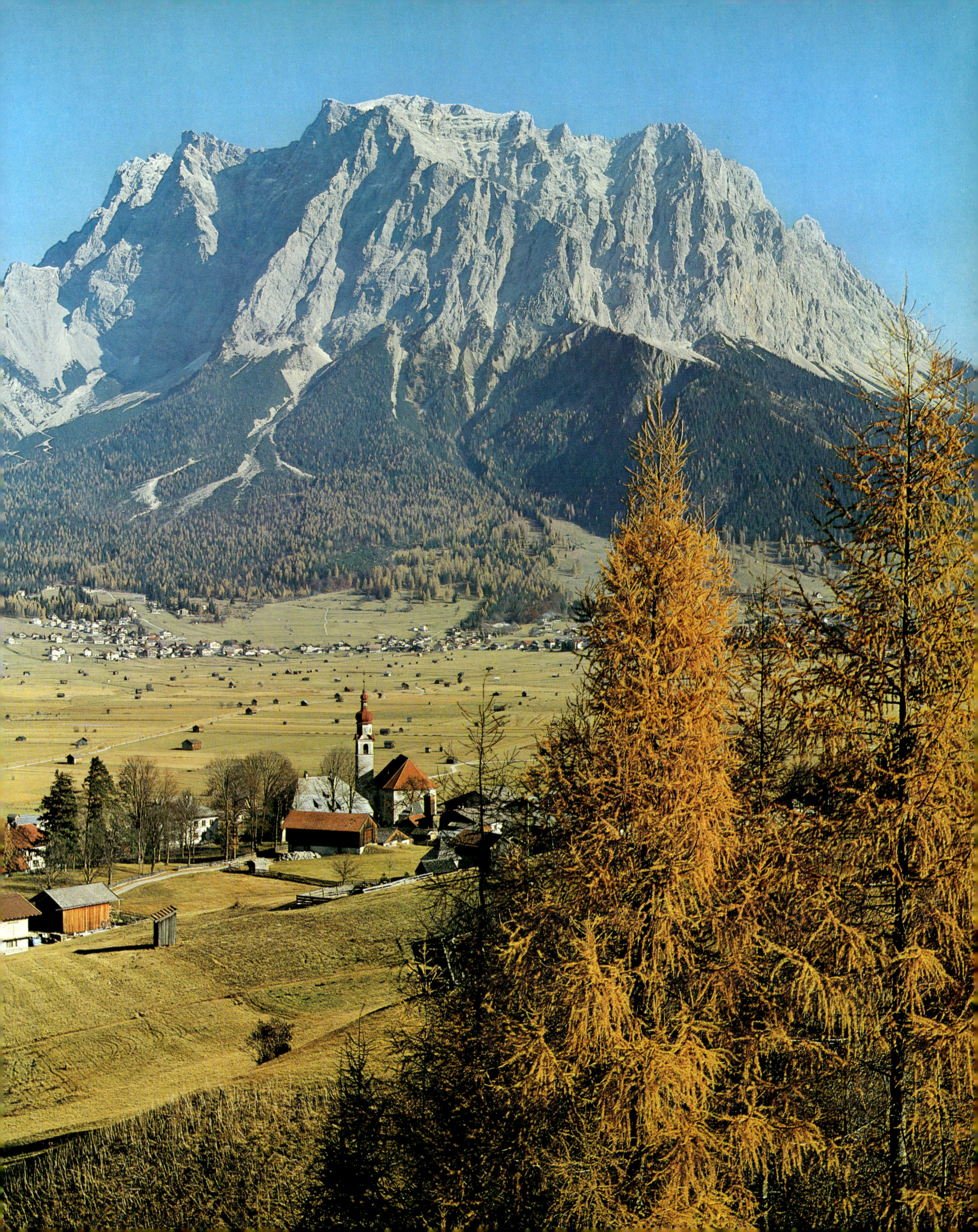

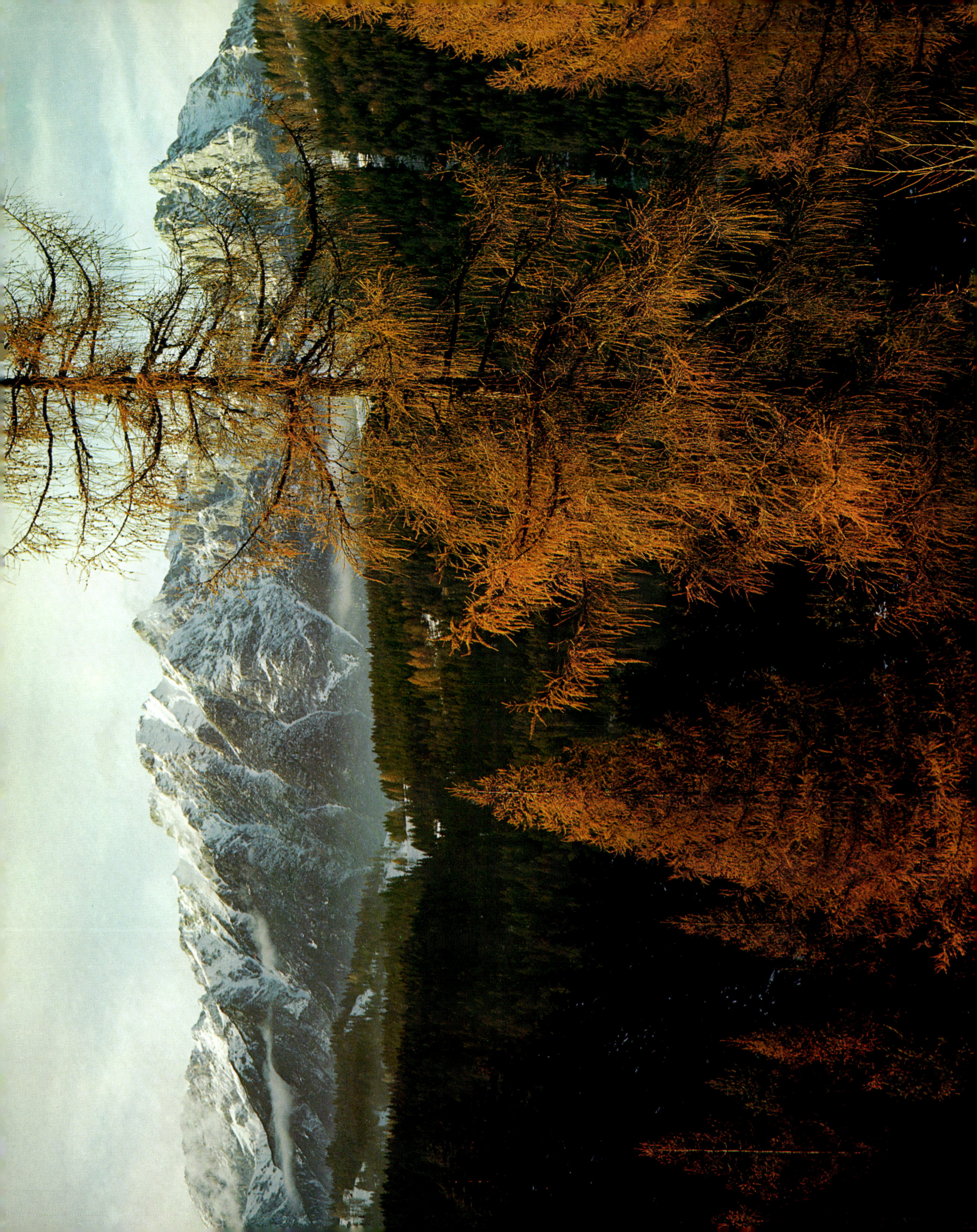

The view from the Wetterstein, near Seefeld

Seefeld is a summer and winter sports resort situated between the Wetterstein range to its north-west and the Karwendel to its east. It lies, at a height of 3,870 feet, surrounded by wooded hills, which provided the course for the ›Langlauf‹ cross-country ski-race of the 1964 Winter Olympic Games. In summer, and especially in the autumn, when the golden hue of the larches enhances the beauty of the scene, the district is a favourite area for extended rambles and quiet walks.

This picture shows one of the great ridges of the Wetterstein range rising above the autumnal larches. On the right are the twin summits of the Öfelekopf (8,170 feet), which yield good rock climbs for the expert. The centre is occupied by the riven massif of the 8,770-foot Leutscher Dreitorspitze, while at the left-hand end rises the broad south face of the Schüsselkarspitze, 8,380 feet high. The total length of the mountain-comb shown in the photograph is about three miles, and it continues for another ten, to end in the Zugspitze massif.

On the Hohe Ifen, in the Allgäu Alps

The Hohe Ifen (7,315 feet) rises above the Kleines Walsertal in the Schwarzwasser range of the Allgäuer Alpen and forms parts of the boundary between Germany (Bavaria) and the Austrian province of Vorarlberg. While it only rises to a modest elevation, its unusual rock structure promotes it to the status of one of the most remarkable mountains in the Eastern Alps. Its higher levels consist of huge expanses of ribbed rock, covering an area of about three square miles, which look exactly like a petrified glacier.

These rocky deserts are not without their dangers for the rambler and the mountaineer; for to move about them in safety one must be not only sure-footed but well and appropriately shod. Moreover, on the Gottesacker Plateau (›God's Acre‹!) the onset of mists can lead to very unpleasant experiences, for it is extremely difficult to find the way, owing to the confusing similarity of its rock formations. In good conditions of weather and rock, however, the ascent of the Ifen presents the practised mountain rambler with no serious problems, the summit being reached from the Schwarzwasser Hut in two and a half hours by way of a marked path.

The photograph shows part of the fine view to the south-east. On the horizon, in the centre of the picture, rises the Trettachspitze, with the broad massif of the Mädelegabel, 8,765 feet, to its right. At the feet of the mountains lies the Kleines Walsertal Valley.

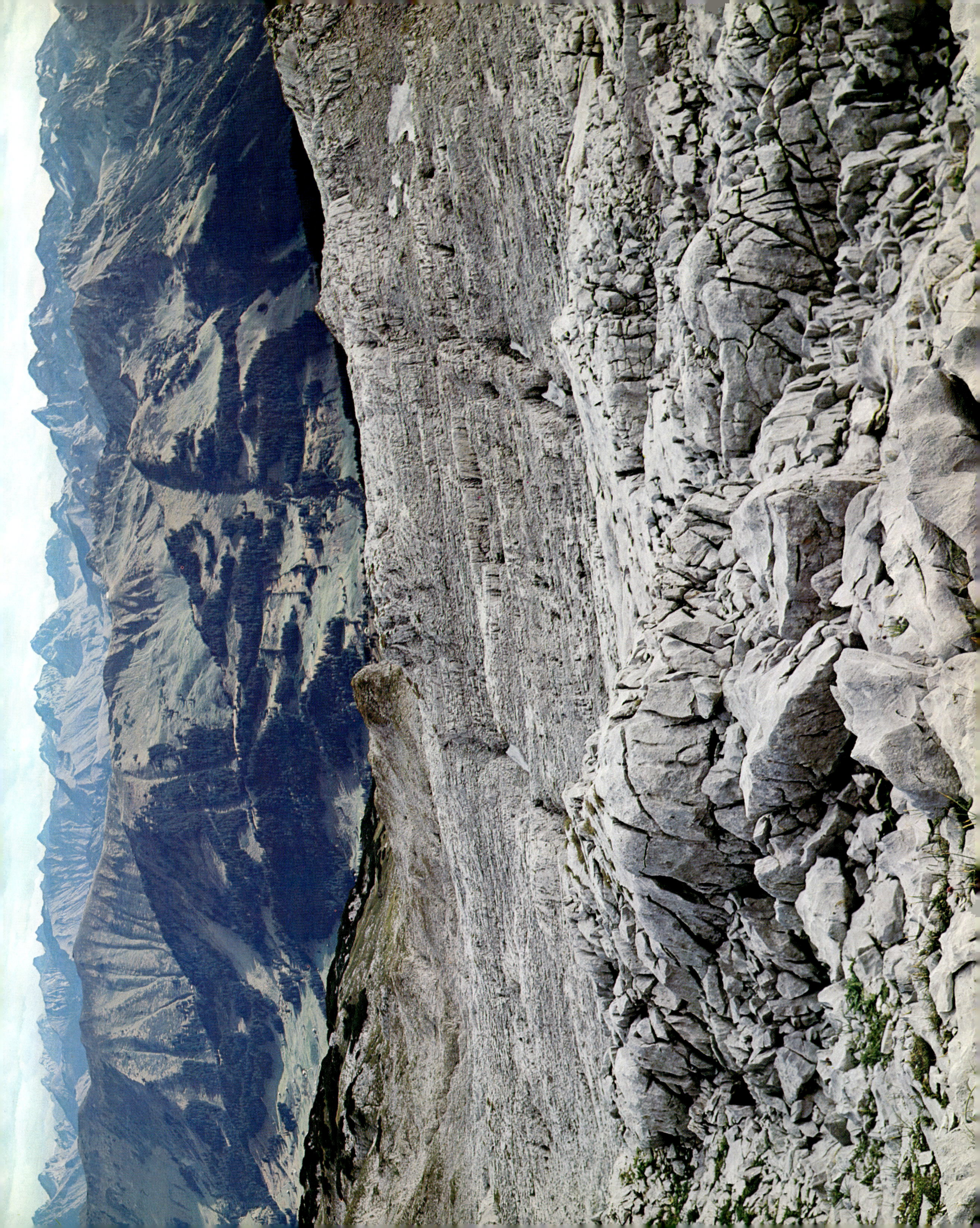

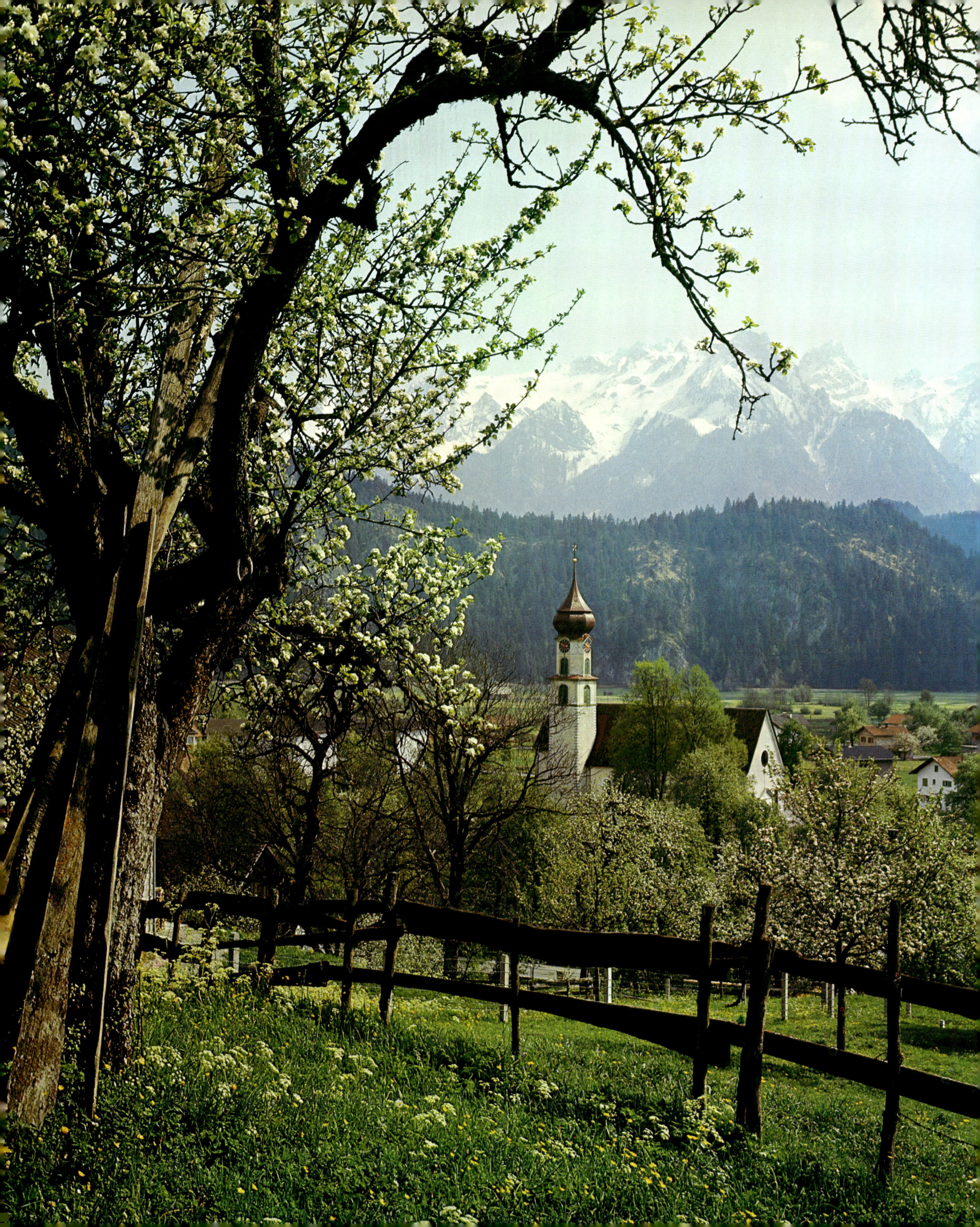

Ludesch, in the Rätikon – Vorarlberg range

The little summer-holiday resort of Ludesch lies, at an elevation of 1,820 feet, where the Grosswalzertal falls into the Walgau, as the district between the Vorarlberg's two regional capitals, Feldkirch and Bludenz, is named. The village is only five miles from Bludenz itself.

This quiet place, lying well away from the main road, and not to be confused with Bludesch, its neighbour only two miles to the west, remains undisturbed by the great rush of tourist traffic by-passing it at no great distance.

In springtime, always so delectable a season anywhere in Alpine regions, Ludesch is at its very best. Little more than five miles away rise the Rätikon peaks, still mantled by the winter snows, forming the frontier ridge between Austria's Vorarlberg, Switzerland and, incidentally, Liechtenstein, the little principality caught up between the two.

In the adjoining picture, the dark mass of the Zwölferkopf (7,450 feet) rises behind a blossom-laden branch, with a part of the long Hüttenkopfstock flanking it on the left, and to its right, behind it, the shapely spire of the 8,680-foot Zimba, known as the ›Matterhorn of the Vorarlberg‹.

Cheesemaker at work in the Allgäu

Even in this atomic age, life and work go on in the huts on the high meadows and green alps much as they have for hundreds of years past. True, electric light is occasionally to be found in a hut up there, but the course of the day's work has seen no material changes.

There are basically two different types of pasture ground up on the alps: store-herd alps (the ›Galtvieh Almen‹, ›galt‹ meaning non-milk-giving), which are concerned only with cattle rearing, though a few cows are mostly kept alongside the oxen and calves, simply to supply milk, butter and cheese for home consumption. There is no difficulty in distinguishing one of these from a cow-alp (›Kuh Alpe‹): it normally consists of only one, or at the most, two huts, in which the meat herds live and the few cows are sheltered.

On the cow-alps there is usually a big main hut, where cowherds, cheese-makers and, it may be, their womenfolk live, and the milk is prepared and processed, with up to fifty stalls and sheds for cows, according to the extent of the alp, surrounding it. Generally, too, the ground of a cow-alp is softer and less steep than the other kind of alp, for young beasts are understandably more mobile than cows.

The milk is heated to 35° Centigrade (95° Fahrenheit) in the great cauldrons and brought to the point where it curdles by half an hour of continual stirring.

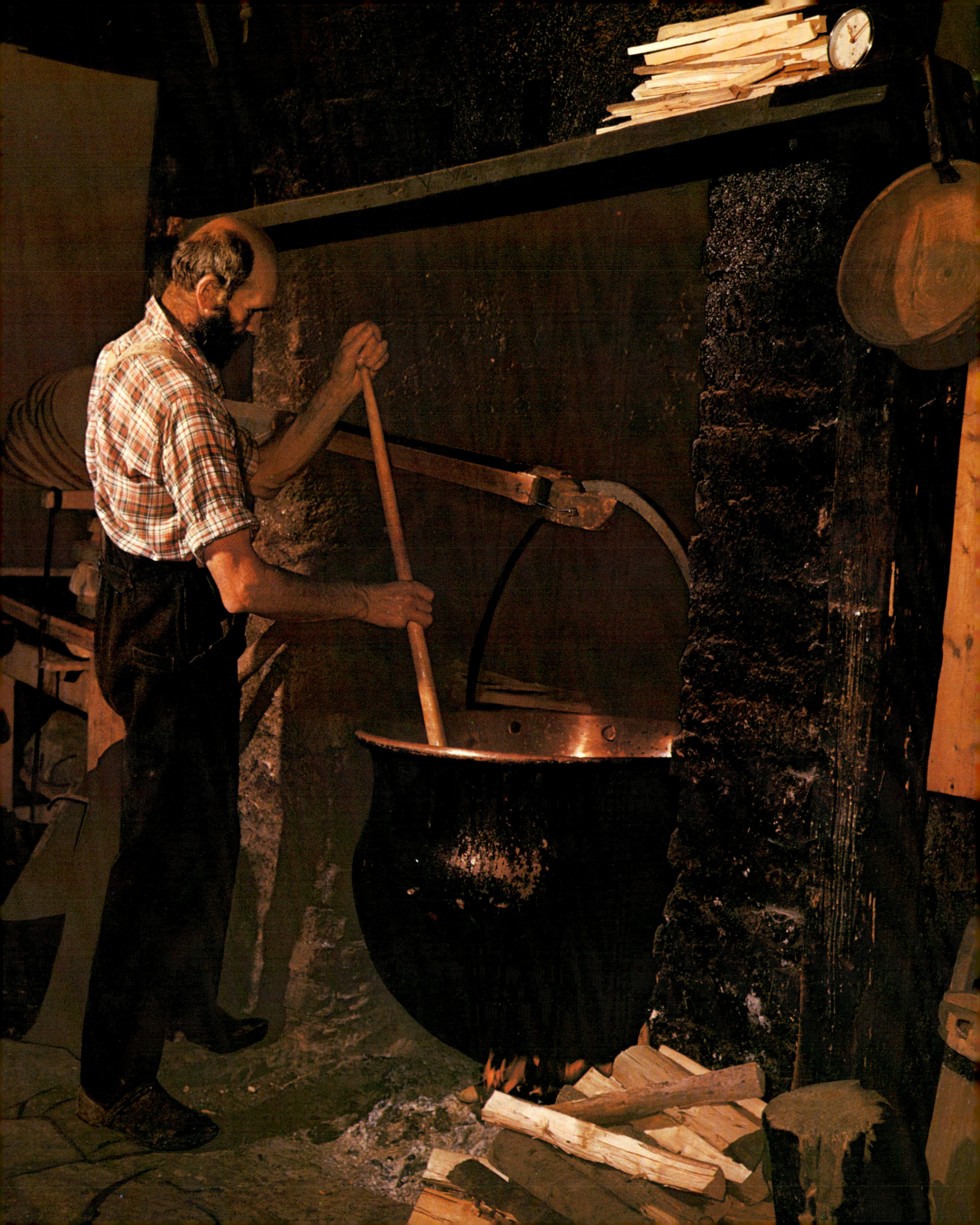

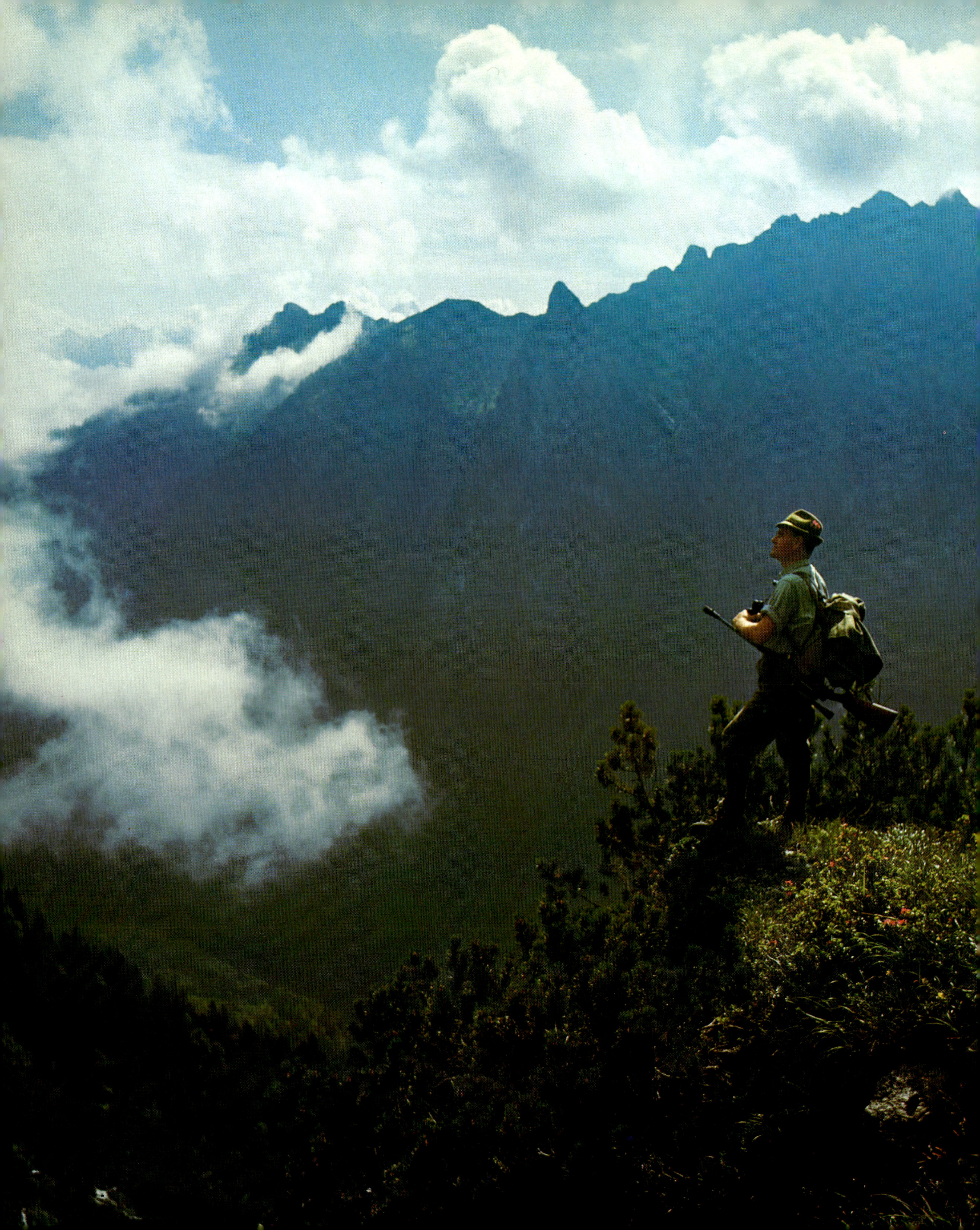

Above the Saminatal, near Feldkirch in the Vorarlberg

The Saminatal, the northernmost valley of the Rätikon, was in days gone by a favourite happy hunting ground for enthusiastic poachers of two different nationalities, for the frontier between the Duchy of Liechtenstein and Austria's western province, the Vorarlberg, runs plumb through its middle. During the difficult years following the Second World War the poachers were joined by smugglers – a clear indication of how wild the valley is, for smugglers and poachers generally choose the loneliest of regions for the conduct of their profession. Today, however, the only people one meets in the Saminatal besides hunters and woodcutters are walkers, ramblers and climbers.

The valley and its stream, the Saminabach, start in the Falknis group on Liechtenstein territory; it is bounded on its western side by the Drei Schwestern group (The Three Sisters, 6,970 feet), the most northerly range of rock peaks in the Rätikon. High up in the valley lies the hamlet of Steg, a quiet holiday haunt of the Liechtensteiners. A ramble from Feldkirch upwards to Steg and down to Vaduz is to be highly recommended to every lover of mountain scenery.

The Karwendel range from the Wagenbruchsee

Almost exactly half-way between Garmisch-Partenkirchen and Mittenwald, a world-famous home of violin manufacture, and a little to the north of the main road, stands the little village of Gerold, close to which lies the Wagenbruchsee, generally known to the locals as the Geroldssee.

It is not a very big lake – not quite half a mile long and 300 yards wide – but it will delight the heart of every nature-lover in search of beautiful scenery; for here he will find meadows, deep-blue water, woodlands and, behind it all, the huge backcloth of the Northern Karwendel range and its peaks. You do not have to look twice to realize that this is an Alpine enthusiast's dream.

In the early winter, when the photographer caught the scene, the high places in this mountain range are out of bounds to all but very experienced mountaineers, but they can still be ›ascended‹ by ropeway, as is, for example, the 7,825-foot Karwendelspitze (at the right-hand edge of the picture), whose top station is sited close under the summit, starting from Mittenwald.

In the picture, the Larchetfleckspitze (7,380 feet), Tiefkarspitze (7,924 feet) and the Wörner (8,070 feet) dominate the ridge to the left, while at the extreme left the base of the Eastern Karwendelspitze (8,274 feet) can be seen appearing behind the tree. The sector of the ridge seen in the photograph is about six miles long; the distance between the Wagenbruch Lake and the mountains about the same.

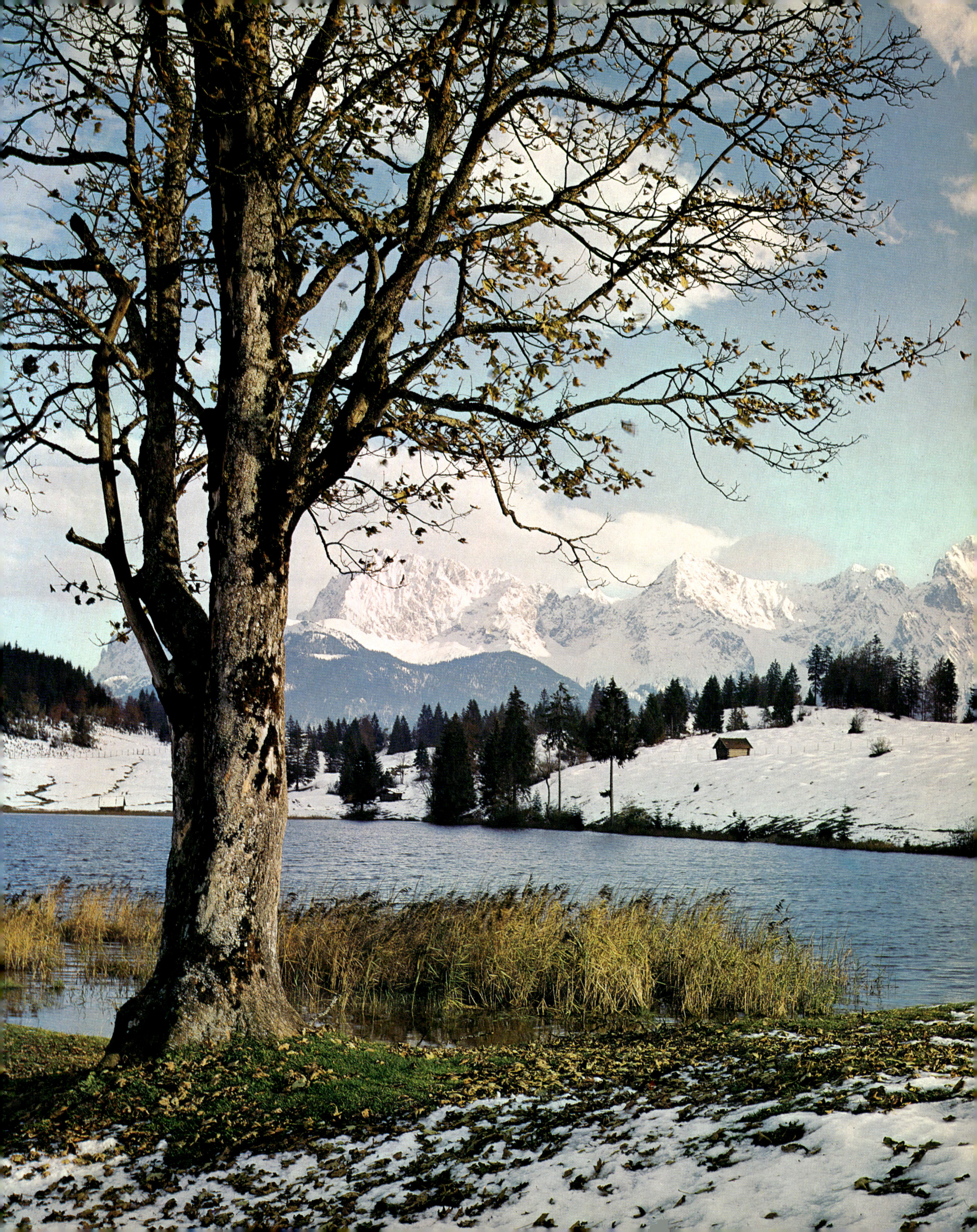

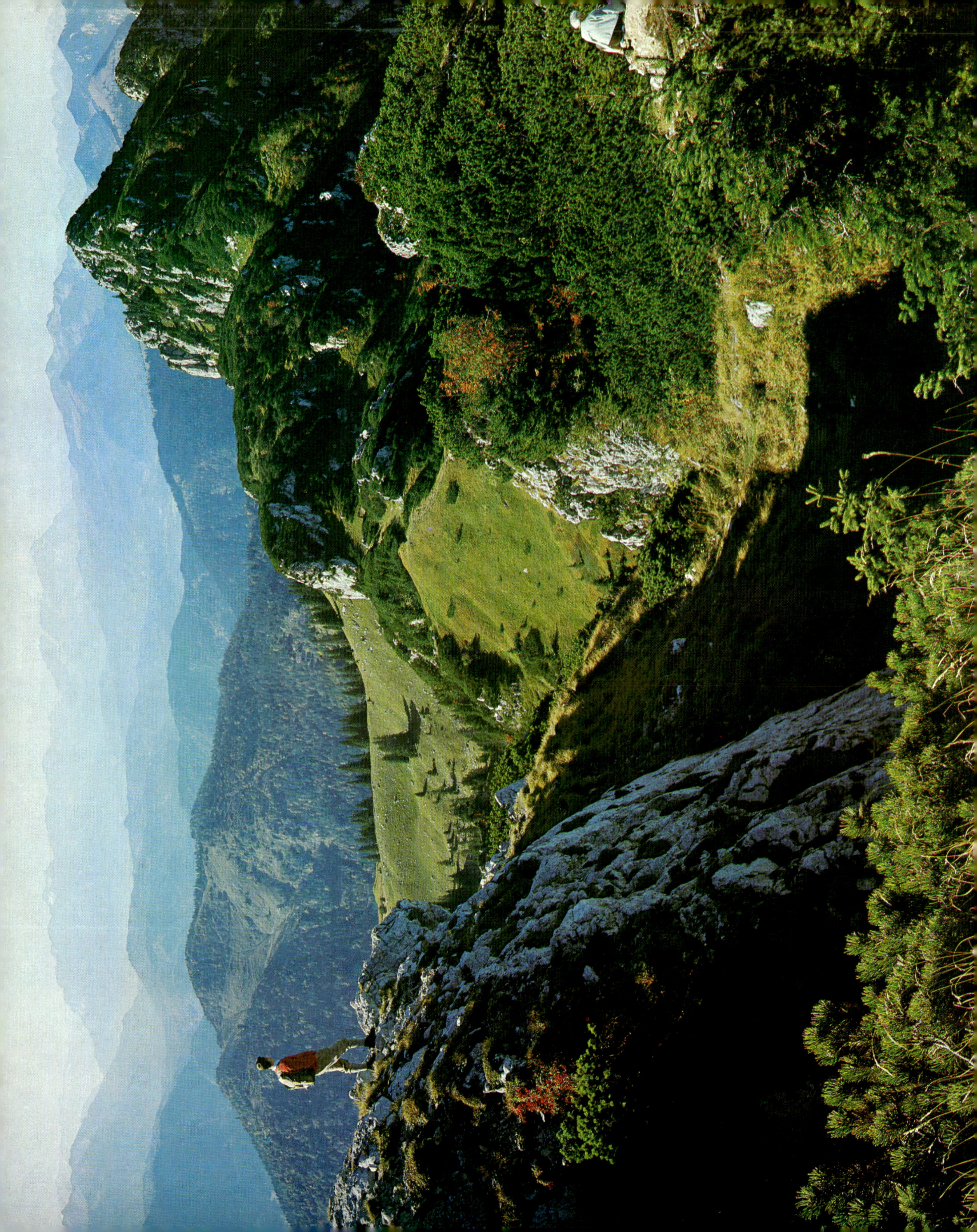

Looking south to the Zugspitze from the Brauneck

The 5,100-foot Brauneck near Bad Tölz is an elevation in the foothills of the Bavarian Alps. It is a perfect ›observation balcony‹ and has the advantage that it can be comfortably reached from Lenggries by cable-cabin. In autumn, when the air is crystal-clear, the main chain of the Alps can be seen, apparently at no great distance from the south.
A dozen or more paths snake their way through woods and between meadows up and on the Brauneck; they are almost all completely free from danger and constitute a rambler's joy. These easy strolls can be prolonged to the west by the more experienced as far as the Benediktwand and beyond it to Kochel on the shores of the similarly-named lake. These longer walks are facilitated by the presence of several huts.
The Brauneck is primarily the province of the Munich ski-addicts; it has even been dubbed ›the Munich Arlberg‹. The two main runs are extremely steep affairs, finishing at Lenggries in the valley.
The western spurs of the Karwendel range can be seen near the top left-hand edge of the picture. Mittenwald lies in the deep valley trench, with the Wetterstein sweeping away to its right. Thirty-five miles away, in the mists of the central background, rises the Zugspitze.

The view towards the Inn Valley from the Zugspitze

This picture can leave little doubt in the viewer's mind as to the magnificence of the view from the Zugspitze. Even those who have won their way to this 9,720-foot summit with the effortless aid of the ropeway can feel little compunction in enjoying it to the full.

The centre of the picture is occupied by the sharp cone of the 9,010-foot Hochwanner, with its sombre north face in deep shadow. Immediately above it rises the Solstein (8,340 feet), already part of the Karwendel range, which stretches away to the left. High up on the extreme right, part of the main Inn Valley is visible, with the Stubaital branching away from it towards the south (see plate 31). The deep bowl occupied by Innsbruck is hidden by the Karwendel and the dark wooded ridge running down to the right of the Solstein. The central and left-hand sectors of the horizon are crowned by the snowy heads of the high peaks in the Zillertal Alps (Hochfeiler, 11,560 feet, Olperer, 11,415 feet, Mösele, 11,435 feet and Gross Löffler, 11,095 feet). Beyond them, on the extreme left, can be seen, at a great distance, the Hohe Tauern range, including the Grossglockner (12,460 feet) and Gross Venediger (12,010 feet), the two highest peaks in Austria and the Eastern Alps.

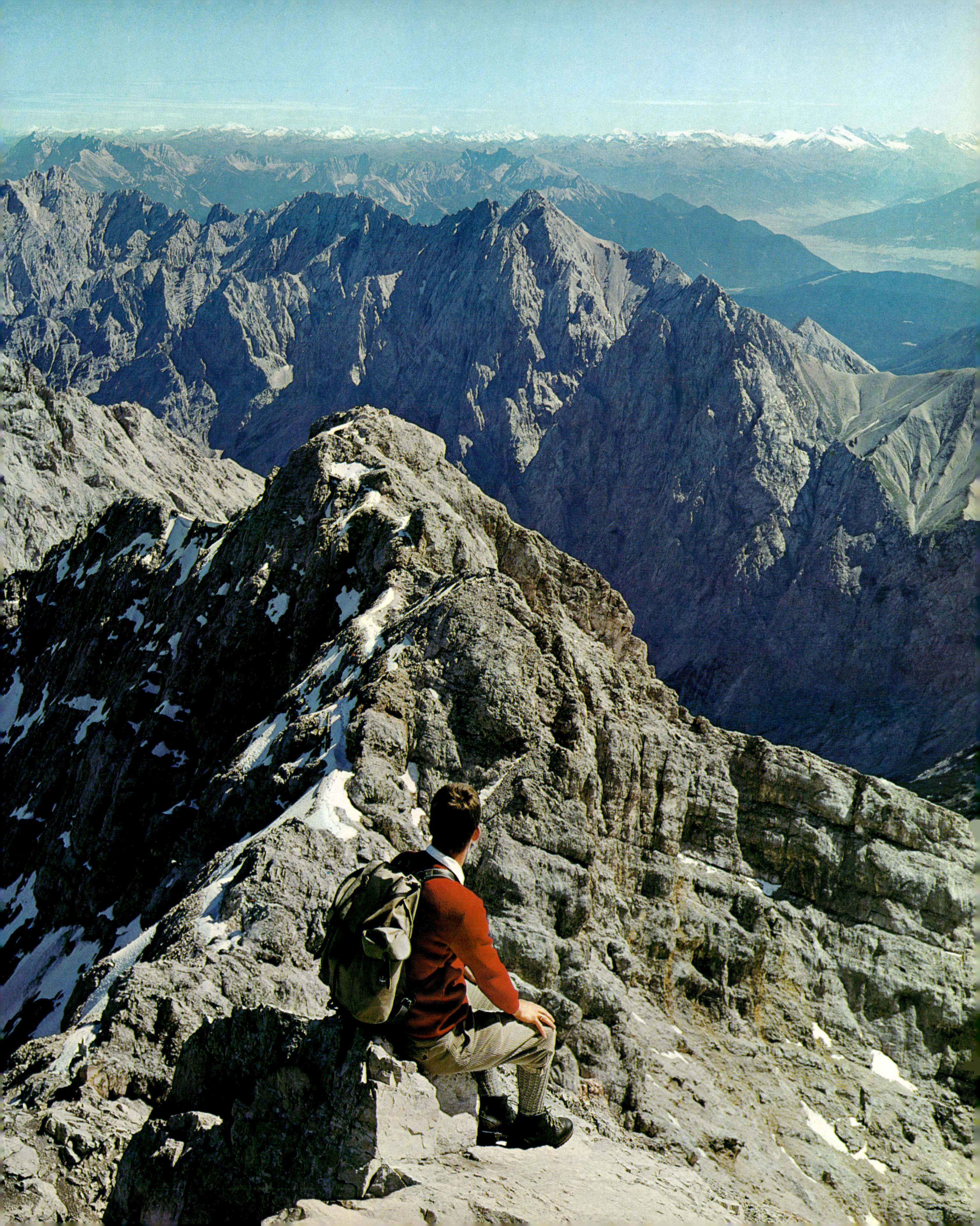

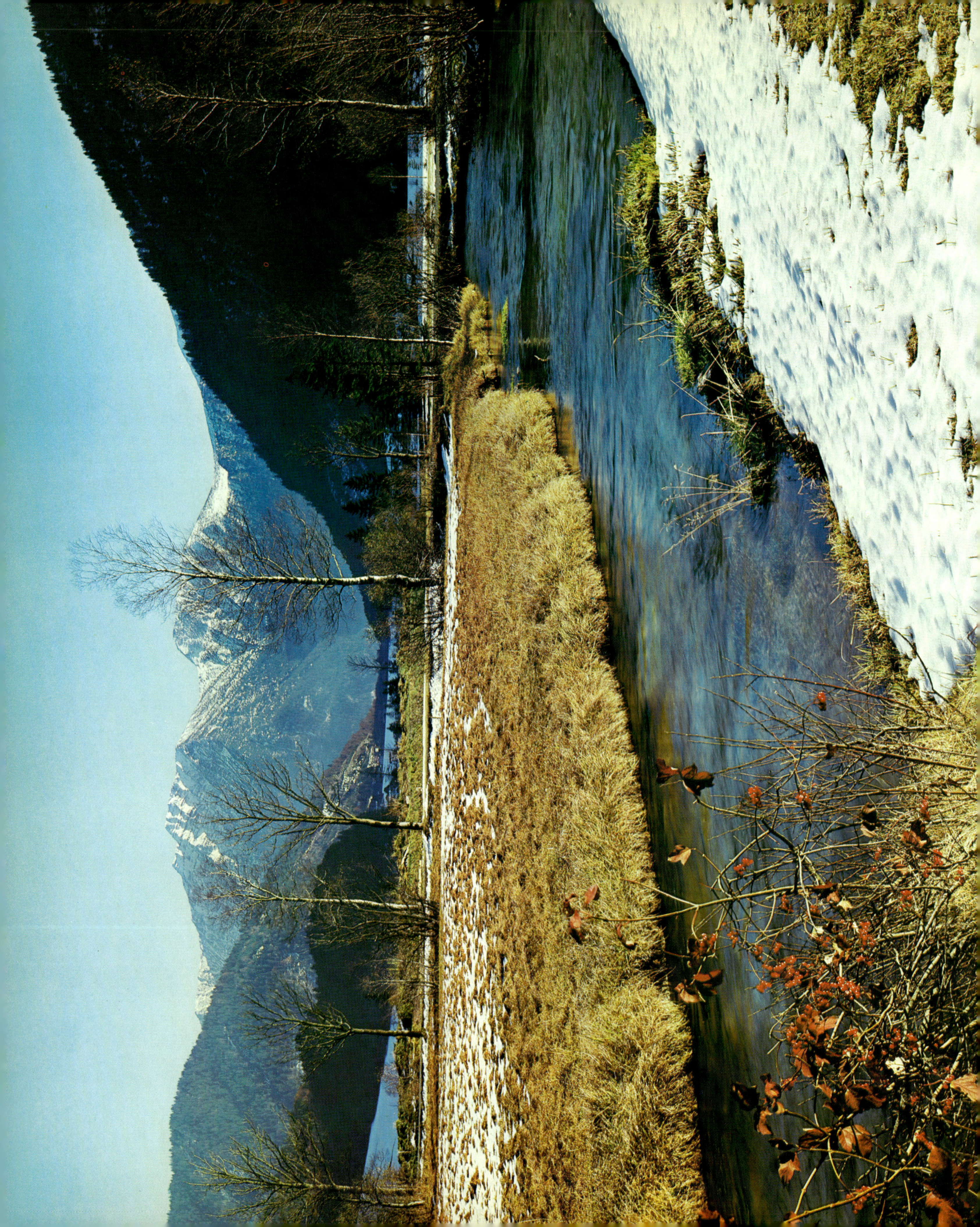

The Estergebirge range, Werdenfels, Upper Bavaria

The motorist driving southwards from Munich along the Olympia Highway comes to the village of Oberau in the Loisachtal, a few miles before arriving at the Winter Olympic city of Garmisch-Partenkirchen. At this point the road to Ettal and Oberammergau branches off westwards. A little way beyond Ettal along this road you bear right towards Linderhof and – if you are wise – stop the car to enjoy the view back to the lovely landscape shown in this photograph.
The Loisach Valley lies at the feet of the gentle mountains in the background. The tall silver birch tree covers the Bischof (6,658 feet); to the left stretches the soft outline of the 6,723-foot Risskopf, two of the highest summits in the little Estergebirge, which runs southwards to near Garmisch-Partenkirchen and is a much-favoured range for extensive rambles, especially as it is now possible to gain height rapidly by chair-lift and so find easy access to not too strenuous excursions.

In the Ahrntal, to the south of the Zillertal Alps

The fifteen-mile-long Ahrntal in South Tyrol (Italy) is to all intents and purposes the continuation of the Taufertal's ten miles to the north of Bruneck, the chief town in the Pustertal.

It falls from the 9,560-foot Glockenkarkopf, which the Italians have ingeniously renamed ›Vetta d'Italia‹ (›the Summit of Italy‹) and which is the most northerly peak in this Italian province[1]. The Ahrntal, an unspoiled summer-holiday region, is contained on the north by the main ridge of the Zillertal Alps. Close on a dozen charming rural villages nestle in the valley, their inhabitants as yet untouched by the hectic bustle of the present day. And for this reason the Ahrntal is a place much loved by those who prefer to spend their leave far from the madding crowd. There are all sorts of delightful walks in and about this valley, which retains its beauty and charm all the way up to the tree-level.

For the experienced mountaineer there are attractive opportunities among the peaks and glaciers of the Zillertal Alps at the head of the valley. These range from easy glacier tours to ice faces of great difficulty, which only trained and experienced experts can safely tackle.

The picture was taken near Luttach, looking up towards some of the Zillertal peaks just raising their heads in the far background.

---

[1] In conformity with Robert Löbl's preference in the original book, the German names in use before the transfer of the South Tyrol have been retained, as have such names as Ortler, Langkofel, Grödnertal, etc., throughout. The Ahrntal is now shown on Italian maps as Val Aurina, Bruneck as Brunico, Luttach as Lutago, the Pustertal as Val Pusteria.

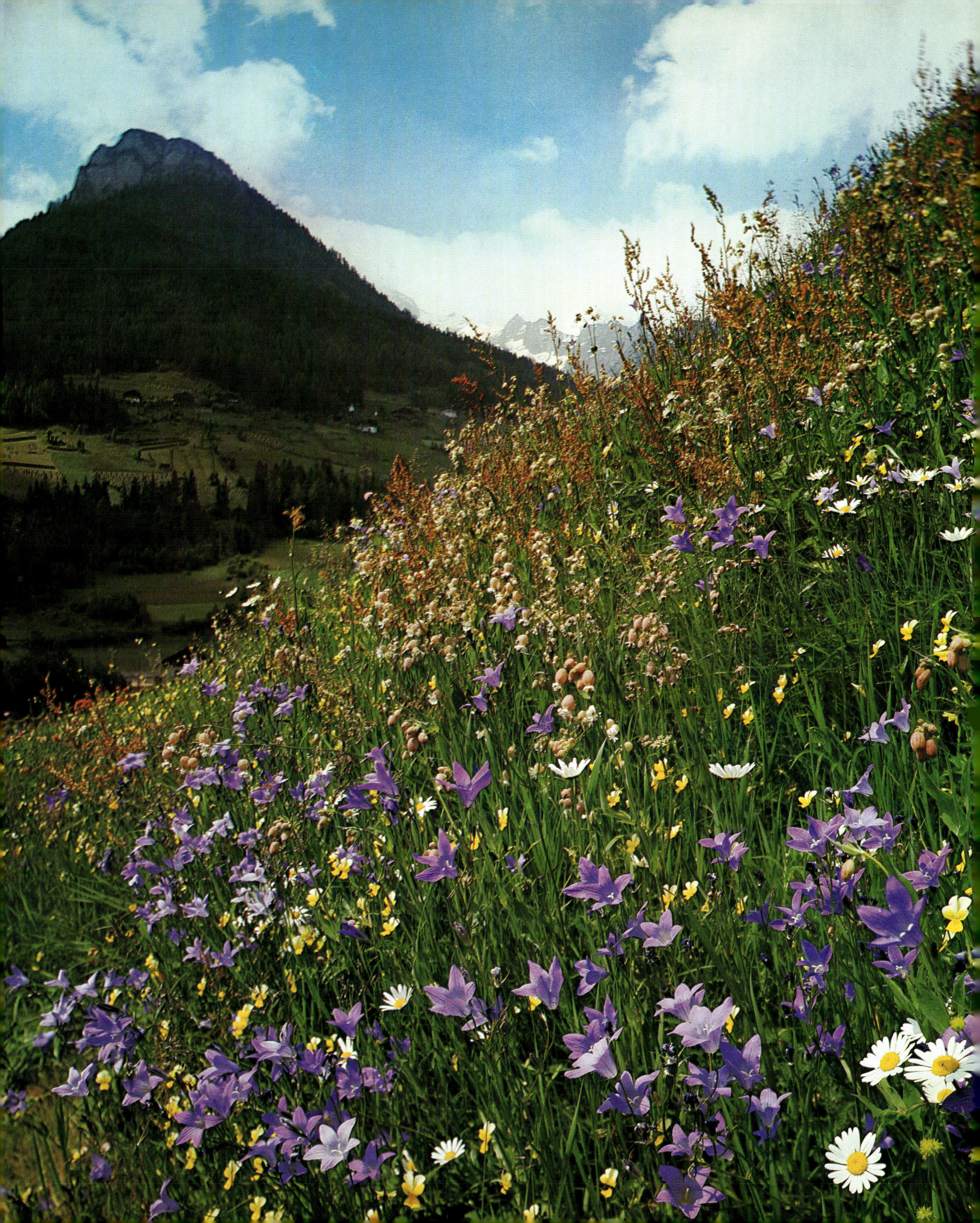

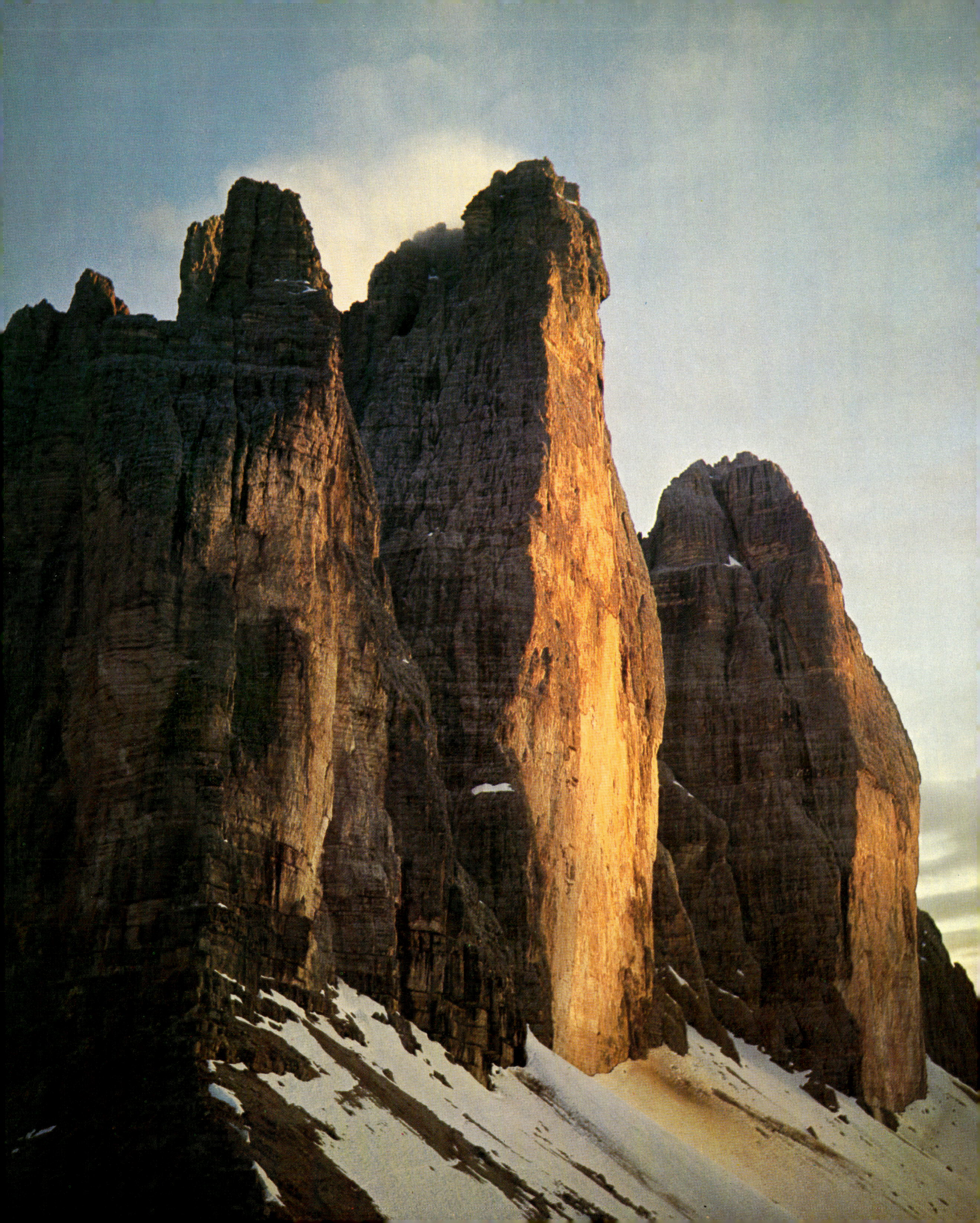

The Drei Zinnen, in the Sexten Dolomites

When, on a summer evening, the light of the setting sun is conjured by low veils of cloud to deepest red, the gigantic pillars of the Drei Zinnen[1] go soaring like enormous torches to the blue sky above.

Actually there are five, not three, Zinnen: to the left, the massif of the Kleine Zinne, which has three summits – Kleinste (smallest) Zinne, Punta di Frida and the Kleine Zinne itself – offering the rock-enthusiast many a rewarding climb.

In the centre the Grosse Zinne (9,850 feet), whose climbing history has been far more exciting, with its north face, smooth as a concrete wall, on which for the last thirty years the world's greatest climbers have fought in summer and winter to open up six separate routes; some of these were mastered in a few hours, others demanded up to seventeen days before the top was finally reached.

On the right, the Westliche Zinne thrusts up its 1,600-foot north face, much of which consists of overhangs and in whose rock can be found nearly 1,000 pitons, for the only way to make progress above the abyss here is with the help of ›ironmongery‹ as these adventitious aids are called in climbing circles.

However, even these two colossal obelisks, besides providing the ›Sextogradist‹ with his supremely severe Grade VI climbs mentioned above, offer the ›ordinary climber‹, in search of the delights of ›normal‹ ascents, ›free-climbing‹ (piton-less) routes on their southern faces to content any mountaineer's heart.

---

1 In the Italian version: ›Le Tre Cime di Lavaredo‹.

The Cadini Group, above Misurina

The Cadini Group, rising to the south of the Drei Zinnen and to the west of Misurina, a pleasant resort with a charming little lake, is one of the ›poor relations‹ of the Dolomites. Its chain of peaks, four miles long and two broad, running from south-west to north-east, is relatively little visited, in spite of the splendid climbing and rambling to be found among them. Those who want to explore unknown rock territory can still find excellent opportunities here; while the genuine rambler will find many delights in this mountain group, though it has lacked a German-language guidebook for several decades. For instance, the whole group can be traversed comfortably from Misurina, and there is a splendid ›club path‹ linking the Zinnen with the Cadini Group. At the heart of the range stands the Fonda-Savio Hut of the Trieste Section of the Club Alpino Italiano (CAI), serviced all through the summer months.

The photograph was taken from near and above Misurina, to the west of the range. On the left, the Cima Cadin dei Tocci and the Torre Wundt (Wundtturm) appear as twin summits; to the right, below cloud, lies the 7,765-foot Passo dei Tocci, on whose saddle stands the Fonda-Savio Hut. The three great summit wedges to the right are the Cima Cadin NE (9,320 feet), the Cima Cadin Sud and the Cima Sötvös; farther to the right, beyond the sharp Campanile Verzi, the wide score of the Forcella della Neve – by which the rambler can traverse the range – faces the viewer, with the Campanile Antoni Giovanni and the Cima Cadin della Neve, topped by cloud, rising to its right again.

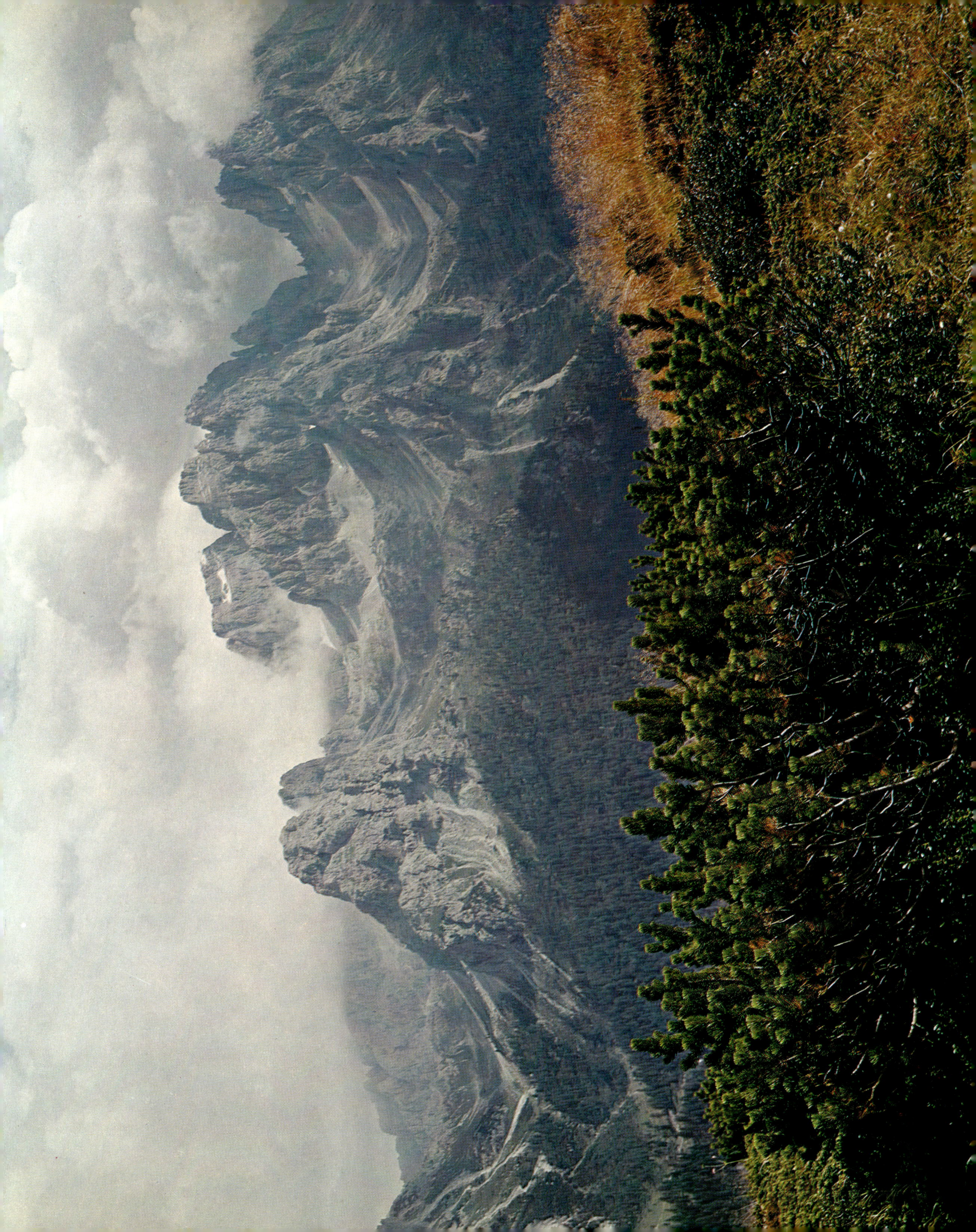

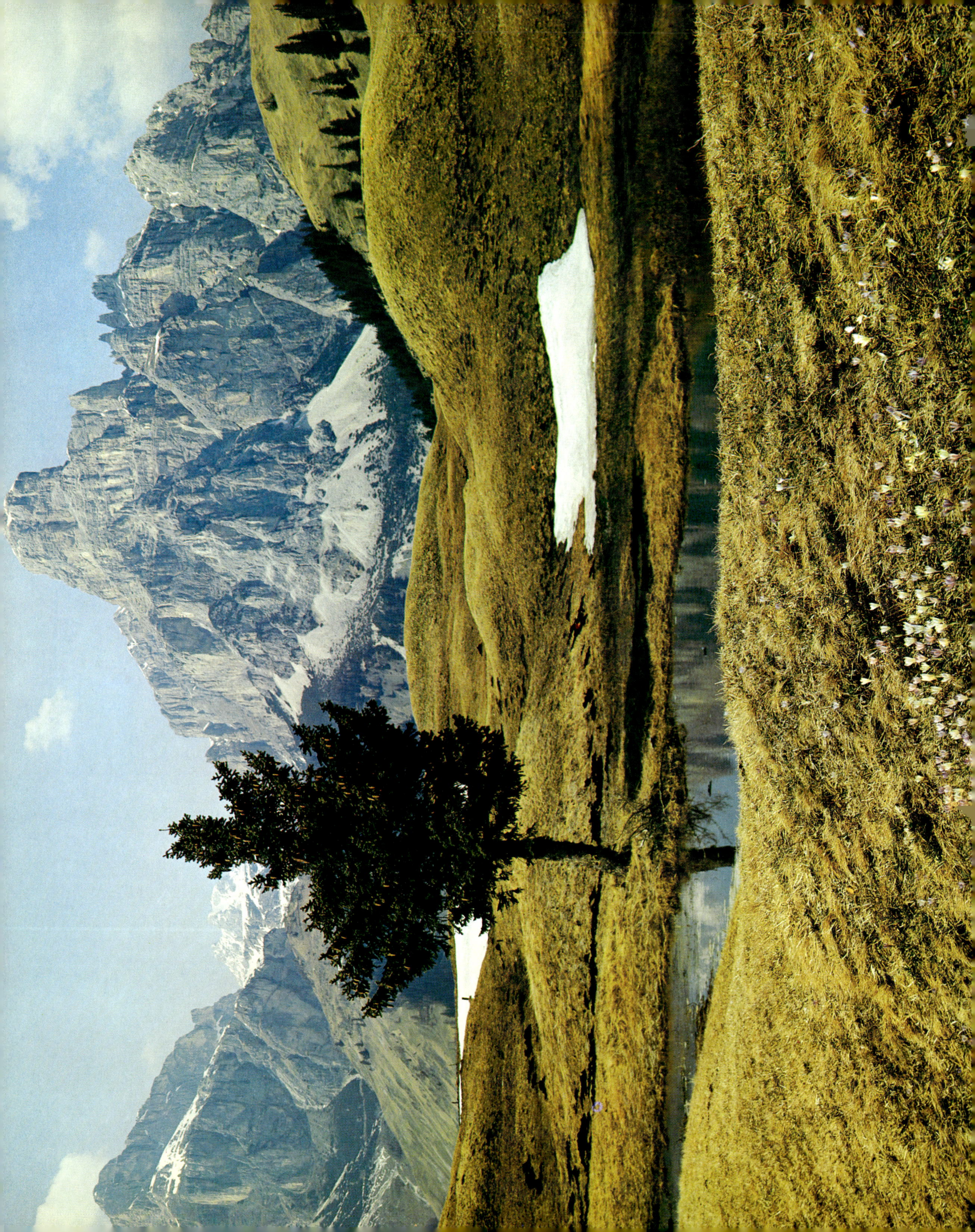

The Sass Songher, near Corvara, Ladin Dolomites

The village of Corvara (5,110 feet), at the eastern edge of the magnificent Sella Group (highest peak Cima Boe, 10,340 feet), has for decades been a favourite summer-holiday resort and for the last twenty years a much-frequented skiing centre, visited chiefly by droves of beginners from the German territories to the north, for most of the runs are extremely easy.

To the north of the village, Corvara's famous landmark, the massive Saas Songher (8,750 feet) goes towering to the sky like a huge ninepin of Dolomite rock, an easy peak to climb in spite of its horrific and hostile appearance. True, the ascent does not lie up its steep south face, with its tremendous precipices, which faces the viewer in the picture, but attacks it from the western (left-hand) side, by a narrow protected track, demanding absolute sureness of foot; this brings one to the summit, not without some toilsome sections, in four hours from Corvara.

The summit is a splendid view-point, the prospect embracing the Zillertal Alps far away to the north and a particularly fine aspect of the Sella Group, close at hand.

In the neighbourhood of the village, and especially to its east, from which the photograph was taken, there are to be found numerous pleasant and safe walks and rambles among the stark rock peaks of the Dolomites which rise all around.

The Langkofel Group, above the Grödnertal

That famous, even lengendary, explorer of the Dolomite region, Hermann Delago, described this compact but incredibly savage group of Dolomite peaks, briefly but trenchantly, in the following words:

> The summits of the Langkofel Group, which arise in a horse-shoe above the Langkofel and Plattkofel coombes, are only accessible, with the sole exception of the Plattkofel itself, by very exacting climbs. The Langkofel is the finest peak in the Dolomites; the early topographer of the Tyrol, J. J. Staffler, wrote of it that everyone from the outside world must surely wish to come and marvel at its magnificence ...

The 10,425-foot Langkofel is called Sass Long in the local Ladin, Sassolungo (›The Long Rock‹) in Italian. The picture shows the group as seen from the north; from left to right rises the huge mass of the Langkofel itself, with the low pinnacles of the Fünffingerspitz crowding below it to the right, half obscuring the Grohmannspitze set back behind them; then follow the Innerkoflerturm, the sharp fang of the Zahnkofel and, forming the whole right-hand end, the flattened pyramid of the Plattkofel, whose south-west (right-hand) ridge can even be ascended on ski. The meadows and woodlands of the famous Seiser Alm stretch away to the north-west of the group.

Motorists who do not care to leave their car can obtain a magnificent view of the group from the summit of the splendid Sella Pass (7,275 feet); when this is approached from the west up the lovely Grödnertal[1], the Langkofel makes its first dramatic appearance as a solitary rock spire shooting up fantastically above the pines.

The upper half of the Grödnertal, continually dominated by the Langkofel, is one long, unbroken skiing centre containing St. Ulrich (Ortisei), Santa Christina and Wolkenstein (Selva) with their variety of runs, from easy to very steep. The World Alpine Ski Championships of 1970 are to be held here.

---

[1] In Italian: Val Gardena.

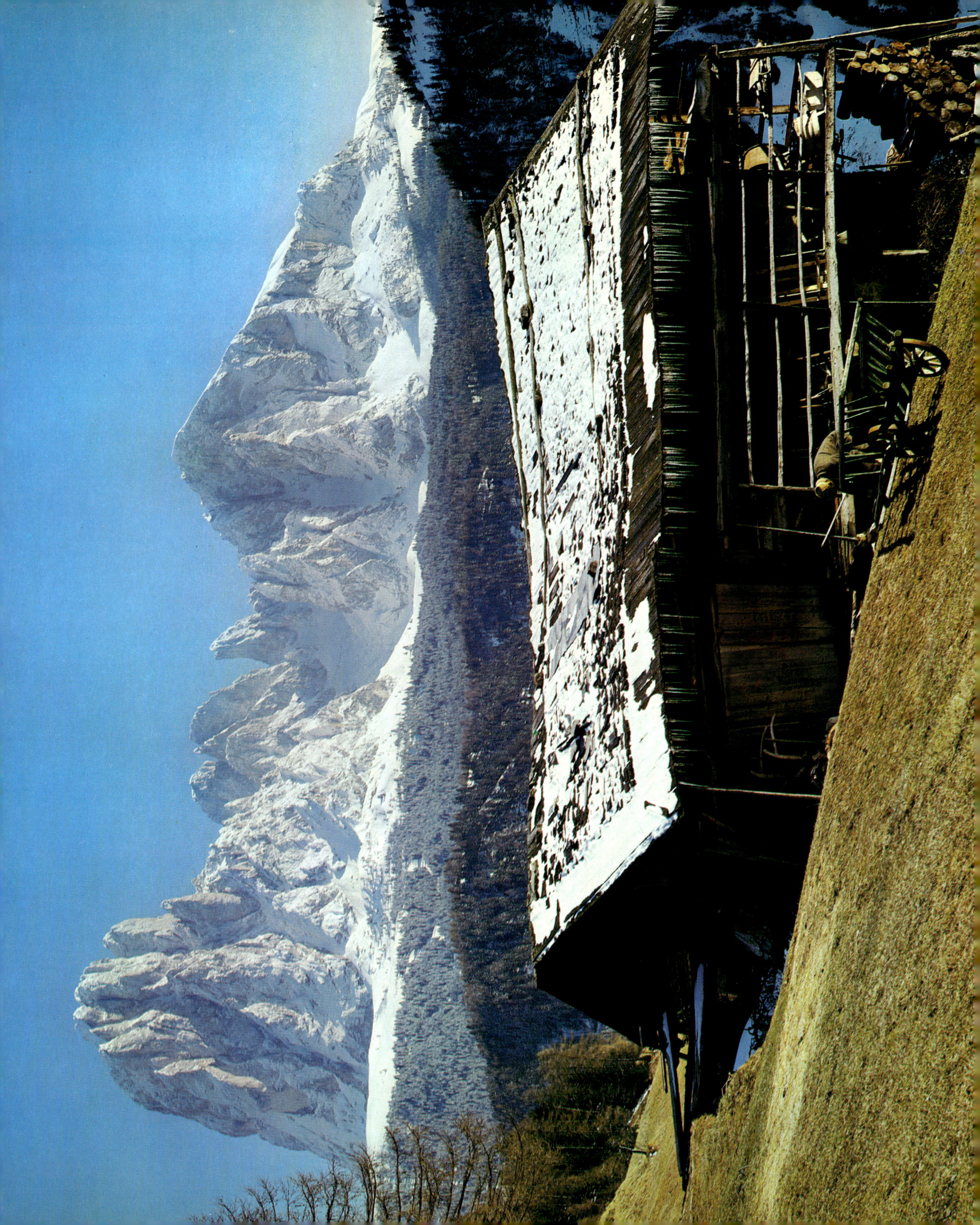

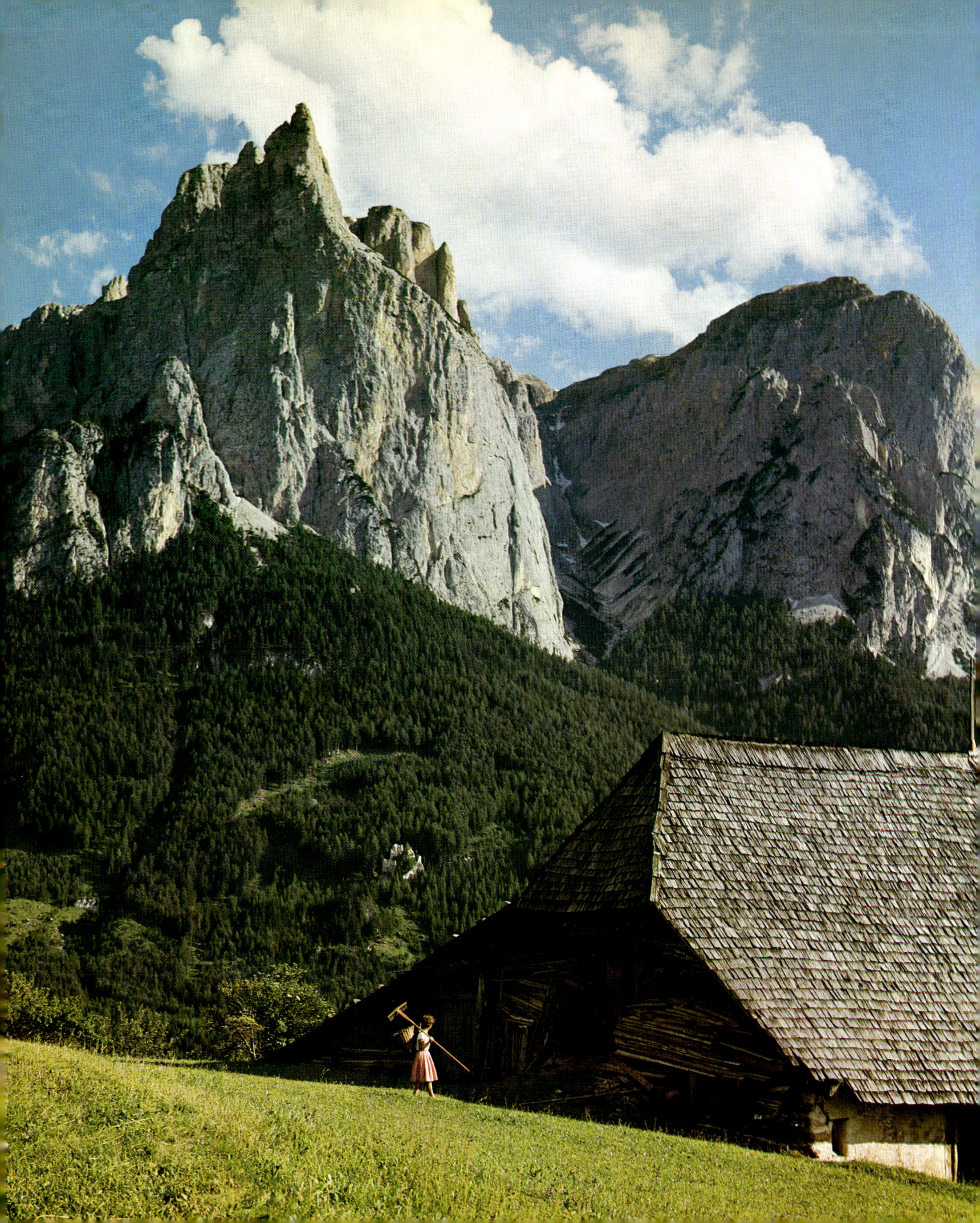

The Santnerspitze in the Schlern massif

The little village of Seis (3,295 feet) in the South Tyrol, to the north of the Schlern massif and to the east of the famous Seiser Alp, is a jewel of the Dolomites. Directly behind the village soars the impressive Santnerspitze (7,920 feet), dominating the whole scene. There are excursions in the neighbourhood to suit all tastes and degrees of skill.

The Santnerspitze itself demands climbing ability and experience, for even the easiest route up the east side (left of the picture) is a Grade III (›Difficult‹) and takes four or five hours. The grayish-yellow north face, more than 2,300 feet high, is suitable only for experts: one does not need much imagination to sense that it entails difficulties of a high order. It was not mere coincidence that till 1880, when that indomitable solo climber, Johann Santner of Bozen, made the first ascent, it was known as the Teufelspitze (›Devil's Peak‹).

To the right, behind the ridge of the Santnerspitze, and appearing lower in the picture, is the slightly higher Burgstall (8,240 feet), while the right-hand side is filled by the dark mass of the 7,830-foot Gabels, with the great re-entrant of the Seiser Klamm in between.

The main summit of the Schlern (the Alt Schlern, 8,405 feet) rises in the continuation of the ridge behind the summit of the Santnerspitze. It can be reached by a path starting at Bad Ratzes, two and a half miles from Seis, leading in three and a half hours by way of the Schlern Plateau to the Schlern Häuser, three huts with accomodation for a hundred, whence an easy path leads in half an hour to the summit. The view is one of the finest in the Eastern Alps, commanding all the Dolomites and the whole main chain of the Alps from the Adamello in the south-west to the Hohe Tauern in the north-east, while beyond the deep trench of the Adige Valley to the south rise the great peaks of the Ortler Group.

There is no need for the summer visitors to Seis to confine his undivided attention to the sheer Dolomite walls of the peaks. The enthusiastic Alpine rambler will also find a wide field for his activities on a well laid-out network of lovely footpaths. So a visit in summer to Seis at the foot of the Schlern is well worth while.

Cima Sappada, with Monte Siera (Carinthian Alps)

If you follow the headwaters of the Piave, on the eastern fringe of the Dolomites, right up to that river's source, you will come upon a charming widening in the valley, with massive pyramids of rock frowning down on it – Sappada.

Sappada is a German-speaking enclave and has been so for nearly a thousand years. A greedy lord in the upper Pustertal (Val Pusteria, now part of Eastern Tyrol) so oppressed the peasants that they decided to escape from his power. The first to go, in 1078, were five families, who crossed the mountains to the south into the upper Piave Valley, among them the Bladen family, after whom the little refugee colony was originally named. This miniature migration of the tribes continued well into the fourteenth century, with the result that Sappada is inhabited almost exclusively by German-speaking families, the Hofers, Krattners, Obertalers and Waschingers among others.

Bladen is a village straggling for several miles on the northern fringe of the Carinthian Alps. The eastern part, lying at 4,264 feet, is called Cima Sappada. Since 1950 the region has seen a heavy influx of visitors, mainly ski-addicts from Trieste and Udine.

The photograph shows the view from Cima Sappada to the riven rock-pyramid of Monte Siera (8,040 feet). To its left rise the 8,020-foot Piccolo Siera and the Cima Dieci or Zehnerspitze (7,238 feet).

This relatively little-visited mountain tract can be explored by a network of excellent paths, though there is a distinct shortage of serviced huts or refuges.

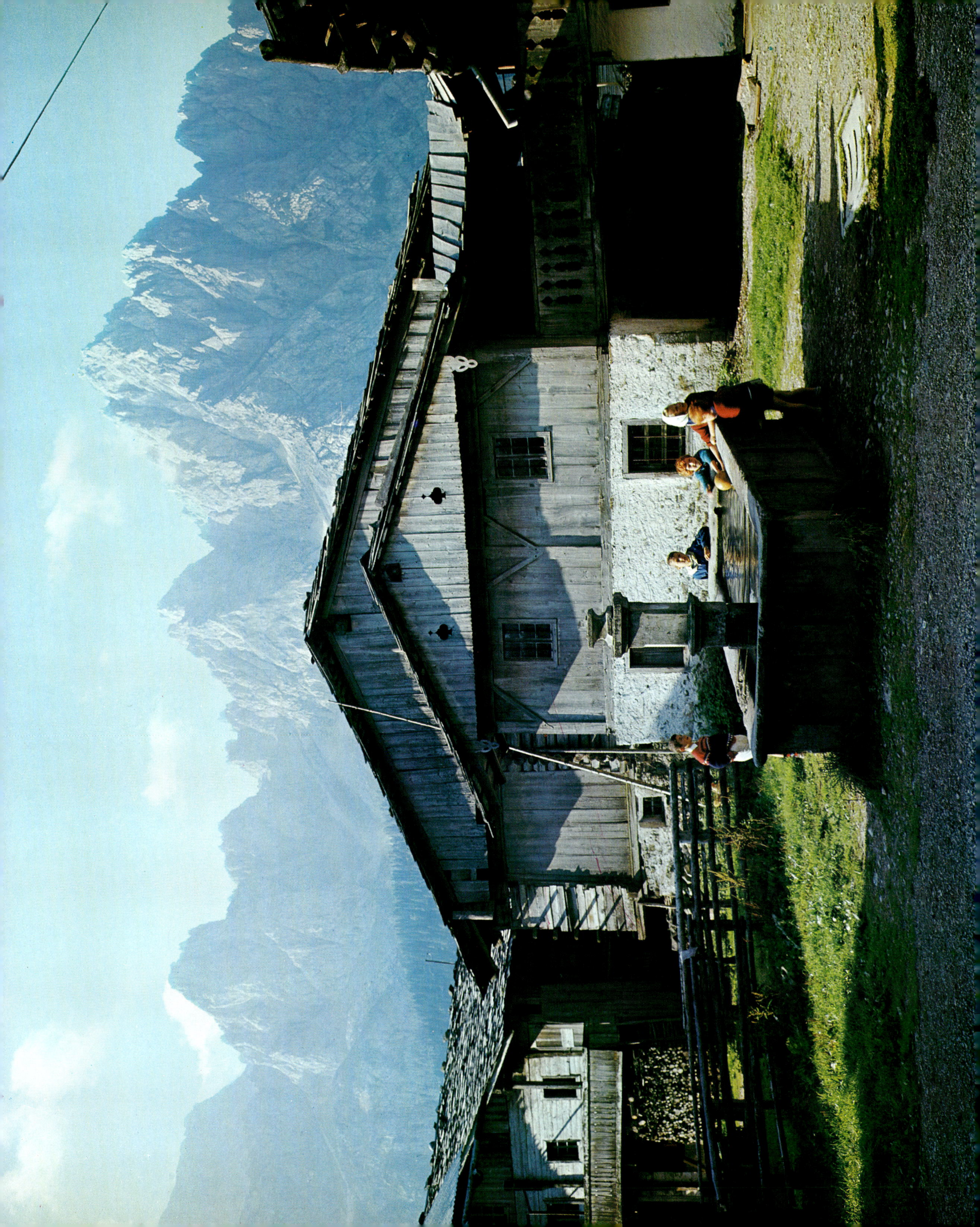

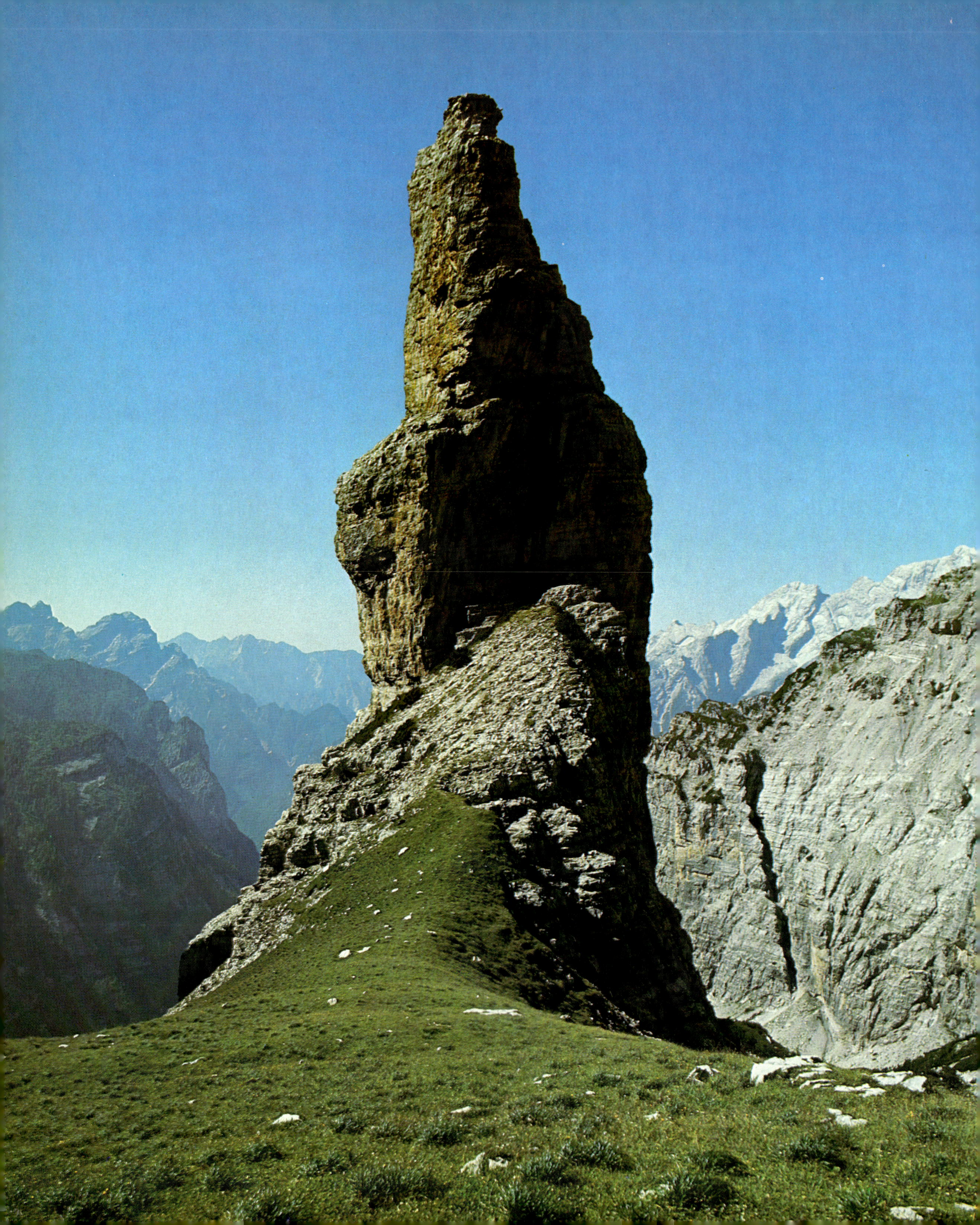

The Campanile di Val Montanaia, Eastern Dolomites

It is in one of the remotest and most deserted of the valleys in the Dolomites that this curiously-shaped ›campanile‹ thrusts up; and though its altitude of 7,120 feet is modest enough and its precipices measure only 250–700 feet, it has nonetheless been a favourite target for first-class rock climbers since the turn of the century.

To the east of Longarone, the scene of the terrible flood disaster in 1963, passing the Vaiont dam and reservoir which caused it, one comes to Cimolais, the entrance to the rugged and beautiful Cimoliana Valley. A journey of eight miles along a somewhat sketchy road brings one to the Rifugio Pordenone at 3,950 feet, and then a steep path leaving the main valley and striking north-westwards leads on into the Val Montanaia, where this gaunt ›belfry‹ stands like a solitary sentinel.

The photograph shows it from the north side, that is, from the direction of the main mountain mass. The normal route, a Grade IV (›Very Difficult‹) climb, goes up the hidden south face and was first ascended in 1902 by two Austrian noblemen, Freiherr von Saar and V. W. von Glanvell. A bell – an appropriate adornment for a campanile – has been placed on the summit.

Till a few years ago the only starting-point for the Campanile was the Pordenone Hut, two hours distant. Today climbers have the use of the Giuliano Perugini bivouac-box, to the north of the tower, quite close to the spot from which the picture was taken – a miniature mountain refuge with room for nine sleepers.

The Tofana di Rozes, near Cortina d'Ampezzo

When you leave the Winter Olympic centre of Cortina d'Ampezzo and drive westwards along the first fifteen miles of the famous ›Dolomite Road‹ towards its first high saddle, the Falzarego Pass (6,945 feet), it is a good thing to stop a while after seven miles or so to enjoy the view towards the overwhelming massif of the 10,565-foot Tofana di Rozes, which is magnificently impressive even if you do not contemplate an attempt on one of the ten routes available on its south face, at this point some 2,700 feet high. For a closer look at the huge yellowish-gray precipices you must leave the main highway after another seven miles and enjoy the still more impressive view from the comfortably appointed Dibona Hut (6,560 feet) about two miles off to the right.

It should be said that the routes up the Tofana are not all climbs of great severity; there is, for instance, an easy ordinary route up the slabby west face (to the right in the picture) at whose foot the Cantore Hut provides a convenient springboard. The photograph shows the Punta Marietta above the highest larch tree in the foreground, with the partly overhanging south face of the Pilastro di Rozes (the ›Tofanapfeiler‹) to its immediate left; both of these demand the most expert climbing skills. To the left, high in the face below the main summit, can be seen the huge re-entrant known as the ›Amphitheatre‹, up which runs the easiest route of those on the south face.

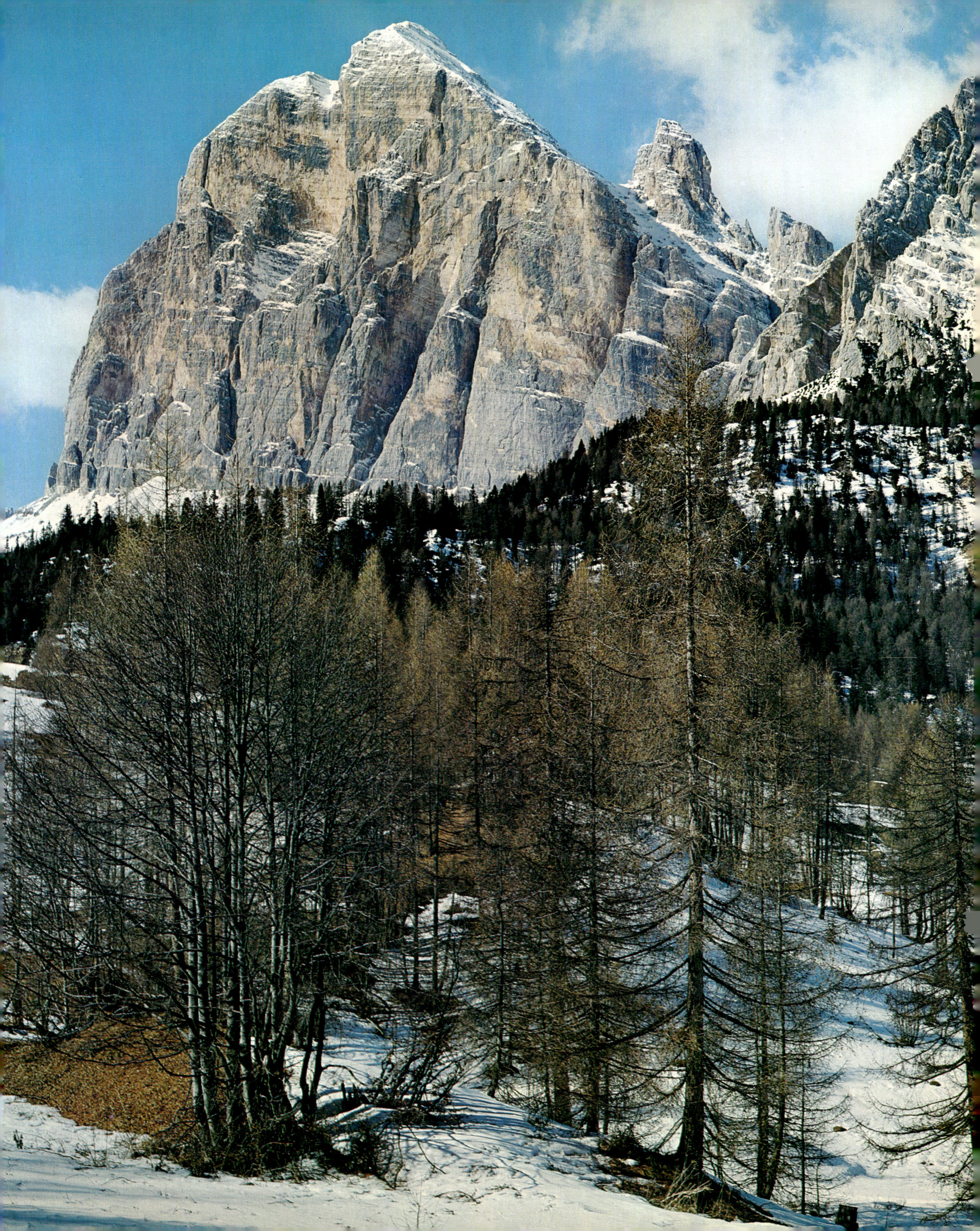

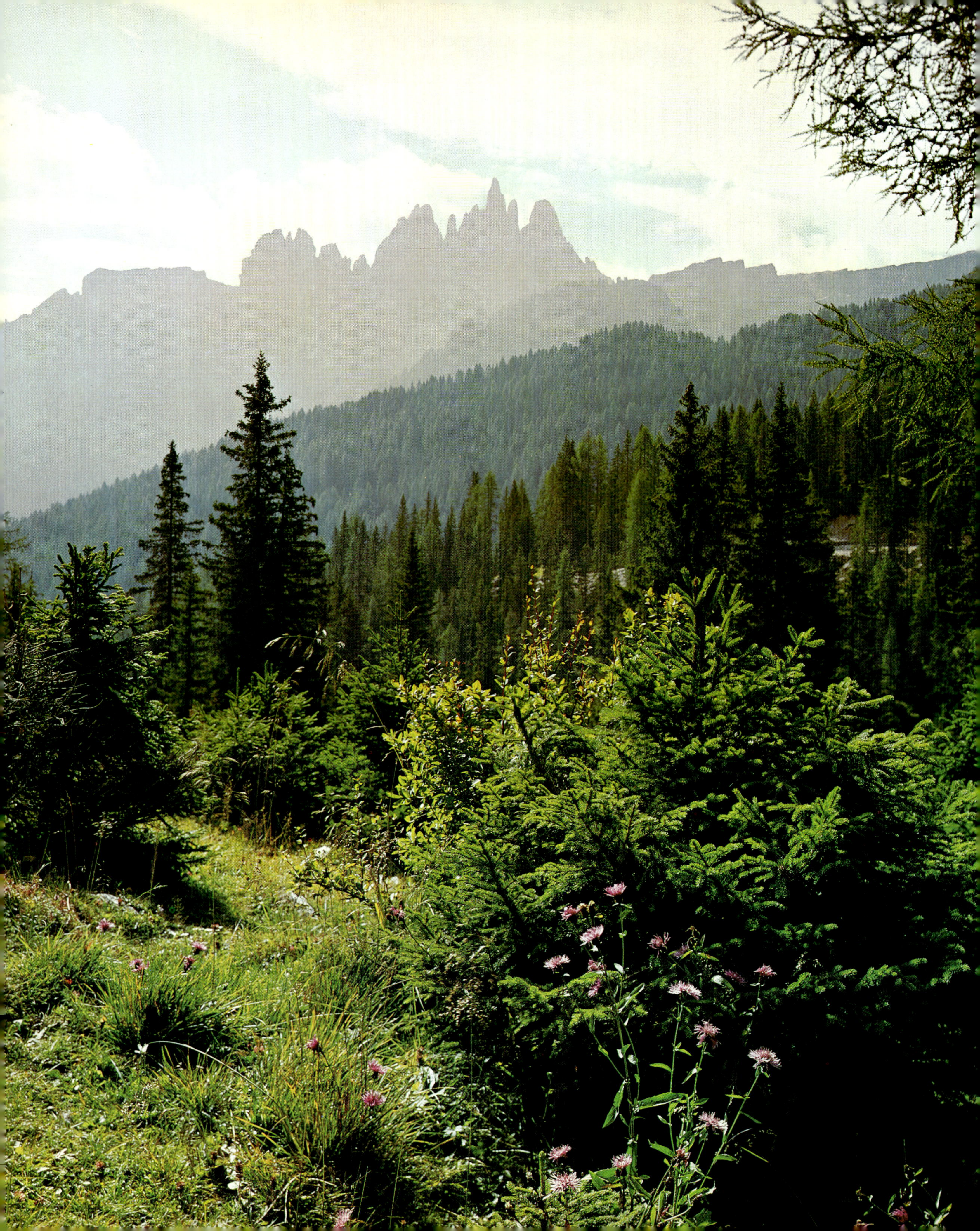

The Croda da Lago, near Cortina d'Ampezzo

This fiercely serrated group, rising to 8,885 feet, is also seen by the motorist on his way up to the Falzarego Pass and the continuation of the ›Dolomite Road‹ over the Pordoi Pass (7,380 feet) through the Eastern Dolomites; but a little sooner, to the south, on the opposite side of the road to the Tofana (see plate 51). Its relatively few towers and spires form one of the smallest of the Dolomite groups, but with its distinctive reddish wine-colour it is one of the most attractive.

The summit ridge is only a mile and a half long and the group is only 700 yards wide at its broadest point. In spring and in the late autumn, when the season has not yet started or is already over in the high mountains, the rock climbers of Cortina can be seen in fair numbers on the Croda da Lago.

Our picture shows it as seen from the north-west, near the Falzarego highway, at a distance of about four miles. The respective peaks, from left to right, are the Croda da Lago itself, Campanile Innerkofler, Campanile Federa, Ago da Lago and Punta Adi.

The group takes its name from the little Federa Lake, which lies to the east, behind the range, on whose shores, at 6,700 feet, stands the Palmieri Hut, the starting-point for the climbs in the group. The hut is some three hours from Cortina on foot, but it is possible to reach it by car if the vehicle is of the hardy mountaineering type.

The Cima Bois, on the Falzarego Road (Dolomites)

The Cima Bois (8,393 feet) is a mountain like thousands of others in the Dolomites and yet it has its own particular charm.

The Falzarego is as well-known to ›pass-bagging‹ motorists as to skiers. The Cima Bois rises above a forest of beautiful light-coloured pines a little to the north-east of the pass, between the Lagazuoi, up which there is a ropeway, and the Tofana di Rozes (see plate 51).

The south face of the peak falls sheer to the road, a wall 1,000 feet high. The north side is a very different affair, its soft and gentle slopes providing easy access to the summit. Very fine ramblers' paths bound the Cima Bois – the Forcella di Lagazuoi to its west and the Forcella Bois to its east, the latter descending into the Travenanze Valley, which again falls into the main Ampezzotal to the north of Cortina.

It is only recently, since the construction of the Lagazuoi ropeway, that one sees a good many ramblers in this area. Before that, the only visitors were occasional members of the Cortina ›Scoiattoli‹ (›The Squirrels‹), a climbers' club which has won world fame, who came to the Cima Bois to start their annual training in the spring on the peak's magnificent southern precipices.

A route, first ascended in 1947 by the ›Squirrels‹ goes straight up the yellowish wall in the direct line below the actual summit (right centre).

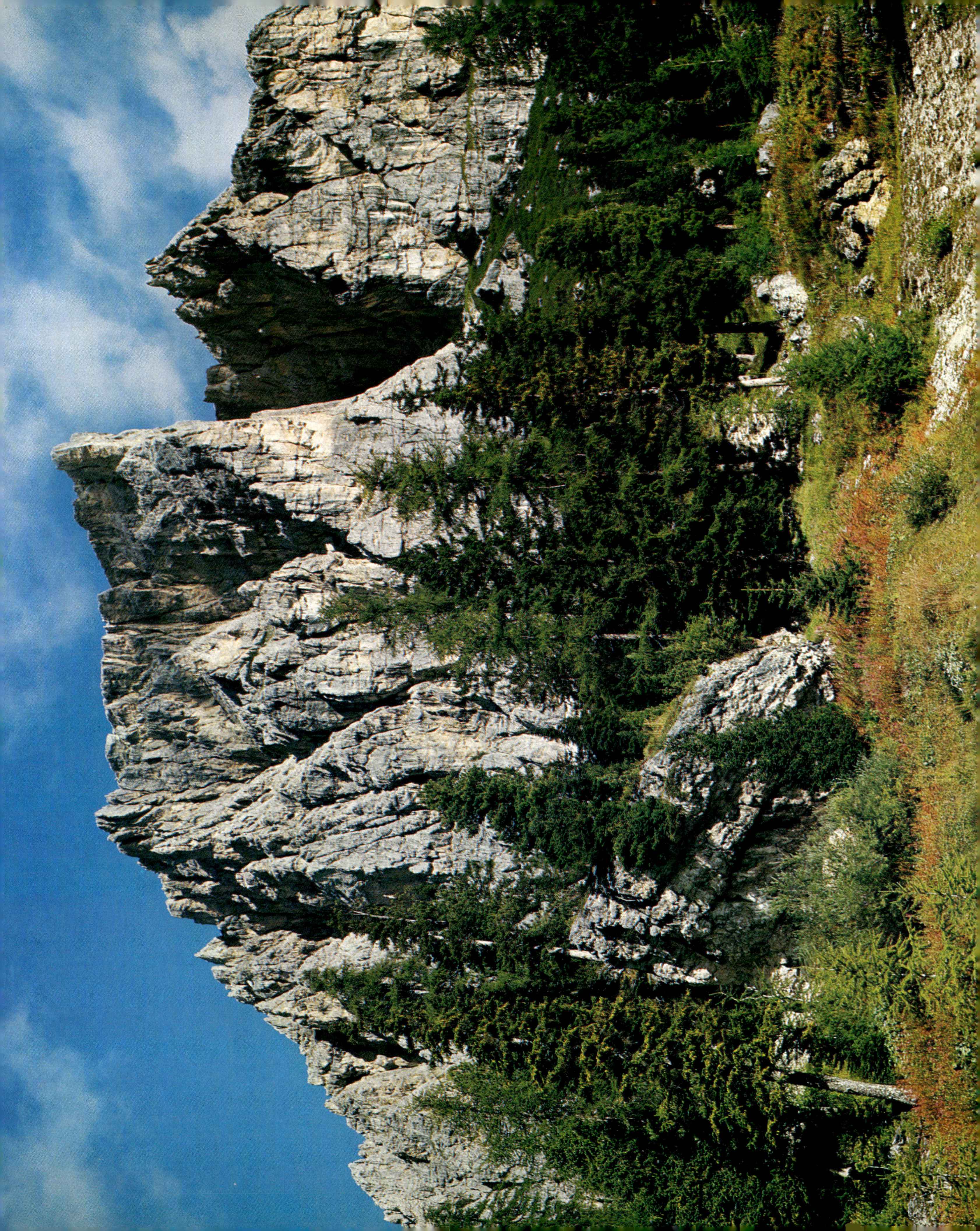

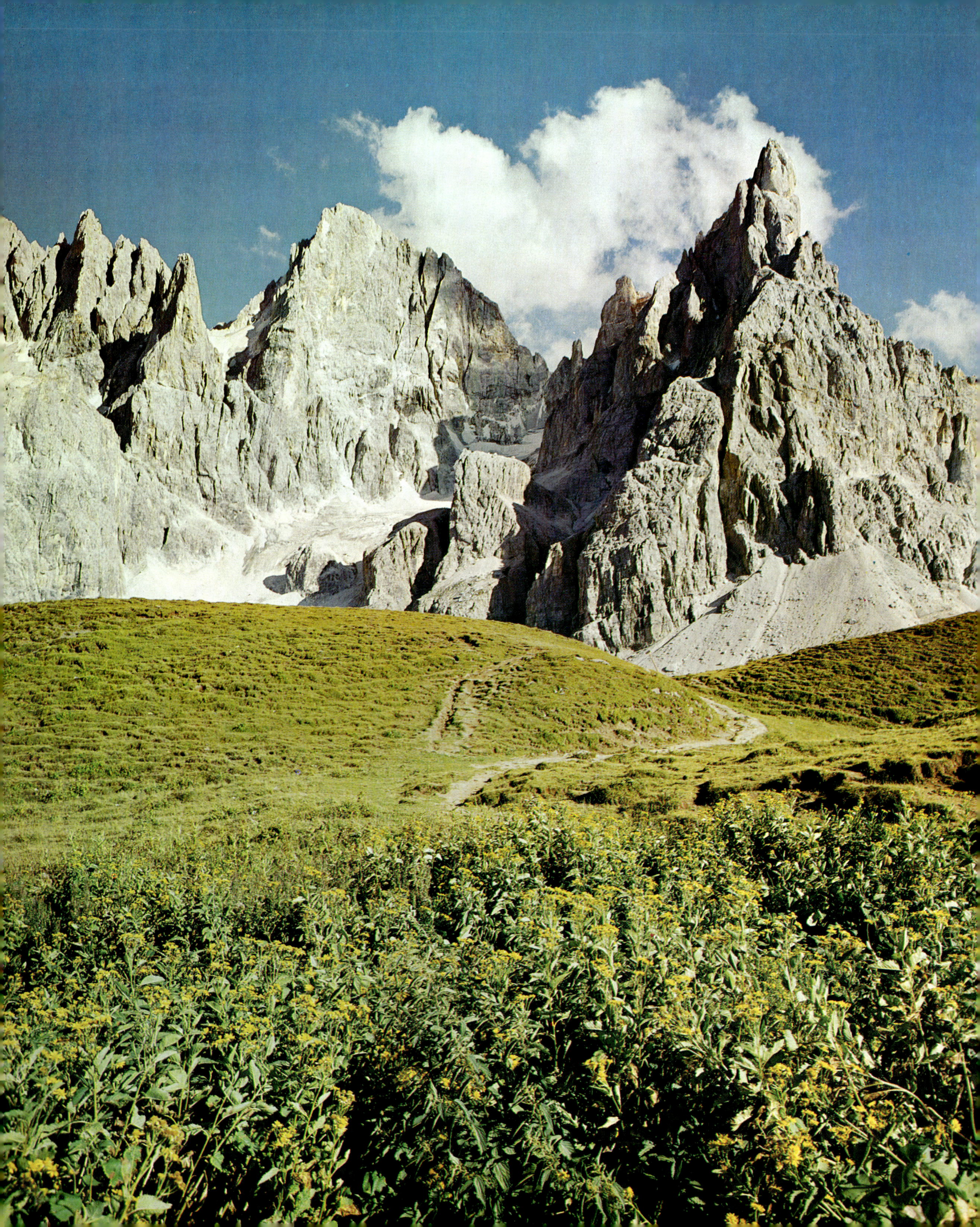

The Cimone della Pala, near the Rolle Pass

The motorist driving the magnificent ›Dolomite Road‹ over the Falzarego and Pordoi passes to Canazei and then down the lovely length of the Val di Fassa, through Vigo di Fassa, gradually drops down to Predazzo. Turning eastwards, to the left, at this busy market town, he finds himself climbing, first through flowery meadows, later through a forest of gigantic dark pines and finally over bare slopes above the tree-line, to the broad green saddle of the 6,510-foot Rolle Pass.

Just before reaching it he will suddenly see, soaring into the sky before him, the fantastic spire of the Cimone della Pala (10,450 feet), a slender needle of gray and yellow rock lifting, apparently sheer, some 4,000 feet above the level of the pass. This is one of the most astonishing ›surprise views‹ in the Alps; little wonder that the peak is known as ›the Matterhorn of the Dolomites‹.

Leaving the car at the pass, one can take a chair-lift, just to its south, up to the wonderfully situated Baita Segantini (named after the great Swiss master of mountain painting), a little hostelry, built in the manner of an Alm hut at 7,400 feet.

The photograph was taken from the Baita and shows the magnificent view commanded by its immediate surroundings; it is no exaggeration to say that one could spend hours up there admiring those incredible rock castles. To the right soars the Cimone, crowned by its sharp spire; horrific and inaccessible as it looks from this aspect, it is in fact quite easily ascended from the Passo di Travignolo, behind it to the left. The centre is occupied by the broad face of the Cime della Vezzana, the highest summit in the Pala Group (just twenty-eight feet higher than the Cimone); surprisingly, the ordinary route up this daunting slab of rock, also starting at the Travignolo Pass, rarely exceeds Grade I (›Easy‹). To its left is the Passo di Val Strutt, from which starts a skier's dream of a run down the far side towards the south-east. To the left of the gap rise the Campanile di Val Strutt and the Cima dei Bureloni.

In winter the traverse of the Vezzana forms part of the high-level Dolomite ski-route, which starts from the charming summer and winter resort of San Martino di Castrozza, five miles southwards down the splendid windings of the Rolle Pass, through some of the finest pine forests in the Alps. Everywhere in the area round San Martino excellent paths provide ramblers and walkers with rewarding excursions, and the 9,000-foot Rosetta, with its glorious views, is now accessible by ropeway.

The Marmolada and Gran Vernel from the Sella Pass

The Marmolada (10,970 feet) is known as the ›Queen of the Dolomites‹ not only because it is the highest mountain in the area and the only one with an extensive glacier system, but because it qualifies even more deservedly than the Dachstein (plate 16) for the epithet ›versatile‹.

For, at the foot of the great mountain mass which constitutes the Marmolada, there are magnificent rambles; its northern side offers unadventurous glacier climbs and also, until far into the summer, enchanting and speedy ski-runs; on its west flank there is an airy ›club path‹; and its southern precipices, in places more than 2,500 feet high, are the home ground of rock climbers whose skills are sufficiently advanced for climbs from Grade IV to VI (›Very Difficult‹ to ›Super Severe‹). To cap everything, since 1968 there has been a ropeway to the summit ridge of the Punta di Rocca (Wintergipfel, 10,855 feet). One could hardly demand more diversified attractions from a single mountain.

The picture was taken from just below the 7,275-foot Sella Pass (see plate 47) and shows the Marmolada's north-western aspect. To the left of the sunlit rhomboid of the summit, and close to it, is the small rocky head of the Punta di Rocca, with its fine snowy northern slopes. To the right, the west ridge, on which runs the protected ›club path‹, falls away into the gap of the Forcella Marmolada, to whose right again rises the Gran Vernel (10,505 feet), hardly less imposing than the Marmolada herself.

In the immediate foreground of the massif stretch the fine slopes of the Belvedère ski area above Canazei, which lies too deep down in the valley on the right to be seen in the photograph. At the extreme left, the dark, craggy, Sasso Beccé (8,325 feet) is seen rising immediately to the south of the Pordoi Pass (7,380 feet), the windings of whose finely-engineered road can just be detected among the dark pine forests covering the centre and right-hand foreground.

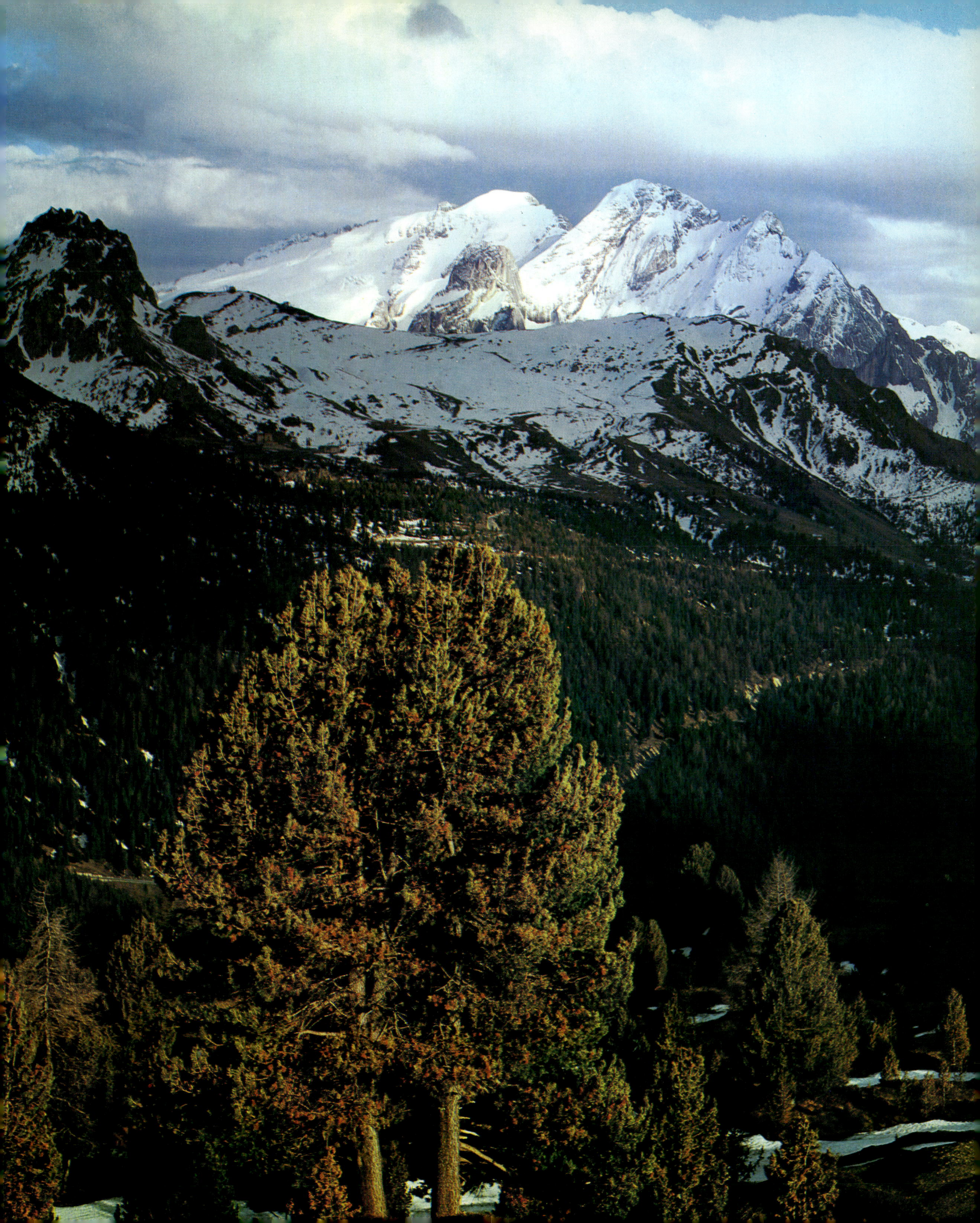

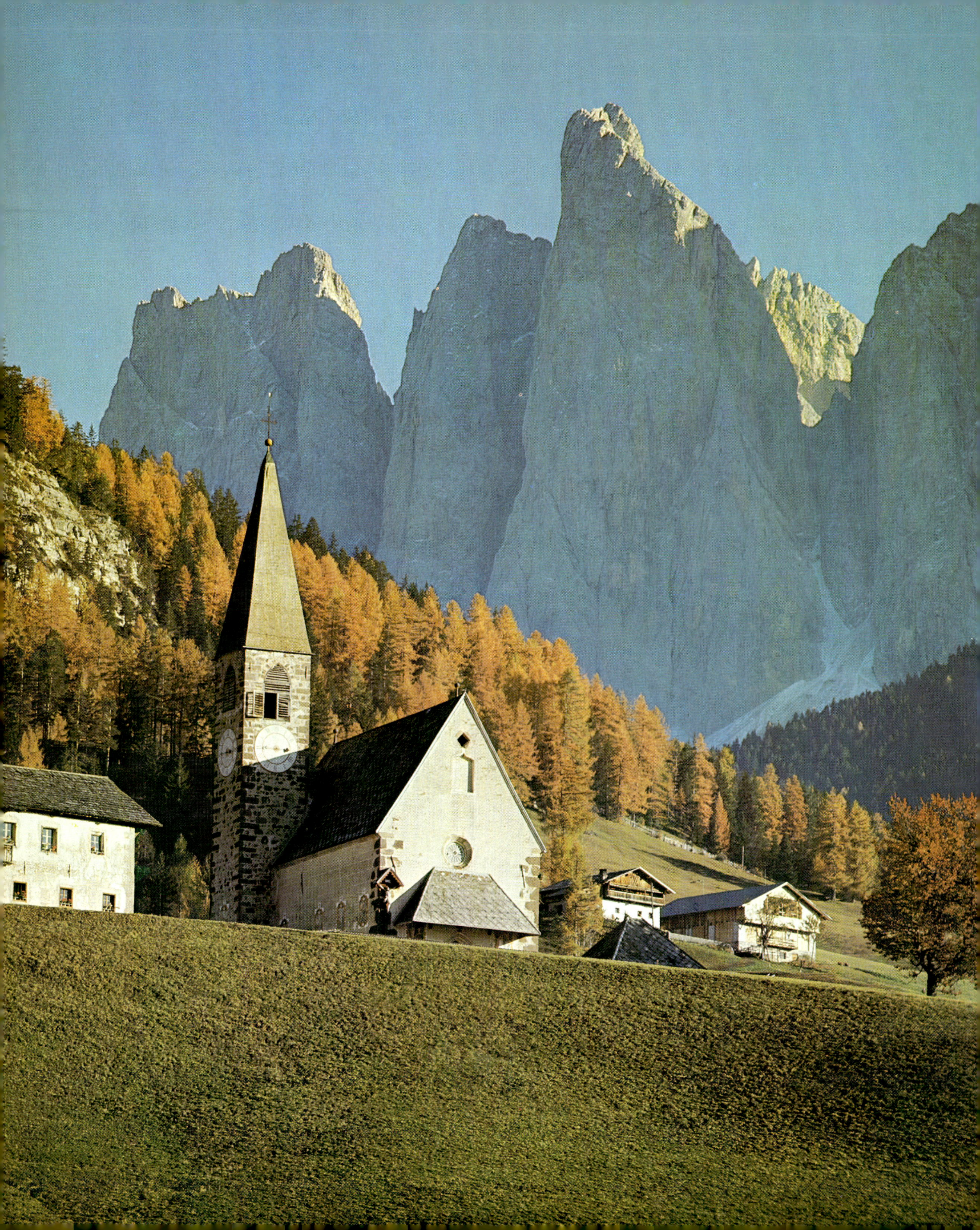

Sta Magdalena and the Geislerspitzen (South Tyrol)

About six miles to the south of the cathedral town of Brixen[1] in the South Tyrol, the highly picturesque Villnöstal falls from the east into the broad main valley of the Eisack[2], with its heavy north-to-south road and rail traffic.

The Villnöstal is some nine miles long and is one of the most attractive regions in the Western Dolomites. Its most important villages are Villnös and Sta Magdalena, which lie between 3,600 and 4,700 feet.

To the south-east of Sta Magdalena, the tremendous Geislerspitzen go streaming to the deep-blue Dolomite sky, presenting one of the most overwhelmingly impressive ramparts in the Dolomites.

The Furchetta (9,930 feet) is particularly striking, for it offers a sheer north face 2,600 feet high, on which none but the most accomplished climbers can set foot, for its difficulties are in the Grade VI (›Super Severe‹) category. This face only feels the light of the sun in the morning, and in the flat light of late afternoon the topmost rocks of the summits alone glow as they catch the low beams. There are, however, less exacting climbs on the Furchetta, such as the Grade I (›Easy‹) ascent, over the west ridge, which takes only an hour from the Geisler Hut. The peak was in fact climbed, and then by a solo climber, as long ago as 1880.

In the picture, the 9,250-foot Odla di Valdussa rises to the left of the Furchetta, the Saas Rigais (also 9,930 feet) to its right.

There is, however, no need at all to be a rock-climbing addict to enjoy the manifold other attractions of this outstandingly beautiful Valley of Villnös.

---

[1] In Italian: Bressanone.
[2] In Italian: Isarco.

Spring on the Mendel above Bozen

The Mendel area above Bozen (Bolzano), lying high to its south-west, is a lovely sun-trap on a ridge with a panoramic view. Eastwards, the mountain wall falls precipitously below it to the broad, fertile plain of the Adige Valley, with its luxuriating vineyards and orchards; to the west, woods and meadows slope away gently to the Valley of the Non.

A finely-engineered road cuts its way up across the steep wooded cliffs to the low Mendel Pass (4,460 feet), where a number of deserted-looking hotels still bear witness to the popularity of this site as a fashionable summer-holiday resort up to the First World War. There is also a ropeway from Kaltern in the Adige Valley.

The wide view embraces a considerable sector of the Dolomites, swinging round to the Brenta group in the south-west, beyond it to the Adamello and to the great white peaks of the Ortler group in the west. It is still better seen from the Penegal (5,700 feet) directly above the pass and the Monte Roen (6,940 feet), the highest eminence in the region, some three and a half hours on foot by a marked path. The view is at its best in springtime, when the orchards down in the Adige Valley are in full bloom, and again in autumn, when the variegated Mendel Woods are aflame with a riot of colours.

The Mendel Pass road winds its gentle way down again south-westwards into the Non Valley and onwards along its pleasant trench to the Carlomagno and Tonale Passes, with their stretches of magnificent mountain scenery – the former passing close to the Brenta Dolomites (10, 420 feet) near Madonna di Campiglio, the latter affording splendid near views of the Presanella (11,690 feet) and Adamello (11,640 feet) on its way to Ponte di Legno (see plates 84 and 85).

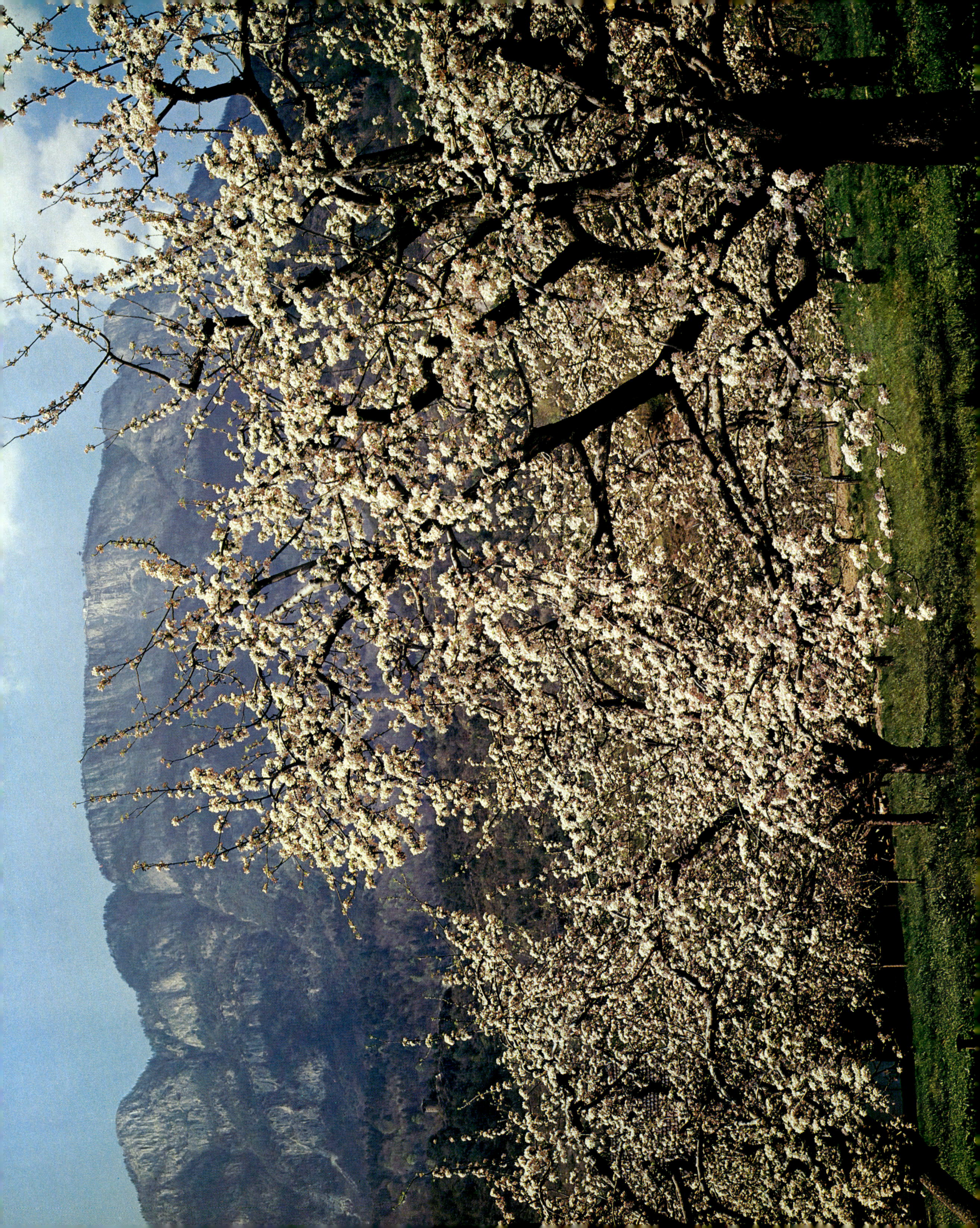

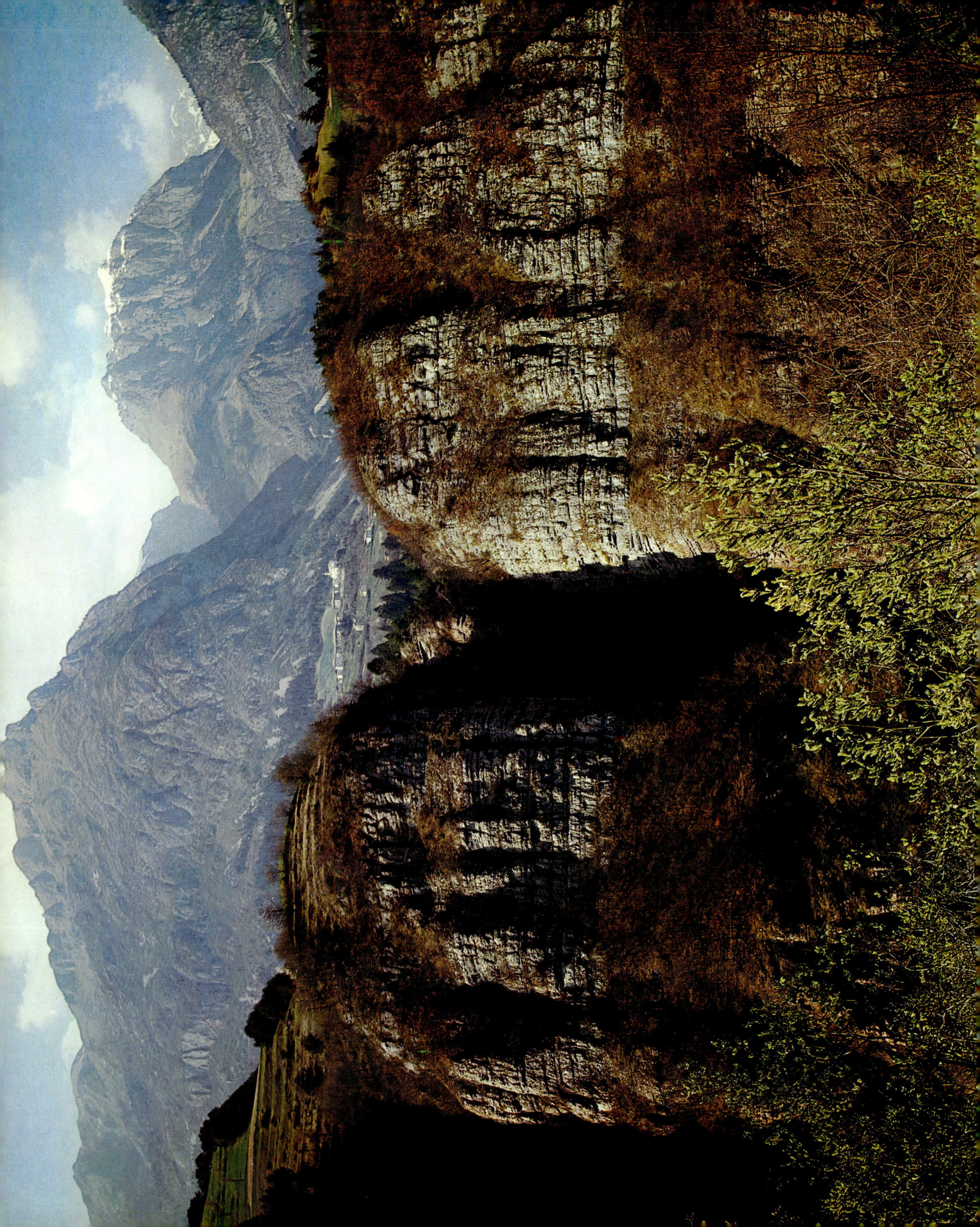

Stenico, on the southern fringe of the Brenta Dolomites

Scientists disagree about the correct allocation of the Brenta Group, twenty-six miles long from north to south and ten broad at its widest points.

The geologists hold that the Brenta consist of almost exactly the same rock formation (Main Dolomite) as the other Dolomite groups to the east of the Adige. On the other hand, the geographers argue that the Brenta Group is so widely divorced from the rest by the broad trench of the Adige Valley that it cannot be considered to form part of them.

Mountaineers will content themselves with the fact that the Brenta is one of the finest and most varied mountain tracts in the Alps, as attractive to the walker and high-mountain rambler as to the ›Sextogradists‹, who for decades past have found among its towers and spires a wealth of supremely difficult climbs.

Our photograph shows the southern spurs of the Brenta, as seen from the Sarca Valley to the west of Trient (Trento), in whose province the group stands. In the centre of the picture lies the village of Stenico, with the broad massif of the Crona (7,616 feet) rising to the right above it and, still farther to the right, the cloud-crowned group of the 10,420-foot Cima Tosa, above Madonna di Campiglio, which is the heart of the whole tract.

The cliffs in the foreground clearly exhibit the sedimentary stratification of the Dolomite base.

The Guglia di Brenta

At the very heart of the Brenta Group, the dark-blue sky is pierced by the incredibly sharp tower of the Guglia di Brenta, perhaps better known as the Campanile Basso (9,540 feet). It is only when one looks eastwards that it presents its most perfect bell-tower aspect, but from whatever side it is approached, the climbing required to reach its summit is never lower than Grade IV (›Very Difficult‹); so the only people one is likely to meet there are highly competent climbers, except on the rare occasions when some adventurous novice lets himself be hauled up on the rope by a guide.

All the same, high-mountain ramblers, sure of foot and absolutely free from giddiness, can derive their fill of enjoyment from the Campanile Basso, for a splendid and exciting ›club path‹ passes directly beneath its vertical upthrust; this is the famous Sentiere delle Bochette, which traverses the whole Brenta Group in seven sections and is at many points blasted out of the living rock.

A sector of it can be seen in the photograph. At the foot of the Campanile Alto (9,635 feet), the great wedge on the right, there is a prominent rock face; the path leads across it to the left, passes behind the two small rock needles and then goes down into the notch at the left base of the Basso. It is inadvisable to loiter at that point, for the climbers who visit the needle on every fine day are apt to dislodge stones on your head.

On the extreme left, the edge of the great Brenta Alta massif is seen surging up in profile.

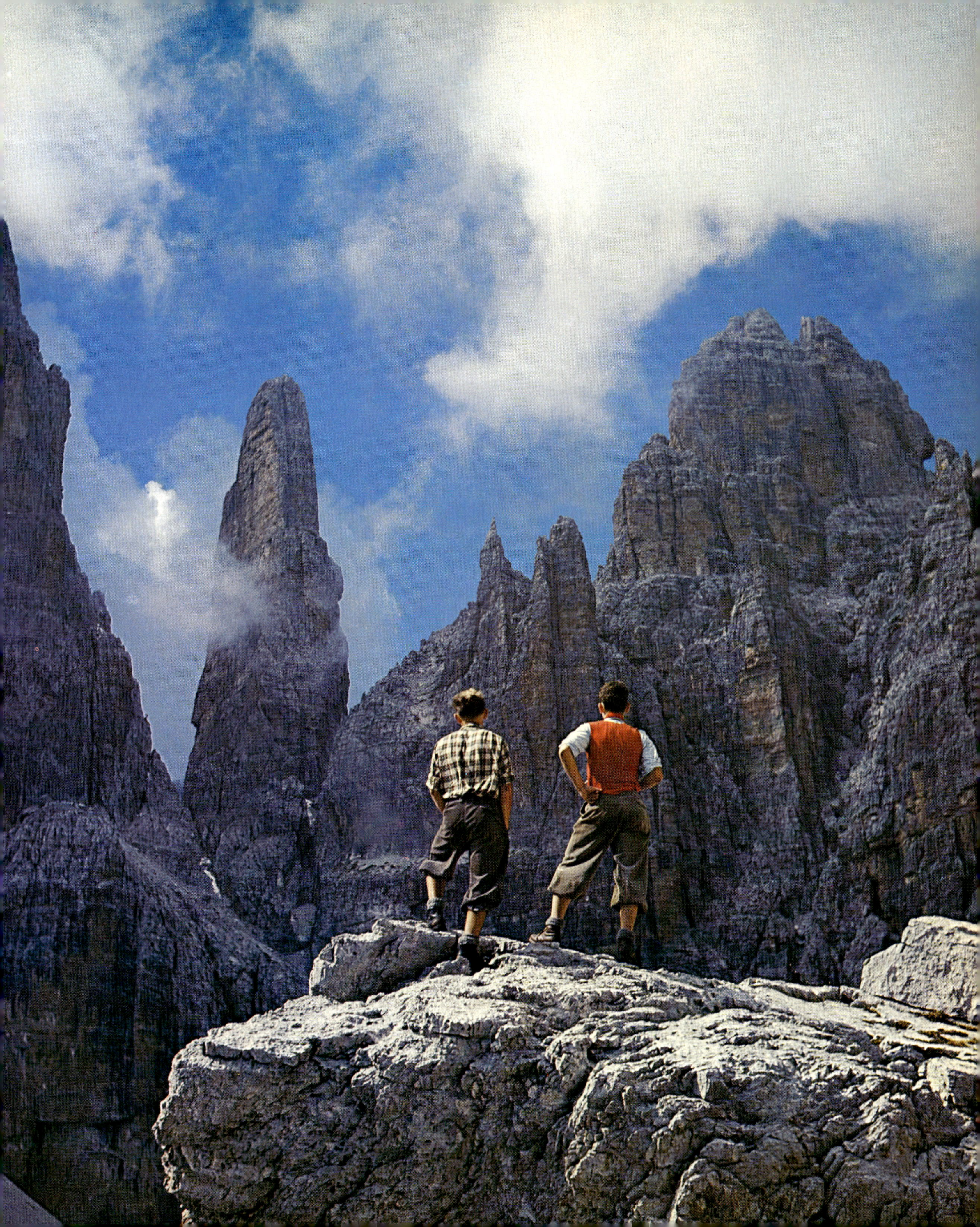

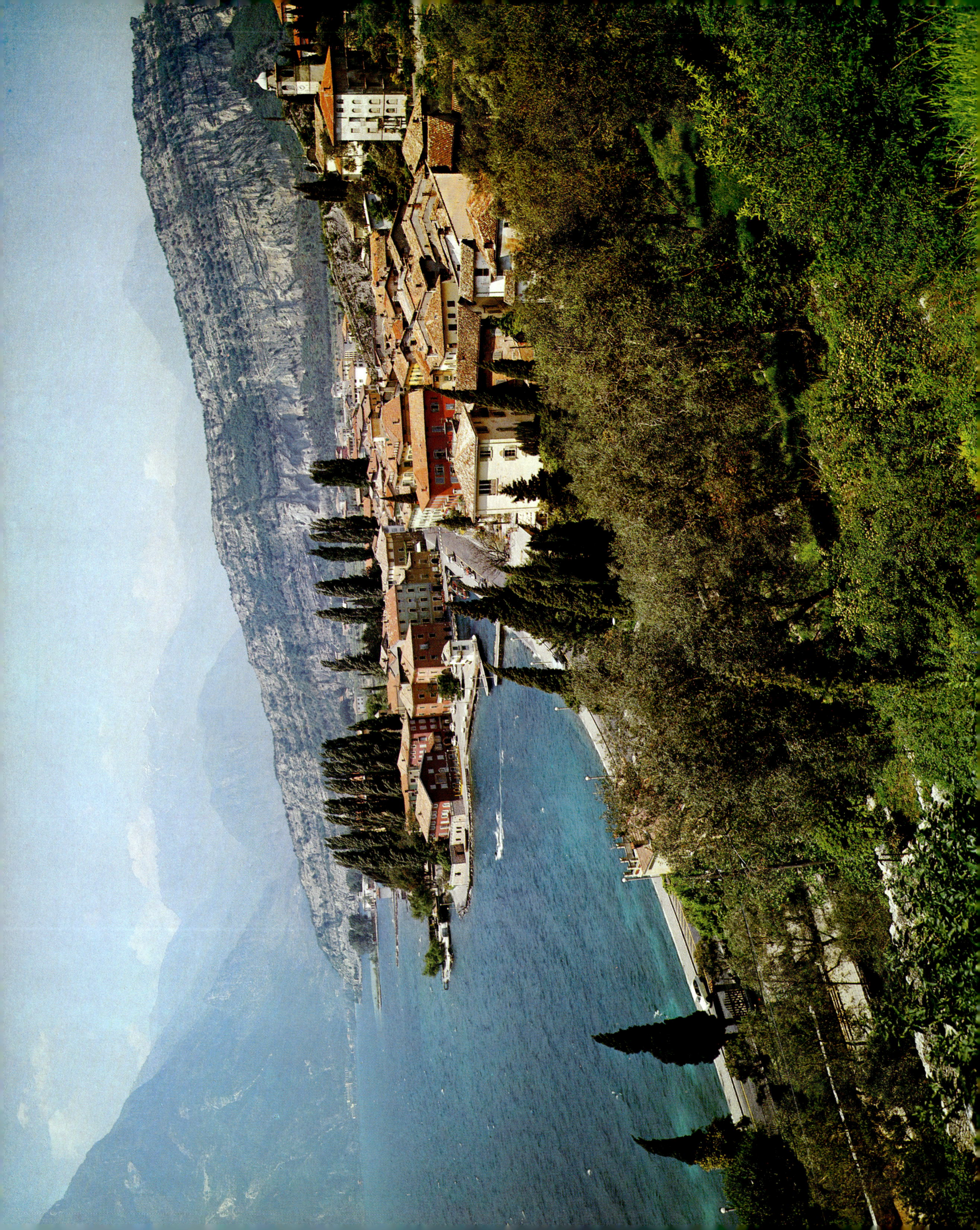

The Lake of Garda, on the southern fringe of the Dolomites

To the south of Trient (Trento) the Alps have carved out an extensive basin, ringed by steep rock walls and gentler undulating ridges. It cradles the lovely lake of Garda, renowned for its clear, blue-green waters; not only Italy's largest lake, but one of the most beautiful in the world.

The lake is more than forty miles long and, in its southern sector, up to ten broad, with an area of nearly 250 square miles; its surface lies only 215 feet above sea-level. It came into being during the Ice Age owing to the tremendous forward thrust of the Adige glacier. Its shores lie in three different provinces, its western bank in Brescia, its eastern in Verona and its northern in Trento.

The Lago di Garda, with its dozen famous and crowded summer resorts, among them Riva, Torbole, Malcesine, Gardone and Sirmione, where two thousand years ago Catullus had his holiday villa on the headland overlooking the turquoise waters, and wrote lovingly of his ›peninsula of all peninsulas‹, is not only a sun-drenched bathing, sailing and water-skiing paradise for the weary city worker. The mountains which look down on its shores also provide endless opportunities for easy walks and longer high rambles, especially on the twenty-five-mile-long range of Monte Baldo (7,220 feet, and accessible by road and ropeway) extending along the eastern shore, with its inexhaustible wealth of flora and its glorious high views over the blue basin of the lake and towards the ridges of the Dolomites to the north. While on the west shore, the hills around 6,488-foot Monte Tremalzo, gentler but no less attractive, are traversed by good, safe marked paths leading to a number of well-serviced huts.

This photograph shows the view northwards over Torbole, at the very north-eastern end of the lake, looking across to Riva at its northern tip, dominated by the steep mountain wall at the left edge of the picture and, seen faintly, rising to the clouds, the southern spurs of the Brenta Dolomites.

A good motor road encircles the whole lake, but for the motorist the showpiece is the magnificently-engineered, fast highway along its west shore, from Gardone to Riva. Here the road forces its fantastic way close above the blue-green waters for more than thirty miles, often blasted out of the precipitous rock faces, swinging over airy viaducts and passing through innumerable tunnels.

The glacier world of the Ortler Group

It is almost impossible to dissociate the magnificence of the 12,800-foot ›King‹ Ortler, from the beauties of the Stelvio Pass, considered by many to be the king of the Alpine passes. For not only does the great ›surprise view‹ of the peak's snowy dome burst on the motorist coming from the south at the summit of that wonderful road (9,042 feet), but the famous half-century of hairpins, by which it wriggles and writhes its way down the northern wall of the mountains into the smiling valley of the upper Adige, passes almost within a stone's throw, beyond a deep, sundering gorge, of the rock ridges, snowfields and glaciers of the glorious peaks which are the Ortler's neighbours and satellites. Each of the many lay-bys thoughtfully provided, as the road falls deeper and deeper into the valley at the foot of the towering range, offers another enchantment for the eye or the camera. There are also several vantage-points high above the road, notably the one just below the 7,290-foot Furkelspitze (accessible by chair-lift from Trafoi), which should tempt even the most car-minded motorist to leave his vehicle for an hour or two in order to enjoy to the full the splendid panorama of peak and valley to the east and south.

In the photograph, taken not far above the Stelvio's summit, the huge glaciated mass of the Ortler itself rises on the left; (it is difficult to grasp that its flanks were the scene of bitter fighting during the First World War). Next, and farthest away, comes the snowy trapeze of the Gran Zebru (12,255 feet), dominating the glacier which plunges into the central depths, followed to its right by the white dome of the Eiskögele (11,710 feet) and the long, keen rock crest of the Thurwieserspitze (11,945 feet). To their right again, the snows and heavily-crevassed glaciers of the 11,600-foot Trafoier Eiswand go streaming down into the rift below the great, dark buttress containing them and slashing diagonally across the centre of the picture. On the extreme right rises the Schneeglocke (11,215 feet) with its spotless mantle of white.

The crest of the great complex of peaks shown in the picture measures more than four miles. Trafoi, the little mountain hamlet, nestling at 5,050 feet at their foot, and from which all climbs on this side of the Ortler range start, lies too deep down in the trench below the Ortler's rocky base to be visible.

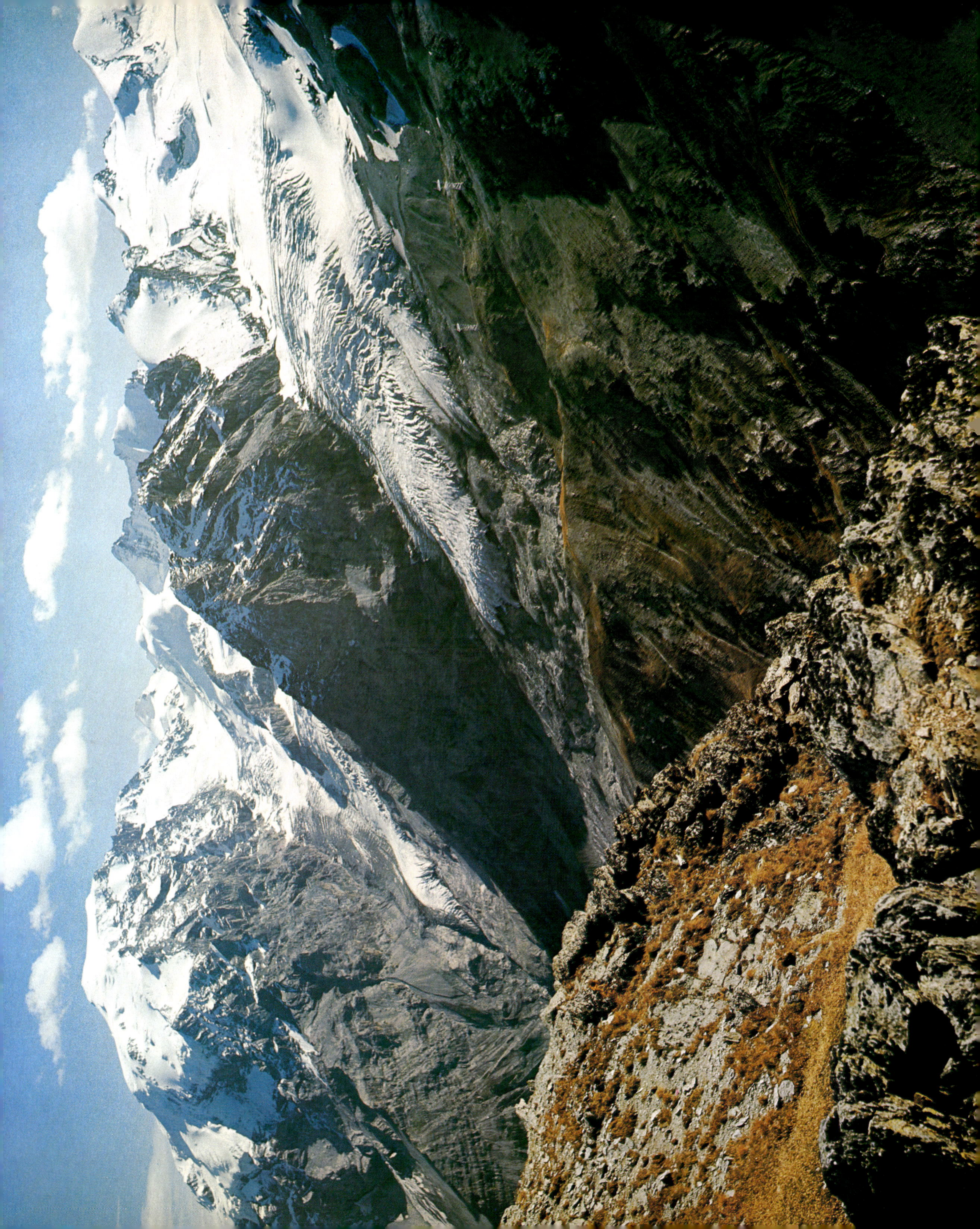

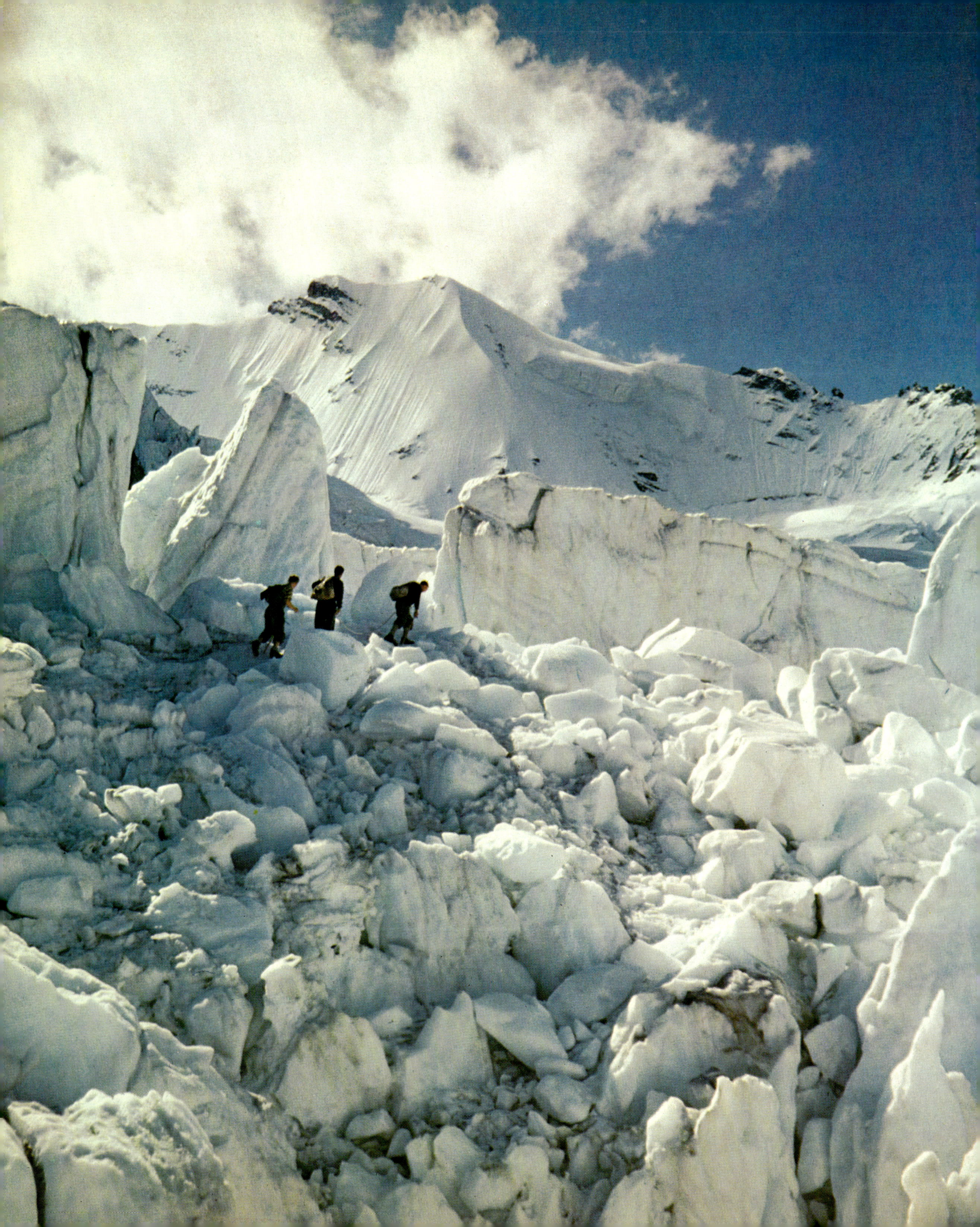

In the icefall of the Trafoier Eiswand (Ortler Group)

The Ortler Group (12,800 feet), and the Bernina (13,295 feet) in the Engadine (Switzerland), thirty miles to its west, are the two loftiest ranges in the Eastern Alps.

Not two miles south-west of the Ortler (see plate 61) rises the heavily-glaciated summit of the Trafoier Eiswand (11,600 feet), whose north face falls away in an ice slope 700 feet high, seen in the left centre of the photograph. This is no target for the ordinary glacier tourist, for its ascent requires both skill and experience of a high order; even the approach through the crevassed chaos of the ›Amphitheatre‹ below it is difficult and dangerous. Needless to say, first-class equipment – ropes, ice-axes and crampons – are indispensable on such undertakings.

One of the disquieting features of this kind of icefall is the possible collapse of a sérac or ice-tower, and this is an unpredictable hazard. An indispenable precaution on such terrain is to keep as far apart as possible, so that in case of an emergency the whole party on the rope is not engulfed by the fall of one of these masses of ice.

The chaotic condition of this type of icefall is caused in the first instance by counter-pressures in the flow of the glacier and by the structure of the bed beneath it. The ice masses frequently move down towards the valley over humps in the rock base underneath them; at such points the ice shatters and an icefall comes into being.

The Churfirsten, in Eastern Switzerland

The traveller, by road or rail, from Buchs to Sargans, passing along the pretty shores of the Walensee, will observe to his north, the peculiar saw-toothed rock chain of the Churfirsten. No Alpine giants these, with a maximum altitude of 7,550 feet, but, for all that, a most interesting area for the rambler and climber.

The photograph shows them from their northern aspect in the upper Toggenburg district, seen across the clear waters of the rushing Thur, which bounds the area on the north. Starting from the left, the peaks are the Hinterrugg, Schibenstoll, Zuestollen, Brisi, Frümsel, Selun and Leistschamm.

This northern part of the Churfirstens' domain is highly rewarding for those who delight in rambling free from danger, or who are interested in climbing summits whose ascent is easy all the way and takes only four or five hours from Wildhaus, the main village in the valley.

The complete traverse of all the summits in the range, however, demands a measure of mountaineering skill and a considerable degree of stamina; while the southern faces of these peaks, which fall towards the Walensee – on the reverse side from that shown in the picture – are only suitable for first-class rock climbers, since their faces, from 1,000–1,600 feet high, offer only very difficult routes, from Grade IV–VI (›Super Severe‹), and are in fact very rarely ascended, and then mostly by local climbers.

The Churfirsten are interesting not only for their walking and climbing attractions but for the geological and botanical discoveries to be made among them.

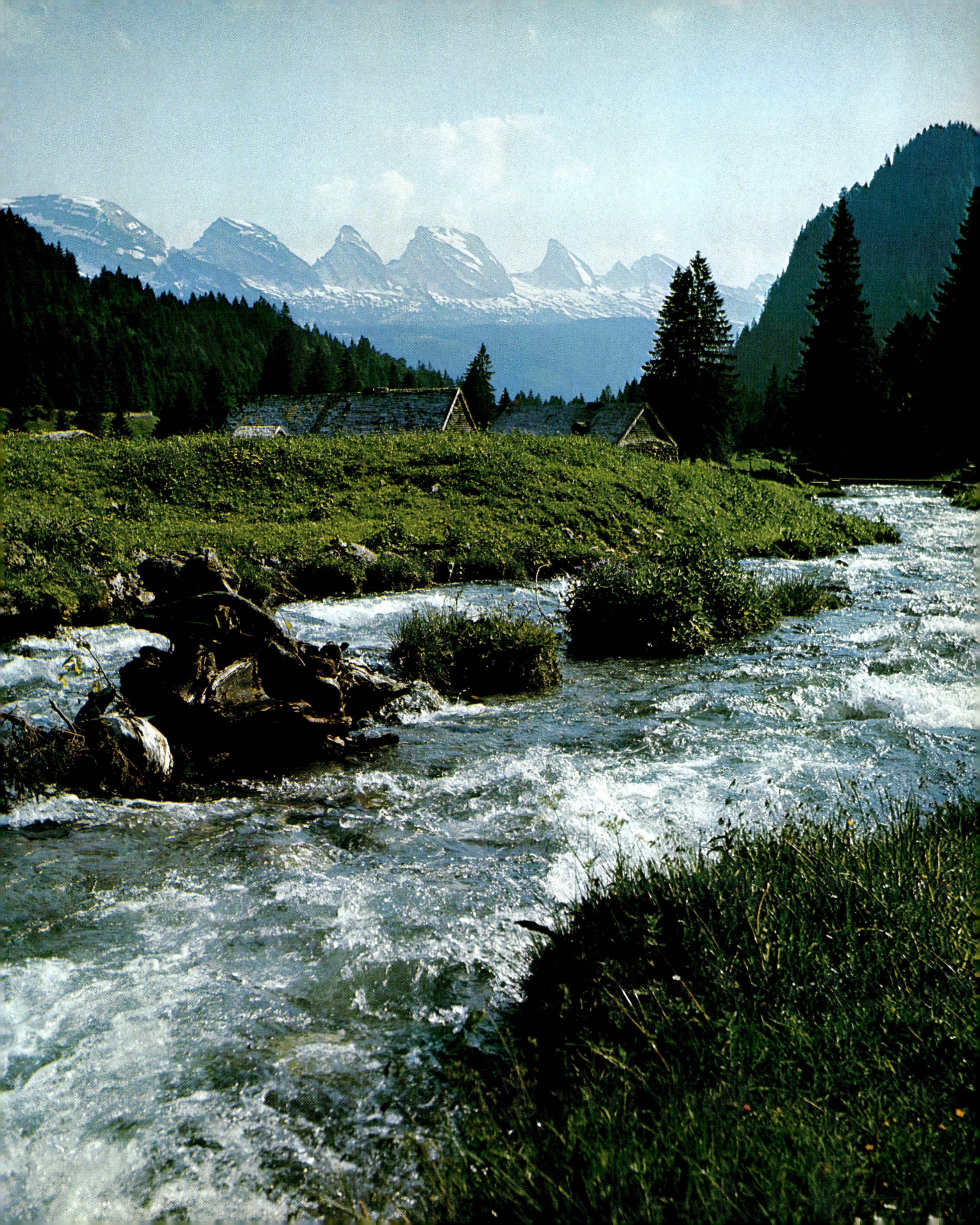

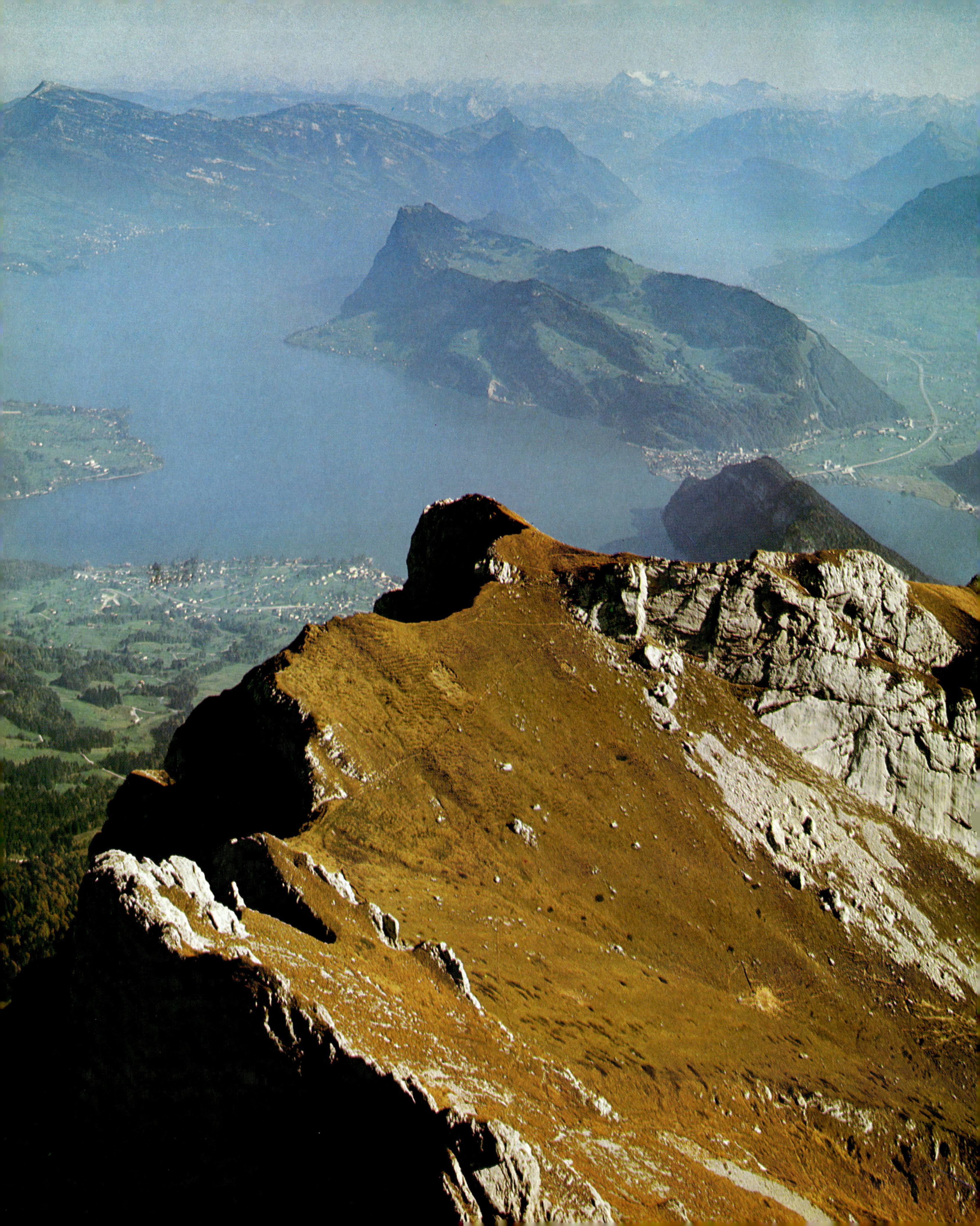

The Lake of Lucerne, from Pilatus

Pilatus (6,995 feet) is Lucerne's own landmark and dominates the lower reaches of the Vierwaldstätter See (›The Lake of the Four Cantons‹), known to us for convenience's sake as the Lake of Lucerne.

The view from the spiky rocks of its riven summit and from the airy paths which span its long ridges, towards the great sweep of the distant Alps and away to the Vosges and the Black Forest is overwhelming; equally impressive is the foreground view, plunging some 5,000 feet onto Lucerne and its beautiful, many-armed lake.

In days gone by, hundreds of thousands made their toilsome and not entirely undangerous way up to the summit. Today there is no need to exert oneself in order to enjoy the marvellous panorama, for the Pilatus Railway has been in operation ever since 1889. This was the first rack-and-pinion line in the world and its opening was one of the sensations of the day. The track is just under three miles long and has a gradient of 43 per cent; the journey takes just half an hour.

Our picture shows only a sector of the great circular view and embraces 55°, looking due east. Down below the brown summit ridge on the left lie Hergiswil and the little hamlet of Rüti on its own peninsula. The centre is occupied by the wooded spur of the Bürgenstock jutting out into the lake, with Stanstadt on the narrow plain at its foot.

In the top left corner, its long wooded ridges and sunny alps stretching away to the right, rises the Rigi (5,905 feet), another famous viewpoint, also accessible by rack-and-pinion railway, from Vitznau. While on the far horizon, a little to the right of centre and directly above the long eastern arm of the lake, the glaciers of the 9,583-foot Glärnisch can just be seen catching the afternoon sun.

The Wetterhorn, above Grindelwald

There are numerous Wetterhörner, large and small, difficult and easy, harmless and dangerous, throughout the Alps, but the 12,149-foot Wetterhorn in the Bernese Alps is assuredly the highest, the most impressive and certainly the most famous of them all.

On its northern (Grindelwald) side it plunges to the valley in a single precipitous leap of rock 9,500 feet high, crowned by hanging glaciers, from which great ice avalanches can be seen cascading almost every day (one of them is shown pouring down the shadowed precipice in the photograph). Prominent to the left of and below the summit, the Scheidegg-Wetterhorn (11,024 feet) is recognizable, crowning the supremely difficult 3,300-foot high north face, which sweeps right up to it from near the Grosse Scheidegg. On the extreme right is the sunlit trench of the Upper Grindelwald glacier, up which runs the normal route to the Gleckstein Hut (7,620 feet) on the rocky comb above, and thence (entirely hidden by it in the picture) by the great couloir to the Wettersattel and on by the final 550-foot summit ice slope to the top. In good conditions this is a long but not excessively difficult mixed snow and rock climb of about six hours from the hut, the steep path to which takes four to five hours from the valley.

The summit is a narrow, airy and superb view-point, with all the great peaks of the Oberland clustering round to the south and east, the lakes and plains of Northern Switzerland stretching away to the blue line of the Black Forest, and Grindelwald's roads and roofs spread like a map 9,000 feet sheer below the toe-caps of one's boots.

For the unadventurous rambler there is the twin chair-lift to First, on a high shelf facing a glorious panorama of snowy peaks, with gentle walks to the beautiful Bachalp See and elsewhere, and a long leisurely descent by path through pine forest and flower-laden meadows; though this should only be undertaken by those who are already walking-fit, for it entails a drop of some 3,750 feet – higher than the summit of Snowdon from sea-level. This can, of course, be greatly reduced by taking the chair-lift down to one of the intermediate stations, Egg or Bort.

There is a network of gentle paths through the lovely woods and meadows on the valley slopes to the north of Grindelwald, and these are even kept clear in winter for the visitor who is more interested in strolling in the sunshine than in the more strenuous delights of the ski slopes.

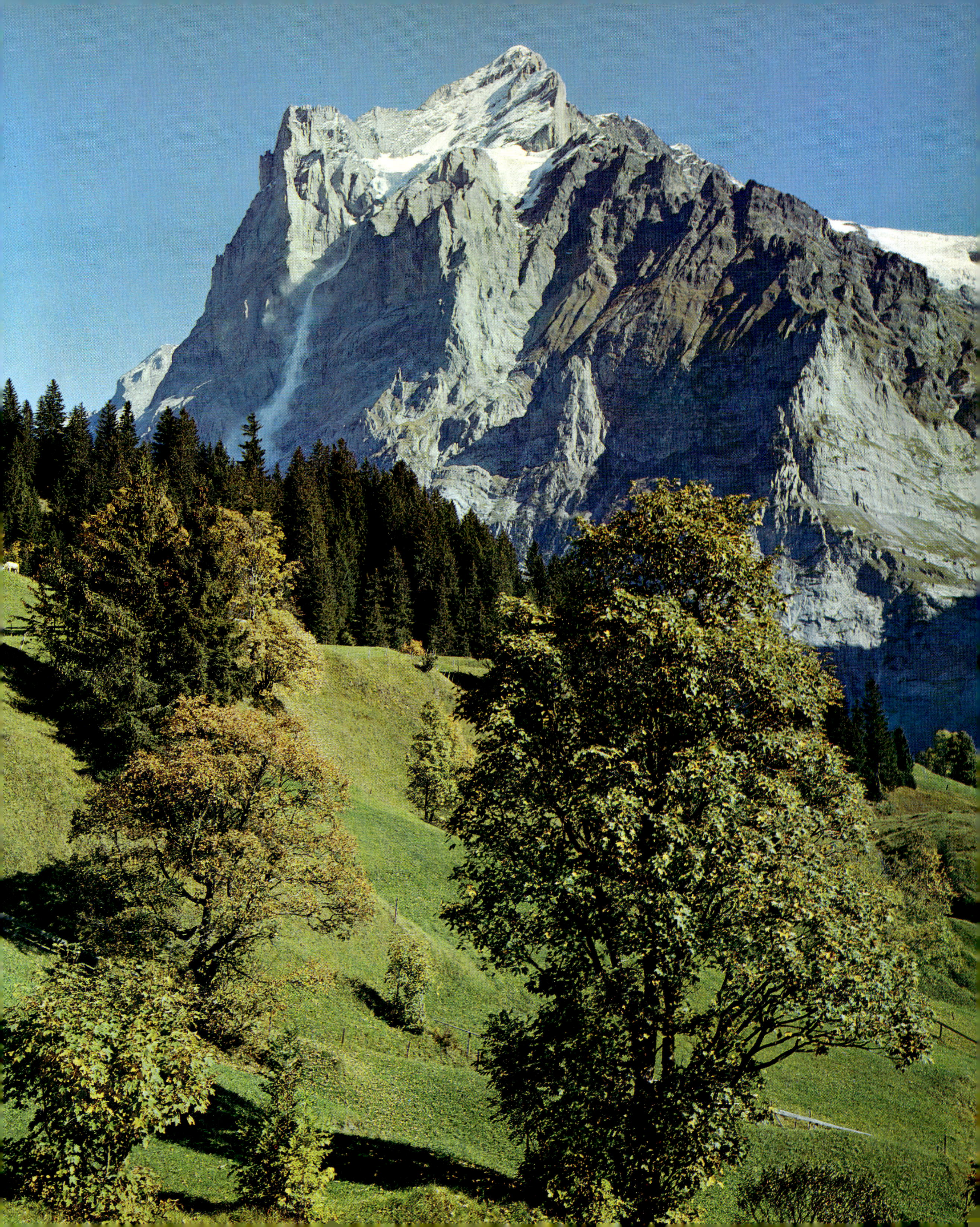

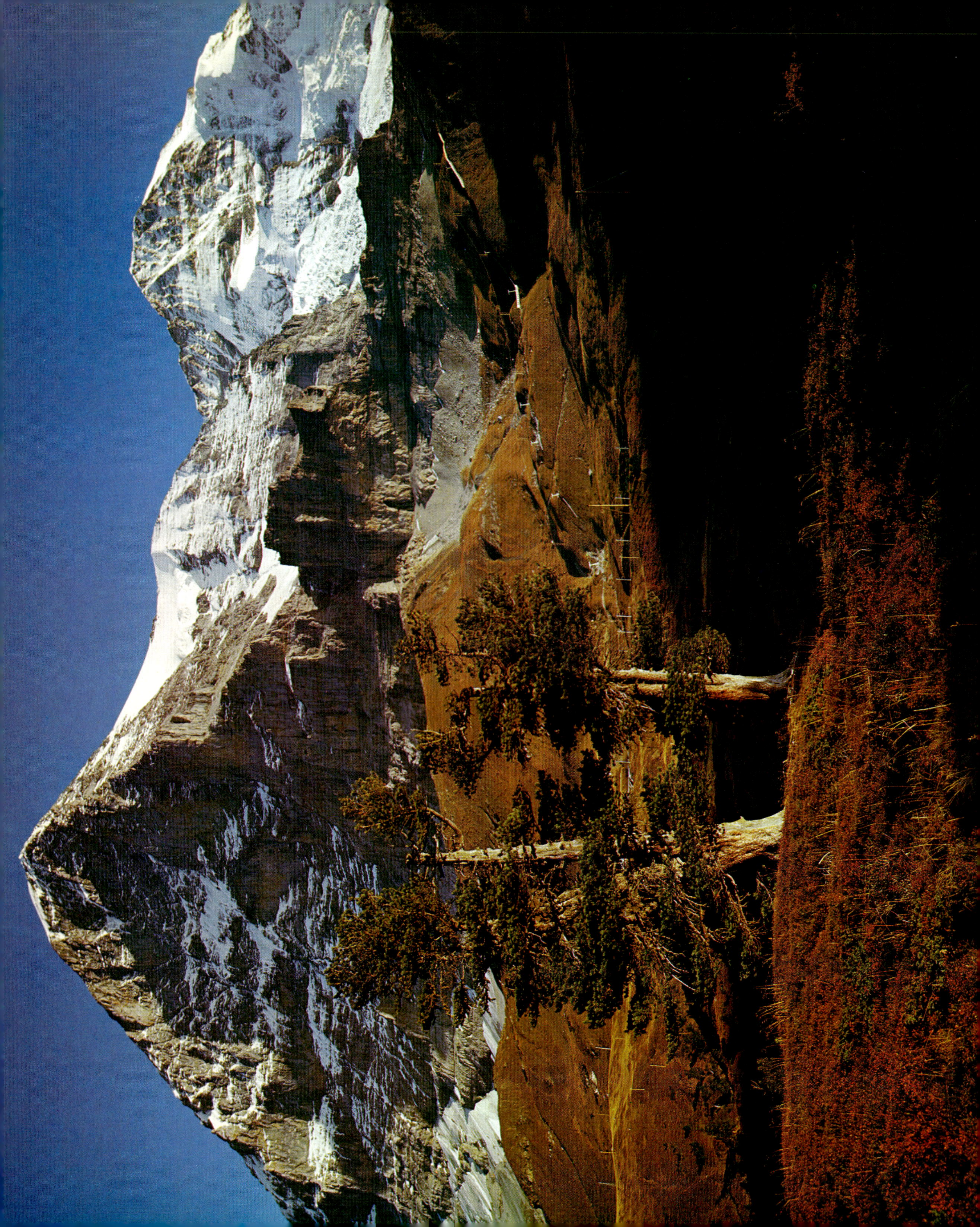

The Eiger and Mönch from the north

The three great neighbours, the Eiger (13,041 feet), Mönch (13,465 feet) and Jungfrau (13,670 feet) – not seen because it lies beyond the right-hand edge of the picture – are famous all over the world, and the area at their northern feet has been opened up to the world for more than half a century by a network of mountain railways.

Of these the Jungfraubahn, whose construction took from 1896 to 1912, is a veritable masterpiece of engineering, starting as it does from the 6,770-foot saddle of the Kleine Scheidegg and entering a tunnel beyond the station of Eigergletscher at the flat spur seen below the Mönch in the photograph, boring its way for nearly five miles inside the Eiger, then swinging back to penetrate the Mönch and reaching its terminus, still inside the mountain, at Jungfraujoch (11,340 feet), the highest railway station in Europe.

The photograph was taken at no great distance below the Kleine Scheidegg and shows the notorious north face of the Eiger, 6,000 feet high, in shadow, directly opposite the viewer. This fearsome gamble with death was first climbed in 1938 and has since been ascended more than fifty times, including climbs in winter conditions and an ultimate ›direttissima‹ route straight up to the summit, at a tragic cost of more than thirty young lives over the years. Some idea of the scale of this immense wall of almost vertical rock can be formed when one realizes that the icefield embedded at its centre is 550 yards wide. Publicity in the press, on radio and television has been such that there can hardly be anyone who has not heard of the north face.

The face is contained on its left by the North Buttress, first climbed in 1968. To its right lies the gentle west flank, which hardly calls for serious climbing except at a few points and provides the normal route to the summit of the Eiger; only in bad conditions is there any danger involved in the climb.

The 2,600-foot high north face of the Mönch has, fortunately, a much less dramatic history than that of its huge and murderous neighbour. To its right lies the curving white ridge of the ›Eisnollen‹, a favourite and oft-repeated climb.

Monte Rosa and Gorner Glacier, above Zermatt

This view of Monte Rosa (15,217 feet, the highest peak in Switzerland) was taken in evening light from the north-west, at a point which can be reached by any fit and vigorous mountain-lover: all he has to do is to take the Gornergrat Railway from Zermatt to its 10,289-foot terminal, there change to the Stockhorn ropeway as far as its intermediate station, Hohtäligrat (10,790 feet) and then walk a little way down the ridge. The keen mountain walker will also enjoy the splendid ridge walk of about an hour from the top station to the summit of the 11,595-foot Stockhorn, which presents little exertion and no danger, and rewards him with a glorious circular panorama of the greatest mountains in the Swiss Alps.

At the left top of the photograph is the Jägerjoch which helps to nourish the huge Gorner Glacier sweeping down to the right past the foot of the Monte Rosa massif. Above the steep ochre cliff to its right, the long, gentle snow ridge lifts to the snowy summit of the Nordend (15,126 feet), down again to the Silbersattel (14,809 feet) and then steeply up to the rocky comb of Monte Rosa's highest summit, the Dufourspitze (15,217 feet), named after General G. H. Dufour, who was responsible for the ›Dufour Map‹, the first great Swiss cartographic effort.

From the summit the ridge falls away to the Sattel (14,285 feet), where the ›boards‹ are abandoned during the ski-ascents possible in early spring. The rocky ridge below the saddle sweeps down to the (unseen) Grenz glacier, behind which, in shadow, rises the Parrotspitze, whose left-hand ridge swings round and up again to the Signalkuppe (Punta Gnifetti, 14,285 feet), Monte Rosa's other summit, on which stands the Regina Margherita Hut of the C.A.I.

The ascents of the Signalkuppe, descending again over the Grenz glacier, and of the Dufourspitze, running down over the Monte Rosa glacier, whose steep white expanse faces the viewer in the centre of the picture, are two of the most magnificent high-altitude ski tours in the Alps.

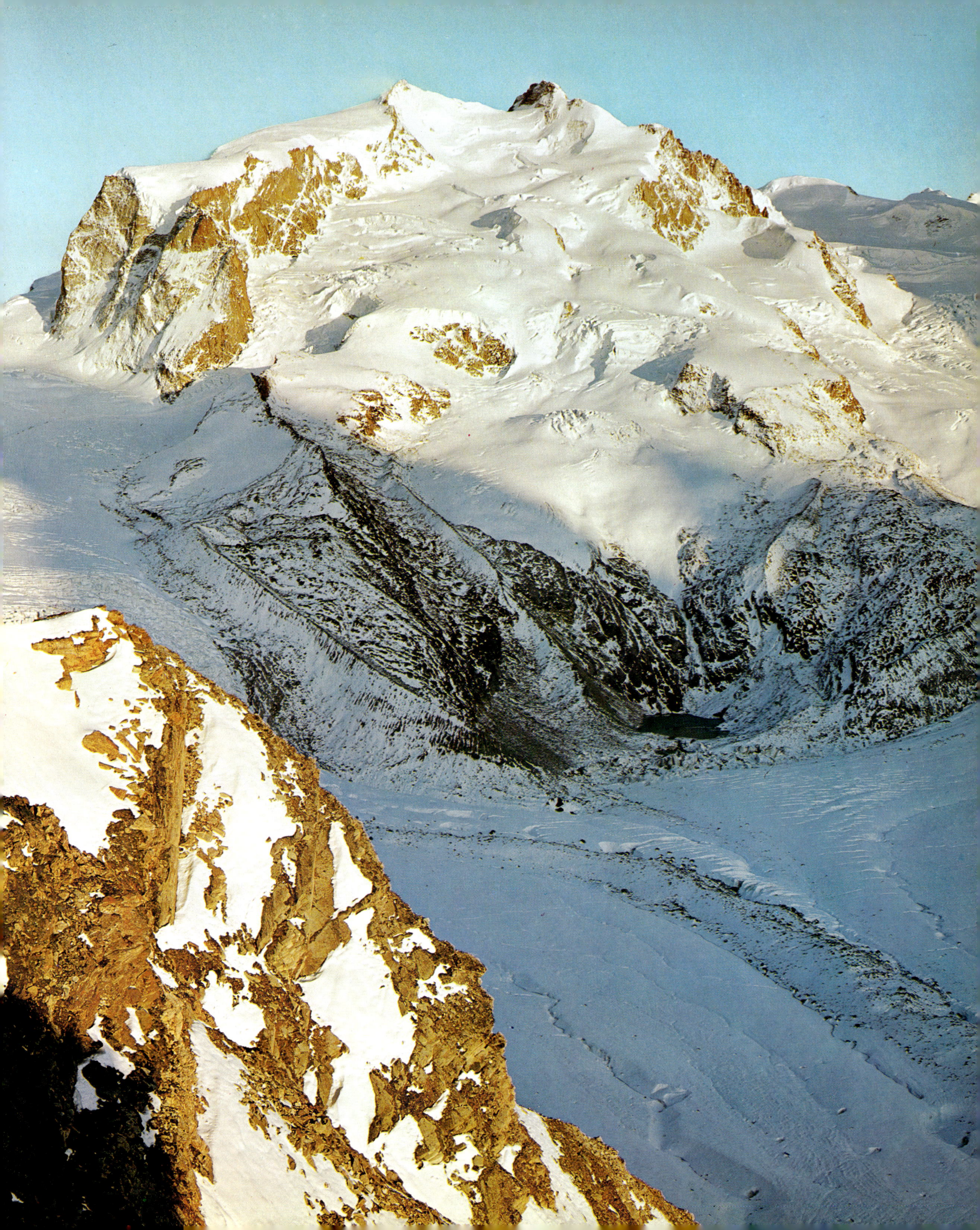

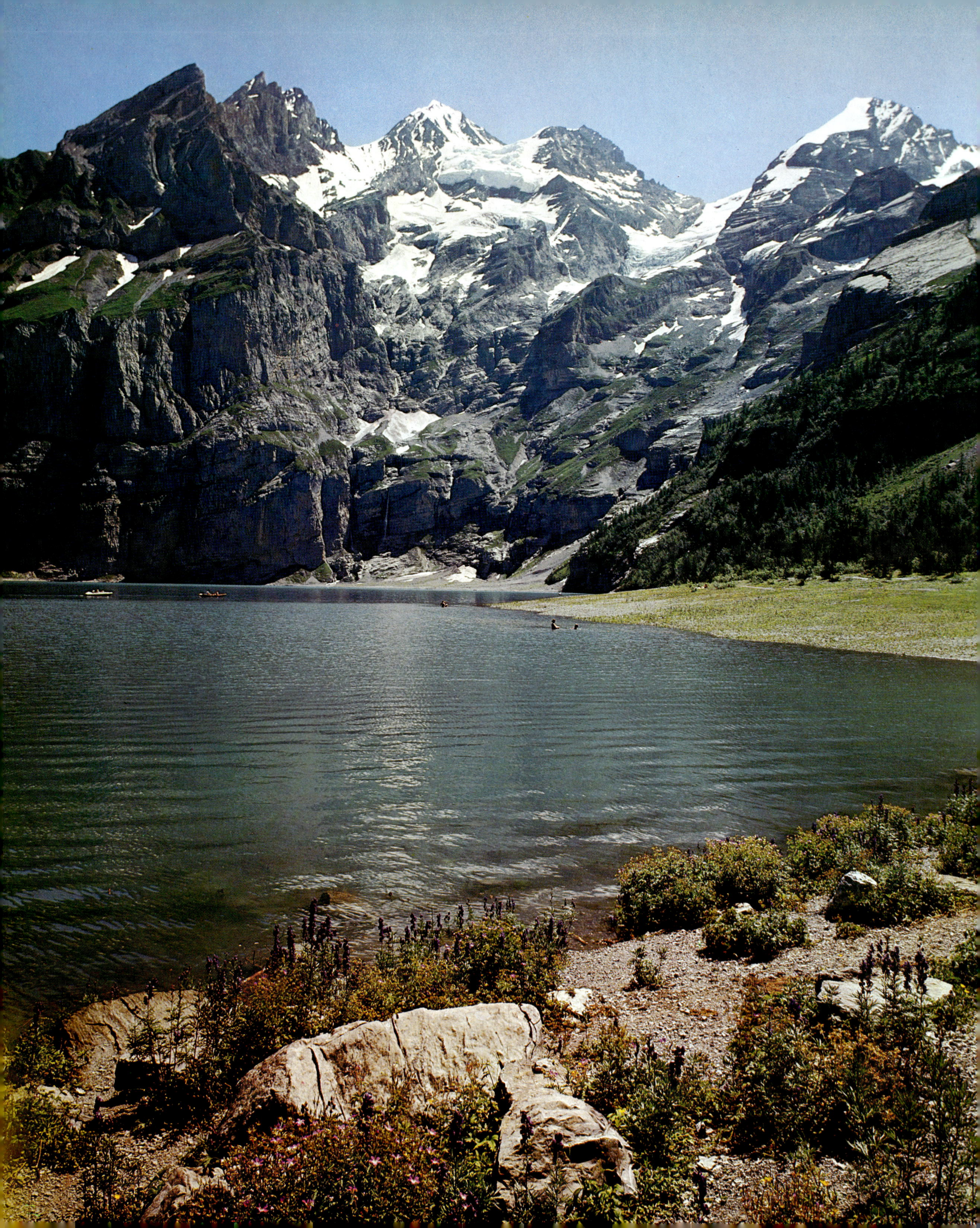

The Öschinensee and the Blumlisalp Group (Bernese Oberland)

The charming holiday resort of Kandersteg, situated at 3,900 feet in the upper Kandertal, whose clear streams flow down to empty themselves in the lake of Thun, lies in a little open plain just before the Lötschberg Railway dives into the great nine-mile tunnel, which bores its way under the high peaks into the Rhône Valley beyond them to the south.

Only a couple of miles to the east of the village, though 1,150 feet higher, at a level of 5,187 feet, lies the small but exceedingly beautiful Öschinensee, a little over a mile long and half a mile wide, surrounded by peaks, most of them glaciated to some extent. The lake can easily be reached on foot from Kandersteg by a comfortable stroll of an hour and a half; if this is considered too strenuous, there is a chair-lift from whose upper end a path descends slightly for a quarter of an hour to the lake shore. Ordinary tourists should content themselves with the lovely view, for the mountain tract above the lake demands mountaineering experience and the appropriate equipment.

To the left in the photograph, rise the sharp rock spires of the Blümlisalp Rothorn (10,828 feet). The crest of the ridge continues through the main summit, the snowy 12,040-foot Blümlisalphorn, the rocky Öschinenhorn (11,450 feet) and the Fründenhorn (11,045 feet) on the extreme right, crowned by a smooth white snowfield.

In the left centre, the icefalls and ice cliffs of the Vordere Blümlisalp glacier descend, ready to break away at any minute; to the right, the narrow stream of the Öschinengletscher sweeps down from between the Öschinenhorn and the Fründenhorn.

The ascent to the Blümlisalphorn's summit, about three miles distant from the camera, presents no great technical difficulties, but takes from six to eight hours, starting from the lake, and calls for a certain degree of mountaineering experience.

The Matterhorn from the Grenz Glacier

When you are on the lower part of the ski-ascent to Monte Rosa's 14,964-foot Signalkuppe (see plate 67) by way of the Grenzgletscher, your eyes are continually drawn westwards to the towering pyramid of the Matterhorn (14,780 feet), the pride of the Valaisian Alps and one of the most impressive and certainly most famous peaks in the world.

In the picture, directly facing the viewer, rises the mountain's snow-plastered east face, so menaced by falling stones that climbers rarely set foot on it, bounded on its left by the extremely difficult Furggen ridge (barely distinguishable as a thin line streaking to the summit) and on its right by the Hörnli or Swiss ridge. To the left of the Furggengrat bulk the dark rock precipices of the south (Italian) face. The peak is usually climbed from Zermatt by way of the Hörnligrat, which is liberally provided with strong fixed ropes; more than two hundred people have been known to reach its summit on a fine summer's day.

In the background, to the left of the Matterhorn, above a sunlit cloud, rises the sharp peak of the Dent d'Hérens (13,715 feet), a summit much less frequently visited, though it is a splendid mountain and offers the ›Sextogradists‹ one of the great north face climbs.

High in the left of the photograph soars the massif of the 13,685-foot Breithorn, with its three rocky summits and beyond them the highest point, a snowy dome, which can be climbed without great difficulty by practised mountaineers in four or five hours from the Gandegg Hut or the Theodule (10,900 feet). Cutting across the whole picture in front of the Breithorn's base is the snow-capped north spur of Pollux (out of sight to the left) and, in the left foreground, the northern spurs of the unseen Lyskamm sweep downwards, crowned by huge ice cliffs, behind the crevassed chaos of the Grenz glacier itself.

The frontier between Switzerland and Italy runs across the summits of the Breithorn, Matterhorn and Dent d'Hérens. The top of the Matterhorn is about eight miles from the camera, which gives some idea of the scale of these giants of the Western Alps.

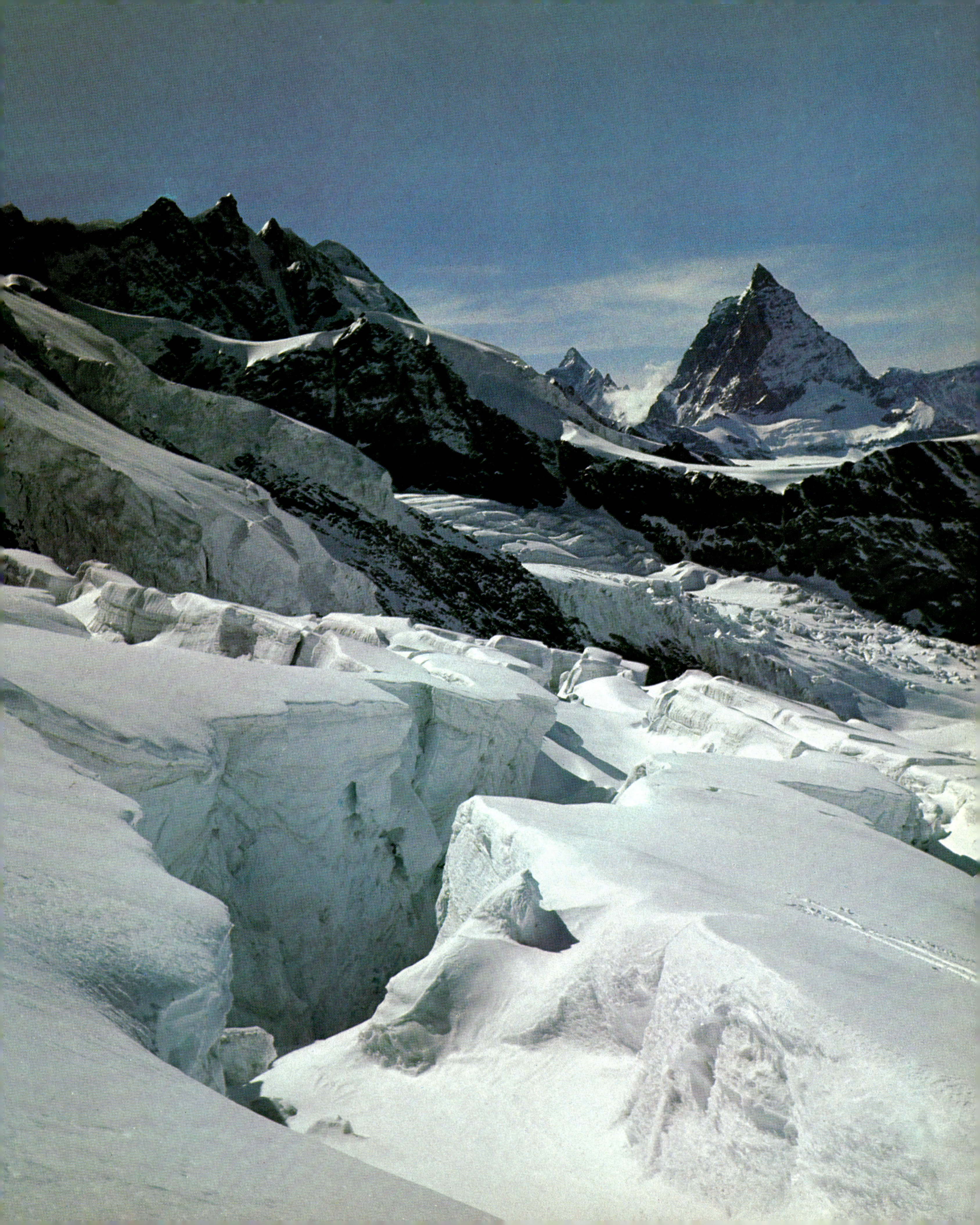

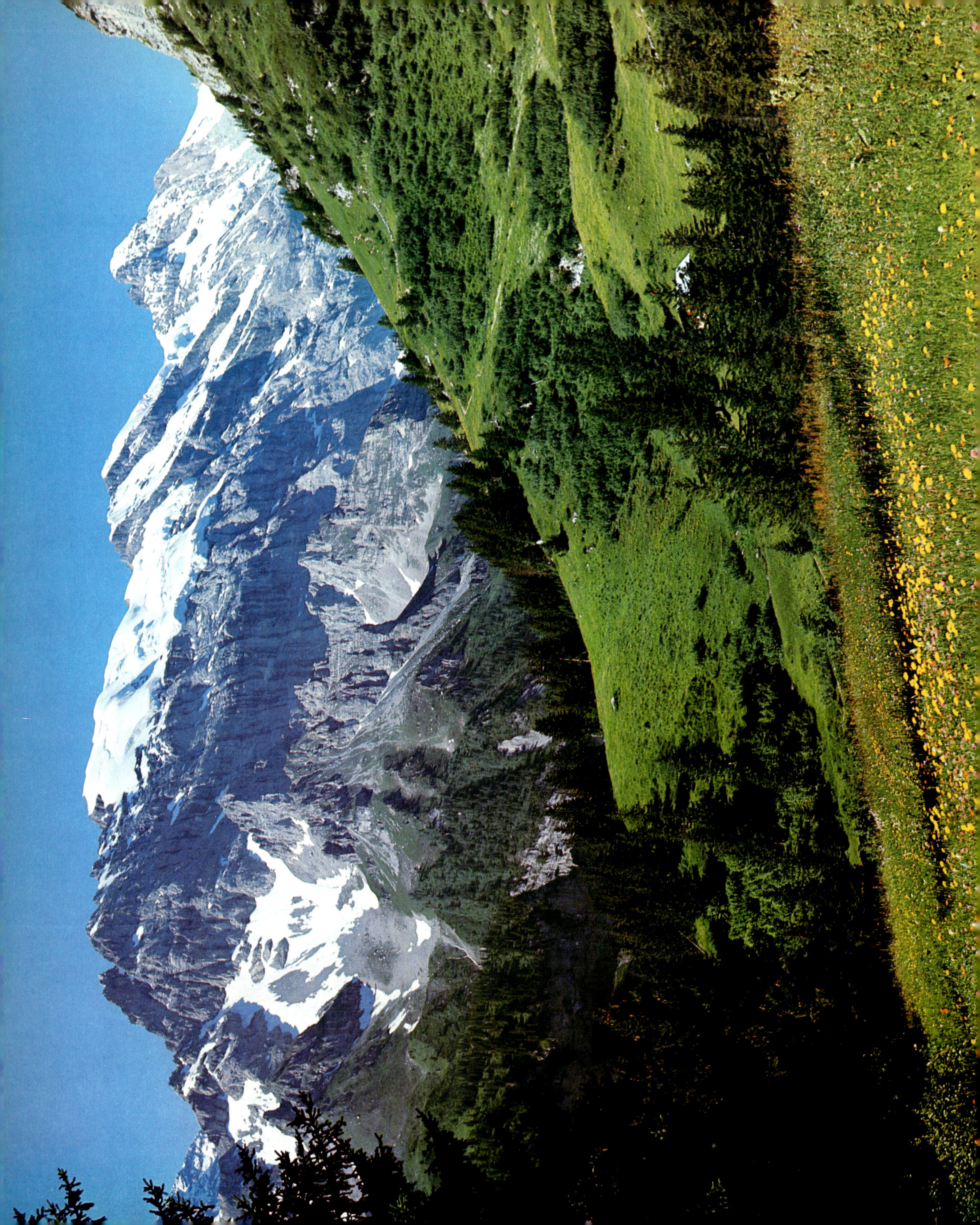

The G'spaltenhorn range from Mürren (Bernese Oberland)

We are all inclined, in this short life of ours, to label some corner of the earth as a paradise, though very often somebody else may show little or no enthusiasm for our choice of a private heaven. There can, however, be no disagreement about the far head of the Lauterbrunnen Valley in the Bernese Oberland, whose primaeval beauty has fascinated every visitor to it for well over a hundred years.

High up above it at 5,500 feet lies Mürren, free from all the horrid sounds of the motorcar, far from the rush and turmoil of these hectic times, surrounded by scenery unrivalled in its beauty by that to be found almost anywhere in the Alps. It faces the north walls of twelve giant peaks of the Oberland, plastered with glittering slopes of snow and ice; torrents and waterfalls ripple and roar through the green, flower-starred meadows dotted with brown wooden châlets. So it is not surprising that the area around Mürren's 9,754-foot Schilthorn, the fabulous prospect from whose summit is now accessible by the world's longest ropeway, has been dubbed ›Panoramaland‹. Moreover, its attractions are no less in winter than in summer, for the great Schilthorn ski-runs are among the finest in the Alps, and Mürren itself provides perfect slopes for the beginner and the expert alike.

The photograph, taken on the outskirts of Mürren itself, shows only a small sector of the vast panorama. To the left rises the Tschingelturm (9,253 feet), whose arête has not yet been climbed, with the Ellstabhorn's still virgin north face flanking it to the right. Then follows the long snow-cushioned ridge of the Tschingelgrat (10,299 feet), beyond which soars the tower of the 11,295-foot G'spaltenhorn, at whose feet lies the Kilchbalm, a gloomy cauldron overshadowed by walls 6,000 feet high, grim and oppressive as if it were the funeral vault of the world.

The Matterhorn

If you asked a child or a North Sea trawlerman, who has never seen a mountain, to try to draw a picture of one, he would almost certainly produce the ideal mountain form – a sharp pyramid with four faces and four ridges. In other words, the exact shape of the 14,780-foot Matterhorn, the ›Lion of Zermatt‹.

There can hardly be a literate inhabitant of the world who is not familiar with the outlines of the great peak, first climbed in 1865, but pictured over many decades since on Swiss (and other) advertisements and posters, chocolate and biscuit boxes, cheese wrappers, watch cases and, even quite irrelevantly, on the wrappings of a great many other articles.

During the last hundred years the Matterhorn has not only enhanced the fame of mountaineers but has proved a veritable goldmine to the inhabitants of Zermatt, for there are few foreigners who do not wish to see the mighty wedge and, of course, it must be from Zermatt, from which it shows itself in its full magnificence.

This photograph shows the peak rising majestically above the stone pines of the Riffelalp (7,300 feet), easily accessible by the Gornergrat Railway if a two-hour ascent of 1,500 feet up an easy path is considered too exacting an undertaking.

In the centre, the north-east ridge, the Hörnligrat, clearly defined between the sunlit snow of the east face and the shadow of the gloomy 4,000-foot high north face, is directly opposite the viewer, with the long, snowy Zmutt ridge faintly discernible above the right-hand pine branches. The left-hand ridge is the Furggengrat, the mountain's most difficult ascent route.

The normal route up the Hörnligrat is today incomparably easier than it was a century ago, for every difficult or exposed pitch on it has since been safeguarded and protected by strong lengths of fixed rope, so that though the ascent is long it is nowadays not technically difficult.

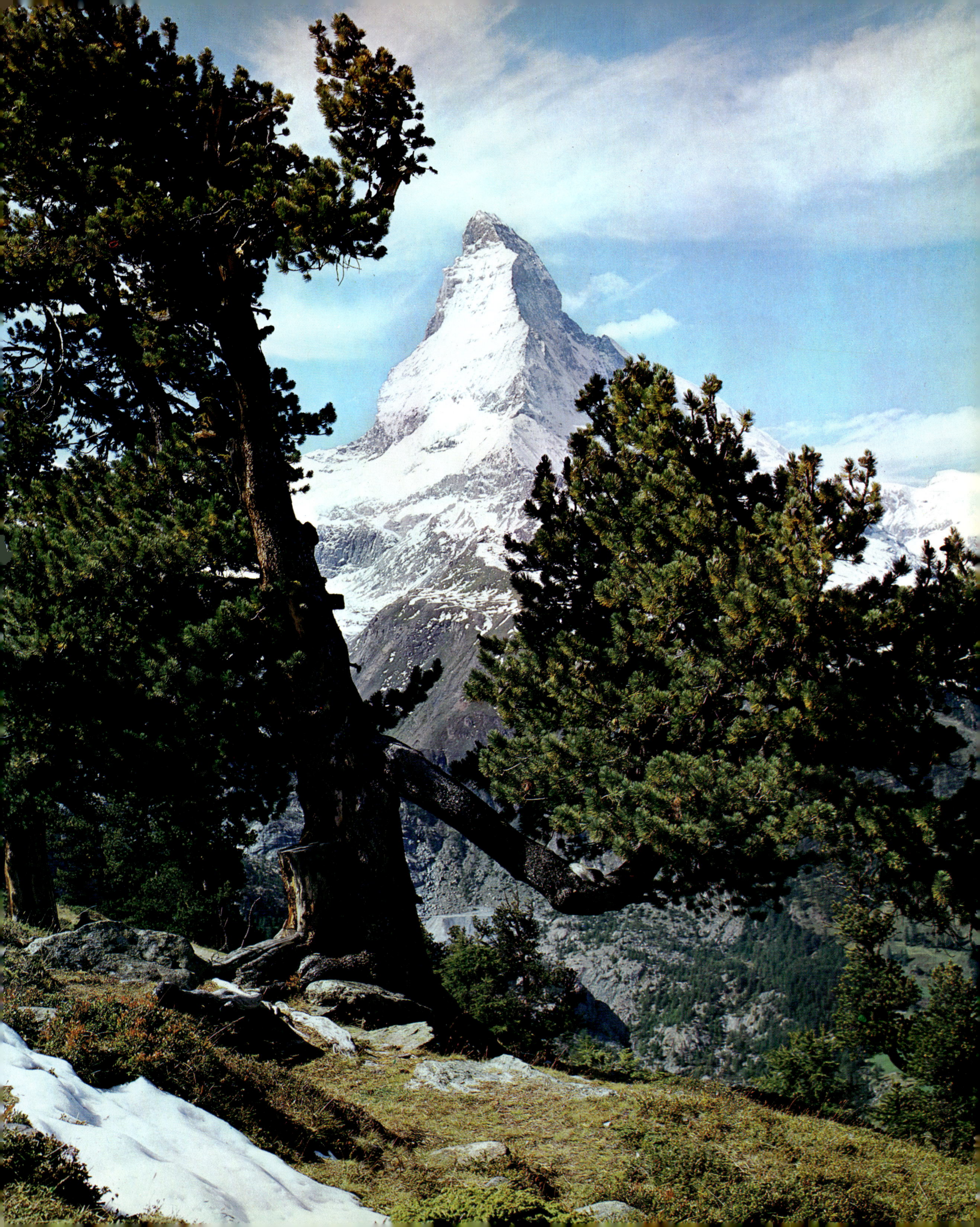

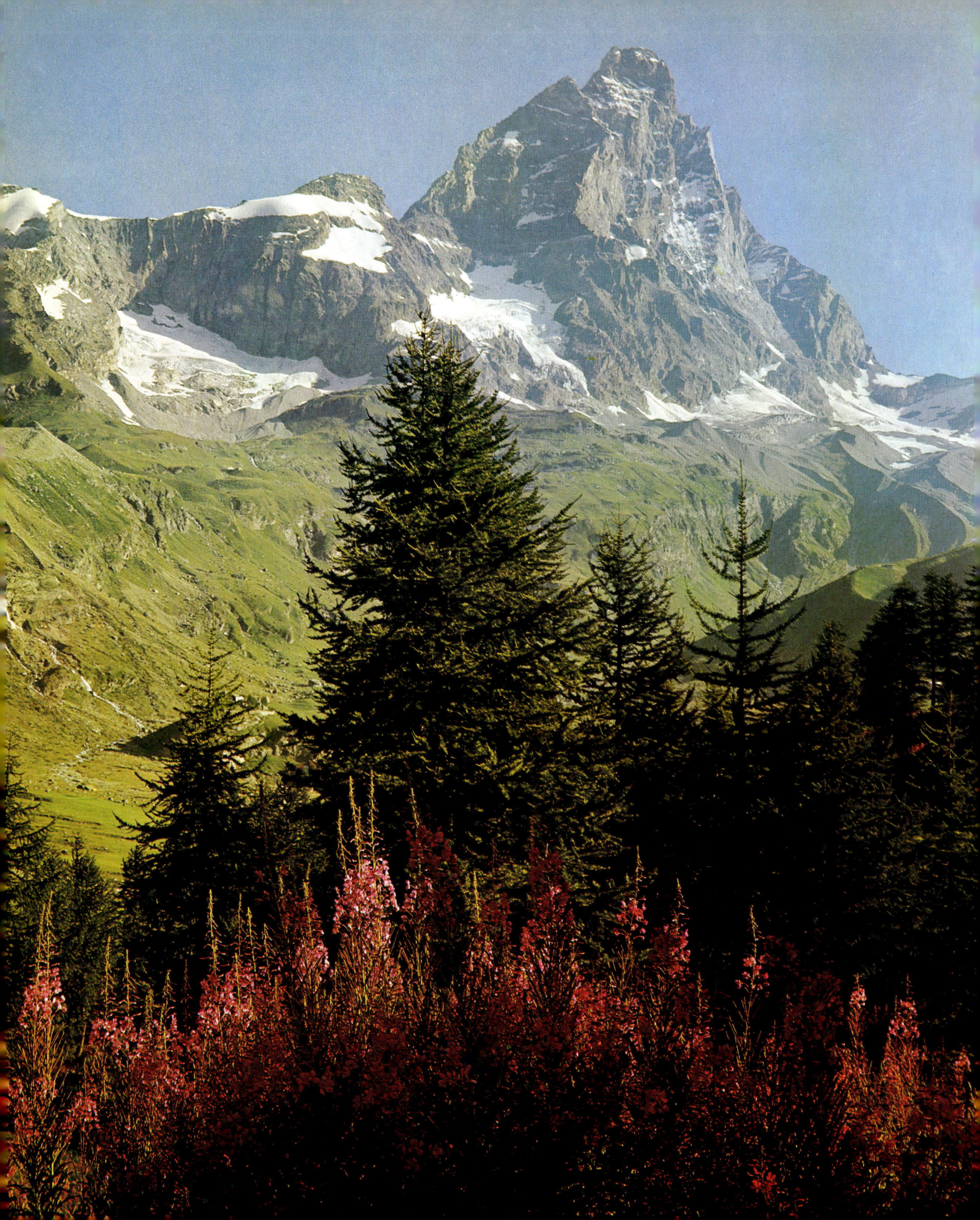

The Matterhorn from the south

A hundred years ago, Breuil, at the head of the Valtournanche, a long lateral valley rising northwards from the main Aosta Valley of the Dora Baltea in Italy, consisted of a few poverty-stricken hovels and an inn to house visitors.

It was not till after the Matterhorn was first climbed in 1865 by Edward Whymper and his ill-fated party from the Swiss side that better days dawned for all those who dwelt in the shadow of the great peak, including the inhabitants of this Italian valley to the south of the Monte Cervino, as the Italians call it.

Since that time, Breuil, recently renamed Cervinia, has become a flourishing ski resort with ropeways running up to magnificent snow slopes at the south foot of the mountain at Furggen and to the broad snowy plateau on the south side of the Breithorn, known as Plan Rosa. Unfortunately, in the process, what was once a picturesque mountain hamlet has been replaced by a veritable city of tall concrete hotels, which to those who knew the quiet, rugged beauty of the valley not so many years ago constitute an affront and an eyesore. In summer, too, the peace of this secluded glen has been shattered by fleets of forty-seater coaches, jamming its long narrow road and unloading hordes of one-day sightseers at its end. Progress is, alas, not always synonymous with improvement.

The photograph shows the Matterhorn's 5,000-foot south face, first climbed in 1931 by the Italians, Enzo Benedetti, Louis Carrel and Maurice Bich. At the base of the huge south-west ridge, generally known as the Italian ridge, lies the deep notch of the Col du Lion (11,735 feet) with the Tête du Lion rising to its left. Most of the ascents from the Italian side are done up this ridge, on which the more difficult pitches, which, on 17 July 1865, gave the pioneers of the climb, the great Jean-Louis Carrel and Jean-Baptiste Bich, so much trouble, have been lavishly provided with strong fixed ropes. The right-hand skyline is the extremely difficult Furggen ridge (see plates 69 and 71). The distance from the camera to the summit was about two and a half miles.

Motorists driving up the valley may be interested to known that, a mile or so short of Cervinia, there lies, completely screened by pines, to the right of the road, an exquisite little emerald of a tarn, whose placid waters reflect the whole stature of the mighty peak – a truly beautiful mountain gem well worth a parked car and a five-minute stroll.

The glacier world of the Bernina

The Bernina Group, rising between the lofty corridor of the Upper Engadine in Switzerland and the deep trench of the Adda Valley, the Val Tellina, in Italy, ranks after the Valais and Bernese Oberland as the third largest glacier area in the Alps. In spite of the heavy glaciation on its northern side, the valleys here lie at a remarkably high average level of 6,000 feet.

The climbers' huts, on the other hand, have been sited at a relatively low average of about 8,000 feet, at least on the Swiss side, so that they can be easily reached by the modest Alpine rambler. Obviously, not every devotee of the Alps, however much he may love the beauties of the Alpine scene, is a dyed-in-the-wool mountaineer. Yet, since the huts are so readily accessible, the Bernese Group is a walker's and rambler's paradise and not only a domain for tough Alpine experts to enjoy.

The photograph was taken from the north, looking across to the western lateral moraine of the Morteratsch glacier. The magnificent prospect includes, from left to right, the rocky summit structure of Piz Bernina (13,295 feet), the highest peak in the group, close to whose short, dark right-hand ridge Piz Bianco, only 167 feet lower, raises its white head – just missing the dignity of being a ›Four-thousander‹ in its own right by a mere two metres. The ice ridge running down from it to the right is the fabulously lovely Biancograt, a narrow crest of ice which is one of the best-loved ice climbs in the Alps. To the right of the saddle at its base rises the modest Piz Prievlusa (›the Perilous Peak‹, 11,500 feet), then, towering above it, the broad ice-crowned mass of Piz Morteratsch (12,315 feet), and finally the triple-headed Piz Boval.

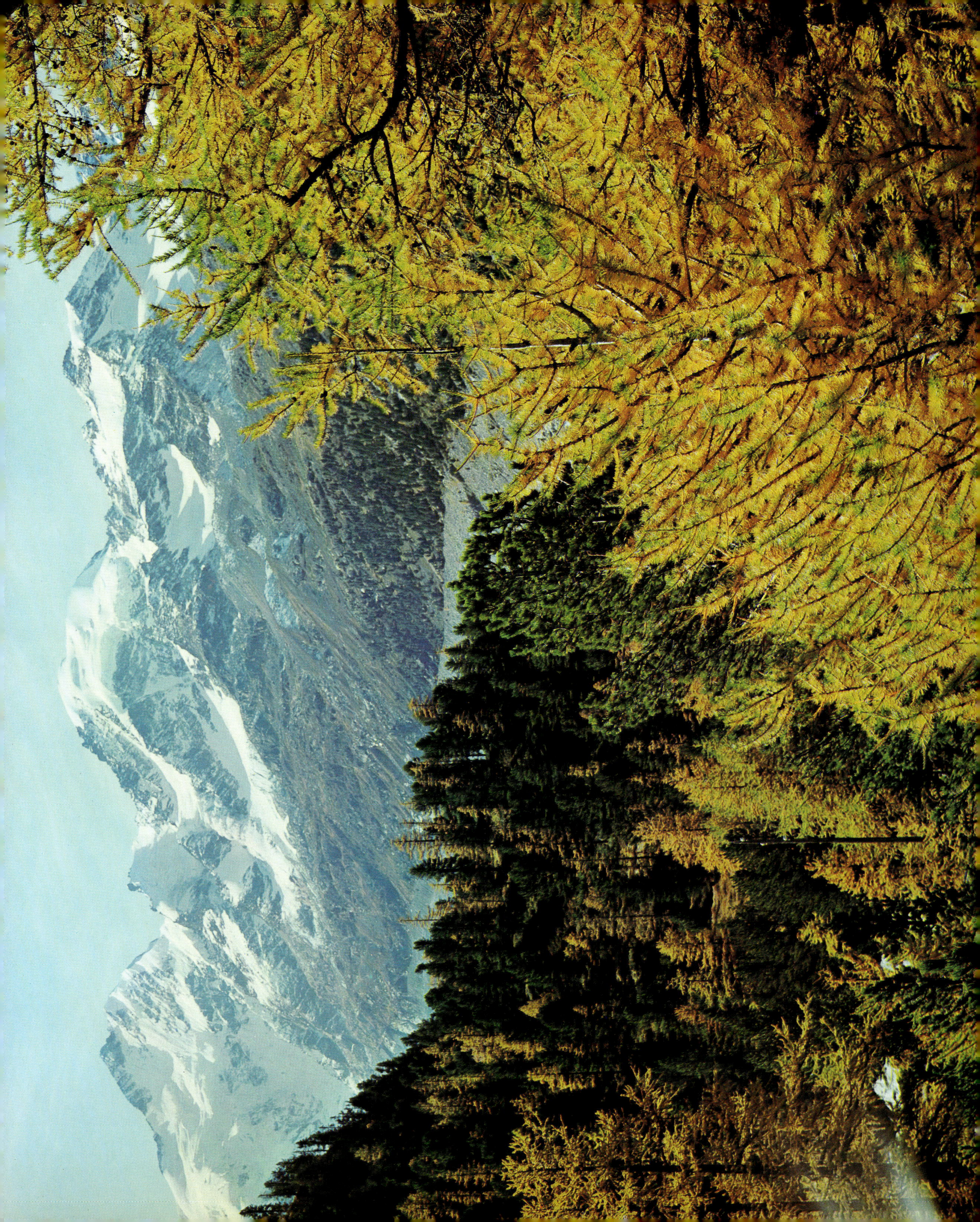

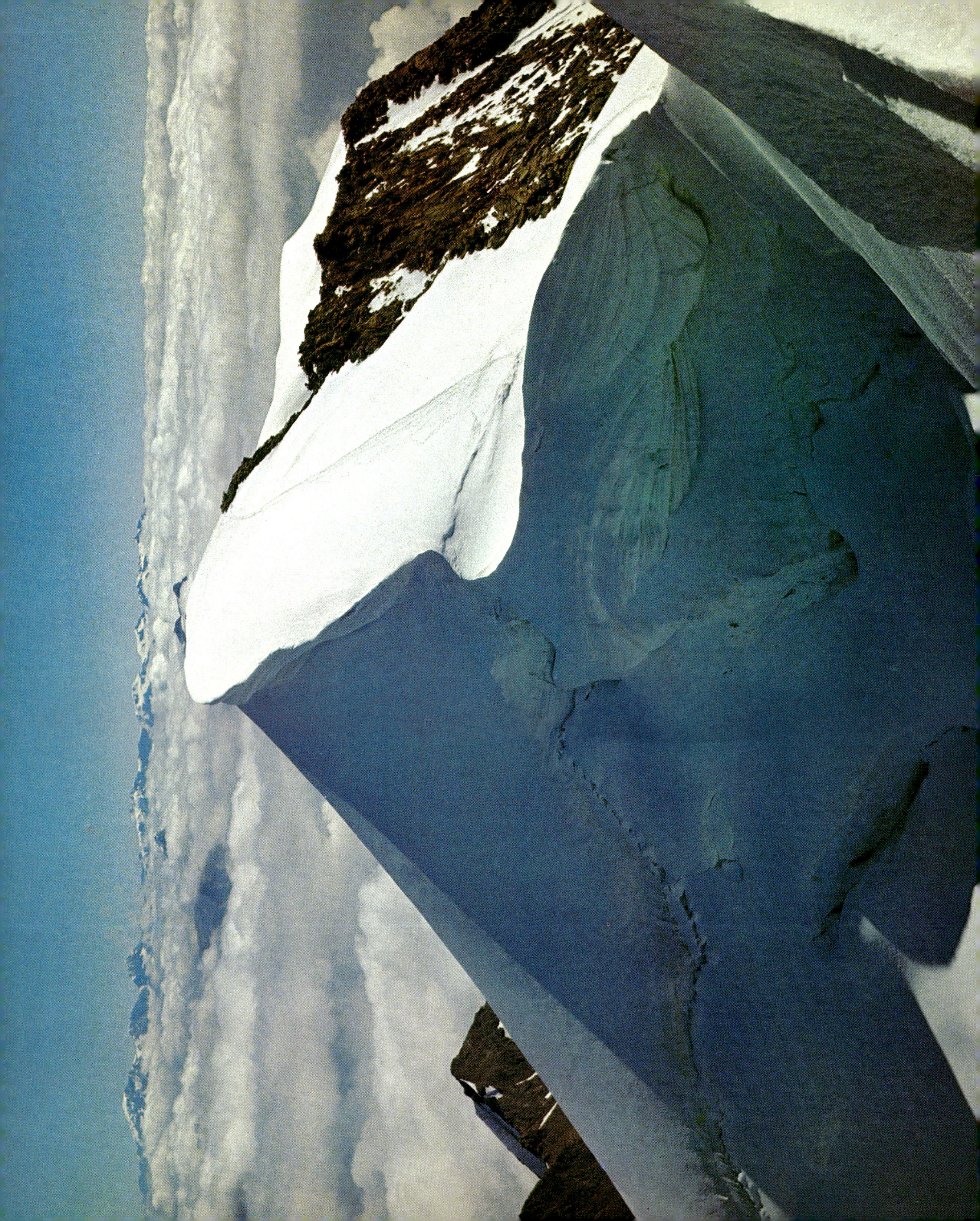

On Piz Palü

The massif of Piz Palü (12,835 feet), with its three almost equal summits is beyond dispute the most imposing peak in the Upper Engadine's Bernina Group which, in spite of its typically West Alpine character, belongs geographically to the Eastern Alps, whose solitary ›Fourthousander‹ is 13,295-foot Piz Bernina.

Seen from the Diavolezza Hut (9,767 feet) to its north, accessible in comfort by ropeway, Piz Palü presents a particularly impressive spectacle. Its steep north faces – in the picture, to the left of the beautiful curve of the summit cornice – are, however, no place for any but experienced climbers, though many years ago they provided the location for a famous film, *The White Hell of Piz Palü*.

The traverse of all three summits from east to west, on the other hand, is a sheer delight for anyone familiar with ordinary glacier tours; and, even if experience be lacking, this glorious progress between light and shade, quite close to the corniced ice rim of the summit ridge, high above the world, can be safely enjoyed in the professional care of a guide.

In the photograph, on the far horizon above the broad expanse of ›cloud-sea‹, the great peaks of the Ortler Group can be seen lifting their snow-capped heads.

The name Palü for this almost completely glaciated mountain is something of a paradox. It is derived from the Latin *palus*, meaning a marsh; and while the Alp-Palü at its feet is inclined to harbour marshy patches, this proud white peak certainly does not.

On the Weisshorn (Valais)

The three ridges and faces of the Weisshorn (14,804 feet) dominate the middle sections of the Zermatt Valley (Nikolaital) above the village of Randa where, with its ice faces, its rock faces, its ridges of snow and stone, it goes streaming to the sky like some huge triple-faced obelisk.

It was first climbed in 1861, four years before the Matterhorn, by John Tyndall with his guides J. J. Bennen and Ulrich Wenger, by the snowy east ridge, which has since in fact become the normal ascent route, and on which the two climbers are seen in the photograph. The climb is a fairly strenuous undertaking – ten to eleven hours from the Weisshorn Hut to the summit and back – but not technically difficult and, above all, relatively safe, for on it there is no danger from falling stones.

The view is overwhelming. Above the broad white expanses of the Jägerjoch and Gorner glacier to the left of the picture, bulks the great mass of Monte Rosa (15,217 feet), with its own glacier falling from it. The next great peak, its famous north face deep in shadow, is the 14,888-foot Lyskamm's long summit ridge, ranging high above the crevassed Grenz glacier at its feet. Beyond the Lyskamm, the ridge sweeps on over the two closely-huddled summits of the Twins – Castor and Pollux (13,848 and 13,432 feet) – to the long rocky crest of the Breithorn (13,685 feet), again in deep shadow, whose snowy summit dome is just off the picture.

The deep trench of the Nikolaithal lies behind the climbers, and high on its snowless slope, directly below the Breithorn, a section of the Gornergrat Railway can be seen glinting as a diagonal white thread; the Gornergrat itself, in the middle-ground below the Lyskamm, is somewhat difficult to distinguish. The Zermatt Valley ends in the far right-hand depths of the picture behind the 11,188-foot Mettelhorn, the low, sharp rock peak partly obscured by the leading climber, itself a fine view-point and a relatively easy climb from the Trift Hotel above Zermatt.

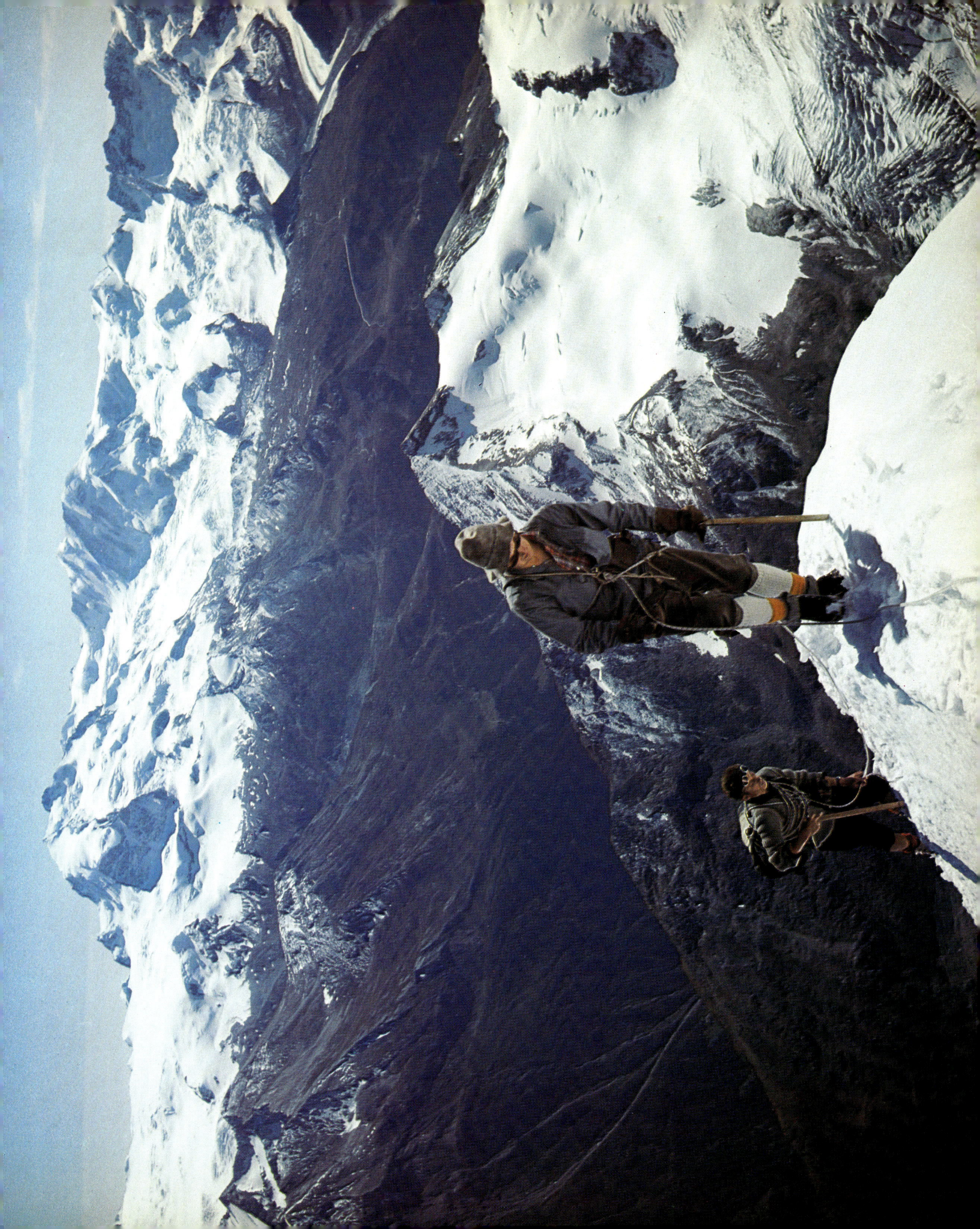

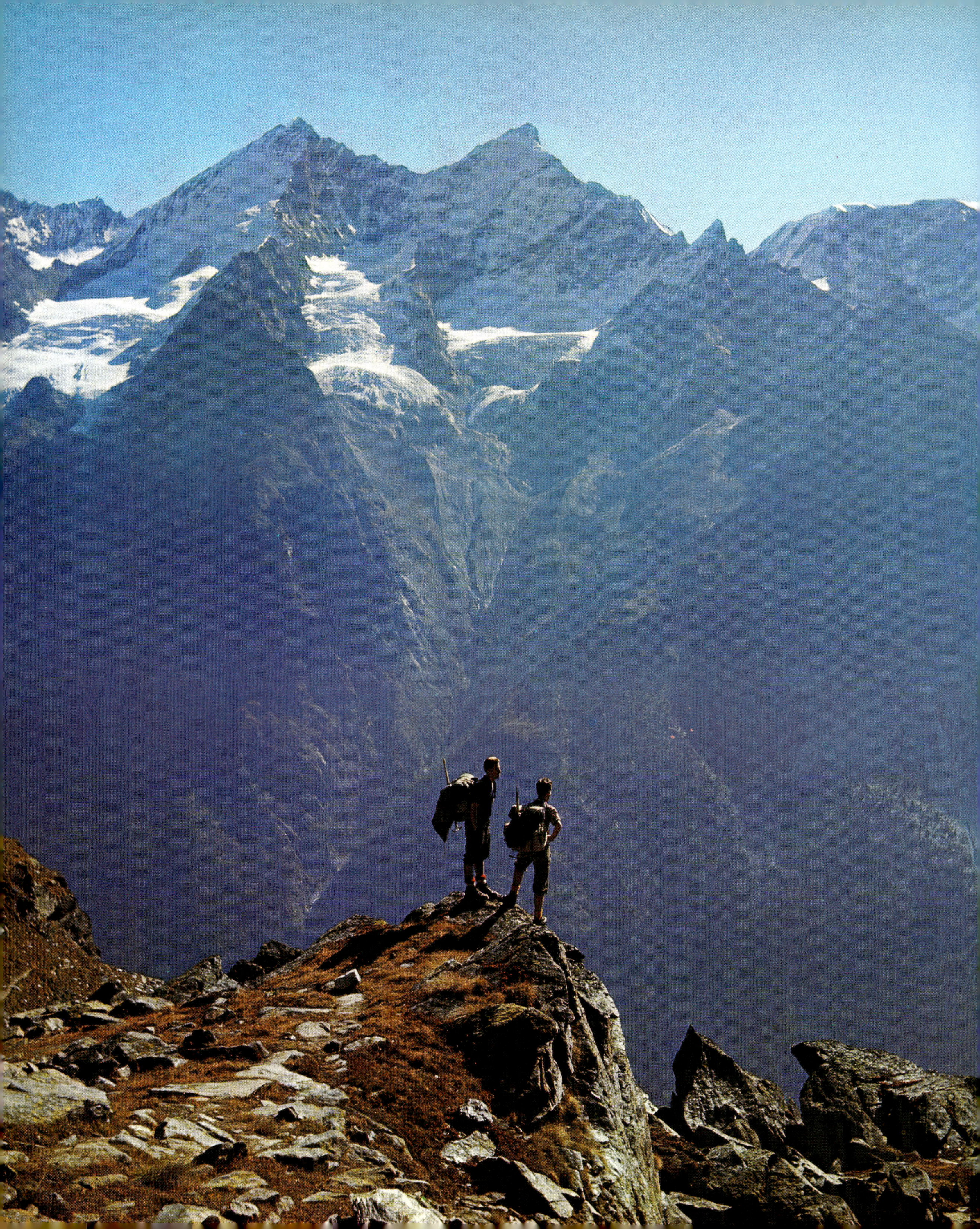

The Mischabel Group (Valais)

This picture shows the great Mischabel Group, dividing the Zermatt and Saas Fée Valleys from one another, as seen from its western (Zermatt) side. Although the peaks look so near, they are in fact about six miles from the camera; the extent of the crests shown is three miles and all five summits are, of course, famous ›Four-thousanders‹.

Touching the extreme top left-hand edge of the photograph is part of the summit of the Nadelhorn (14,220 feet). From it the ridge falls slightly to the Nadeljoch, then rises a little again to the low-contoured Lenzspitze (14,108 feet) and down again to the Lenzjoch, from which it shoots up in a smooth, regular diagonal to the 14,942-foot summit of the Dom. This is not only the highest peak in the Mischabel Group, but the loftiest mountain rising entirely on Swiss ground, for the summit of Monte Rosa, though higher, is shared with Italy.

Continuing to the right, the ridge descends into the Domjoch (14,060 feet) and then steeply up again to the tilted belfry of the Täschhorn (14,758 feet), to the right of which again, the famous and difficult Teufelsgrat (›The Devil's Ridge‹) sweeps downwards.

At the extreme right, lying somewhat withdrawn, is the broad summit of the Alphubel (13,803 feet), whose reverse side, above Saas Fée, provides splendid ski tours.

The three glaciers falling steeply from the Dom and Täschhorn towards the viewer are, on the left, the Festi glacier and, to the right of the huge, dark rock rib, the twin Kin glaciers, nearly bisected by a lesser rib of rock.

The Grand Combin, the western corner-stone of the Valais Alps

The Grand Combin (14,164 feet) with its four great summits, is the highest mountain in the Western Valaisian Alps, and lords it over the forty-mile long main crest of the Alps running from the Grandes Jorasses in the Mont Blanc group to the Dent d'Hérens and the Matterhorn.

To the west of the Combin Massif lies the Val d'Entremont, up which the Great St Bernard Pass, recently equipped with a three and a half-mile tunnel 2,000 feet below its saddle, on which stands the famous Hospice, climbs to a height of 8,110 feet. To the east lies the gentler Val de Bagnes, whose main villages are Lourtier and Fionnay.

The northern flanks of this dazzlingly-beautiful group are, as seen in the photograph, completely ice-clad and the huge summit mass rises from the Corbassière glacier, about five miles long. Most of the climbs, especially in late winter, when done by ski climbers competent to deal with the dangers of this icy tract, are accomplished by way of this ice-stream.

In the photograph, taken high above Fionnay – working for once from right to left – rises the ice-trapeze of the Petit Combin (11,343 feet), with the beautifully-sculptured pyramid of the Combin de Corbassière (12,212 feet) to its left. Beyond the deep indentation of the Col du Meitin (11,697 feet) stand the Grand Combin de Valsorey (13,724 feet) and the highest peak in the group, the 14,164-foot Grand Combin de Grafeneire.

The Panossière Hut (8,745 feet), the starting-point for all climbs on this northern flank, lies hidden behind the rock ridge in the middle of the picture; it is a matter of some four hours from Fionnay to the hut.

Some of the finest views of the Combin, its satellites and the eastern aspect of the Mont Blanc group are to be had in the neighbourhood of Verbier, the much-frequented summer and winter resort lying on a high, sunny terrace a little to the south-east, and reached by a fine hairpin motor road from Orsières in the valley. Magnificent vantage-points can be attained by taking the chair-lift up the high ridge behind Verbier and then walking on a number of unsensational paths which contour the slopes.

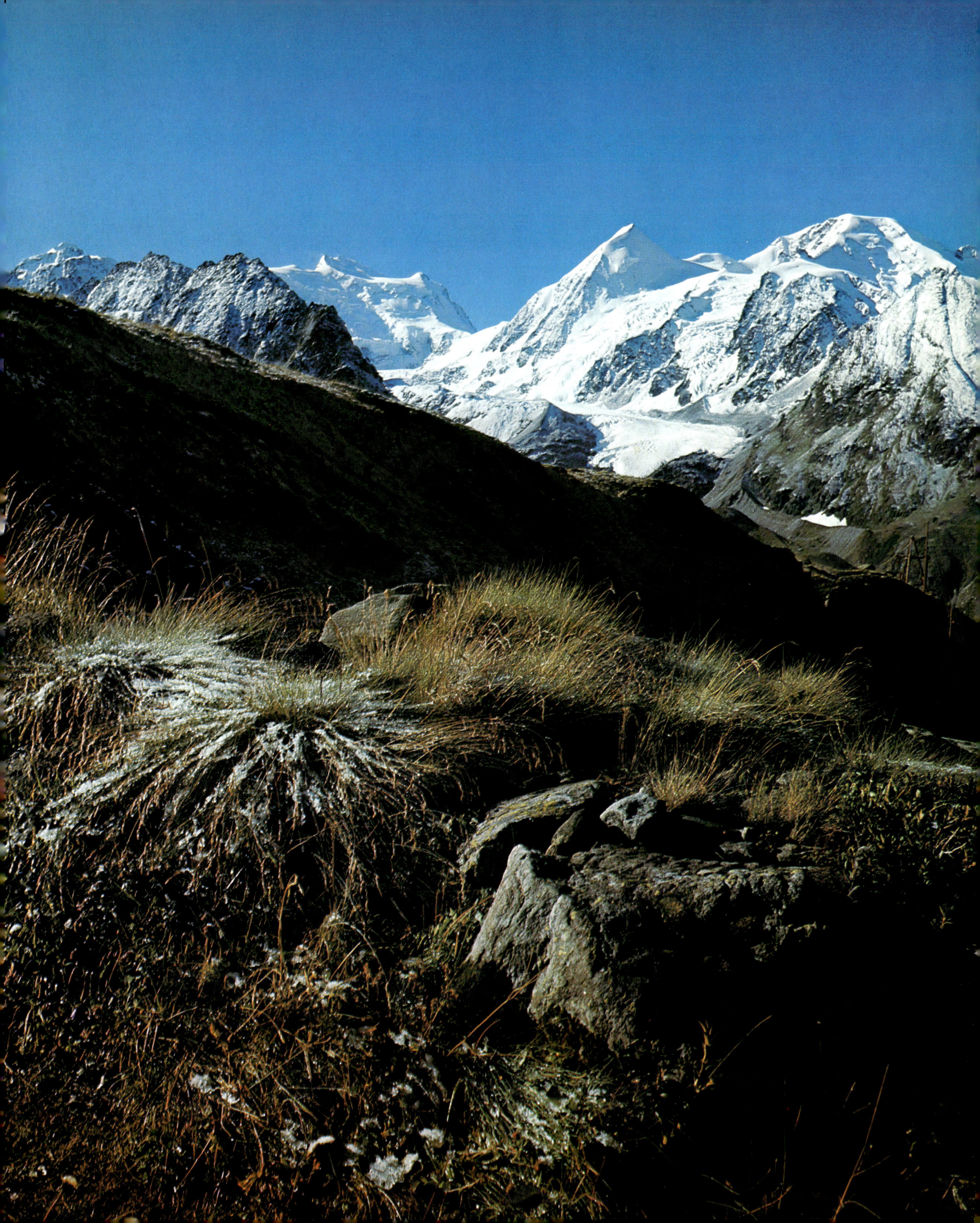

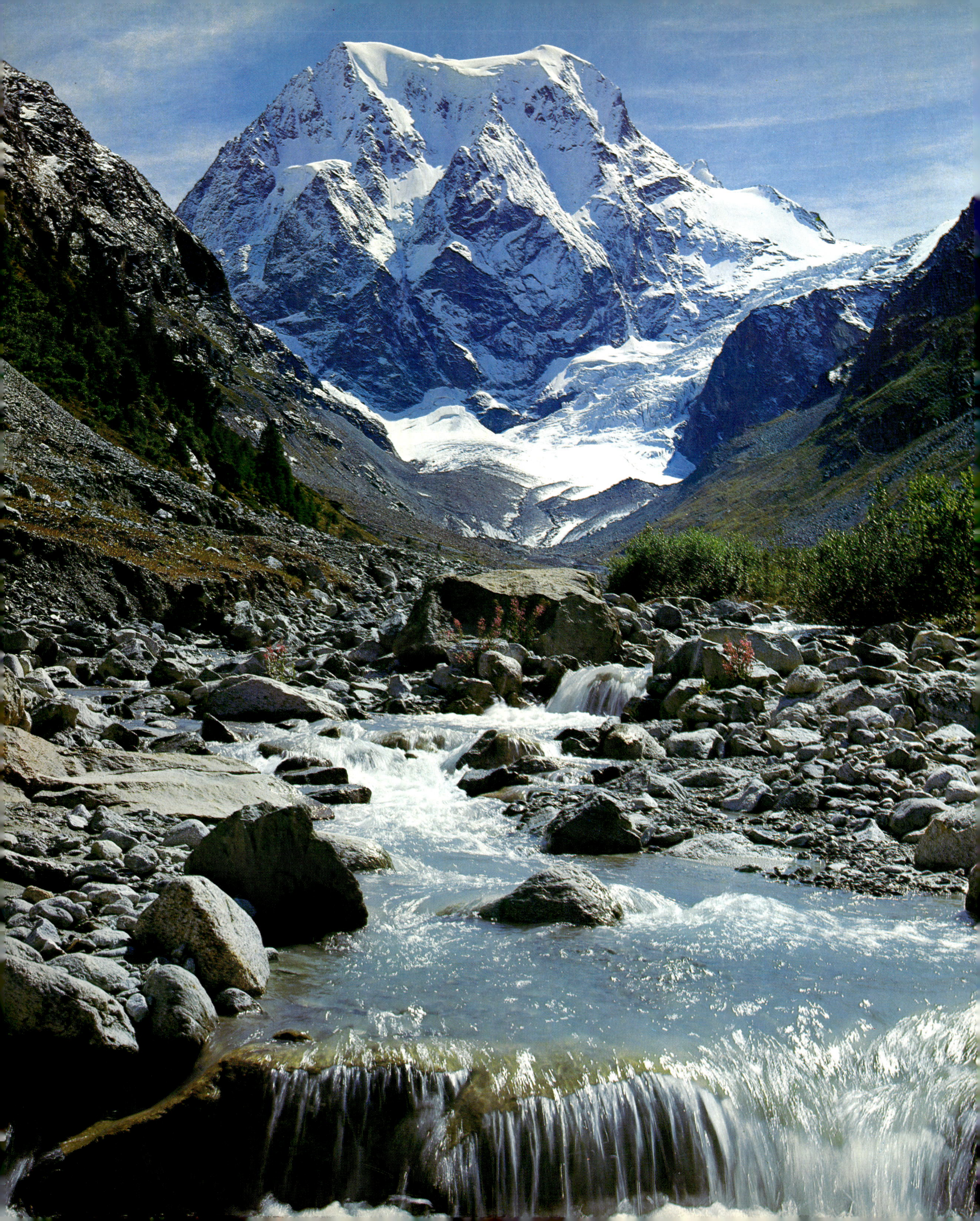

Mont Collon, above Arolla (Valais)

To the south of Sion, which lies in the broad, fertile sub-Alpine trench of the Rhone Valley, a lateral valley, itself at first quite wide, then narrowing as it gains height, the Val d'Hérens, climbs southwards towards the main chain of the Valaisian, or Pennine, Alps. Passing the curious earth pyramids of Useigne, the road winds its way into a high, almost level sector, through the charming little resort of Evolène, with a fine distant view of the Dent Blanche (14,318 feet), to Les Haudères, about twenty miles from Sion. Here it divides, the left-hand arm ascending to Ferpècle at the foot of the great Mont Miné glacier, dominated by the Grand Cornier (13,020 feet) and the huge wedge of the Dent Blanche. The right-hand arm climbs steeply into the wild, high Val d'Arolla, to reach the unspoiled climbing centre of Arolla itself (6,437 feet) in another five miles.

Arolla (named after its stone pines, ›Arolles‹) is a favourite summer resort for walkers, ramblers and climbers whose preference is for the rugged grandeurs of the high-mountain scene.

The tongue of the Arolla glacier lies only two miles away to the southeast and can be reached in three quarters of an hour by an excellent path suitable for ordinary walkers. Here they can enjoy a wonderful view of the broad mass of Mont Collon (11,955 feet), soaring high above the crevassed ice-stream, though its snow-plastered precipices are the preserve of experienced mountaineers; indeed all the ascent routes, even from its southern side (behind the mountain, as seen in the picture) are difficult undertakings. The tip of l'Evèque, its slightly taller neighbour, can be seen lifting above the snowfield half-way down Mont Collon's right-hand ridge.

For those with sufficient experience, there is one of the most attractive glacier tours in the Alps, by path and a steep but easy glacier to the loftily-perched Bertol Hut (11,155 feet), where the night is spent, and then over unsensational snow slopes in two to three hours to the broad snow dome of the 12,354-foot Tête Blanche, with a superb close-up view of the Matterhorn's north face and all the giant Valaisian peaks which tower round this wonderful *belvedère*.

Soglio in the Val Bregaglia

The village of Soglio (3,570 feet), perched like a swallow's nest on a shelf high above the Val Bregaglia (German: Bergell), is undeniably one of the most beautiful corners of the mountain world; certainly one of the most photographed.

This picturesque little huddle of a community consists of a few peasants' dwellings, along a tiny, unique main street, gay with window boxes; three palaces belonging to the one-time overlords of the region, the de Salis family, one of which is now a famous hostelry, where Rainer Maria Rilke wrote his great poems, and died; a church with a beautifully slender campanile, and a graveyard. The setting of meadows, woods and towering rock peaks is one of the loveliest in the Alps.

As you drive southwards from the Engadine, first down the windings of the Maloja Pass and then descending successive steps in the Bregaglia Valley below, the very narrow road to Soglio (priority to the Postal Motor) branches off to the right at Promontogno. The village lies 1,000 feet above the valley floor and the road is just two and a half miles long. The whole area around Soglio abounds in delightful path-walks on the high slopes behind it, and the higher you mount the more splendid the prospect.

The photograph shows the view across the main valley to the great horseshoe of granite peaks at the far head of the Bondasca valley opposite.

To the left centre rise the many spires of the Sciora group (10,633 feet), with the remarkable pale face of the Sciora di Fuori, the trapeze-like tower of the Pioda, the sharp needle of the Agio and the broad snow-crowned mass of the Sciora di Dentro. The Bondasca glacier, in deep shadow, cascades between the Sciora peaks and the 10,692-foot Pizzi Gemelli, the Twins, one of them almost hidden behind the dark wedge of Piz Cengallo (11,070 feet). On the extreme right towers Piz Badile (10,854 feet), its north-west face lit by the sun and its celebrated north ridge, so prized and loved by climbers, clearly defined between the brightly-lit face and the blue shadow to its left, in which the even more famous north-east face, 3,000 feet high, lies bathed. The ascent of that huge, smooth cliff, nowhere technically less than Grade V (›Very Difficult‹), is one of the very greatest among Alpine rock climbs.

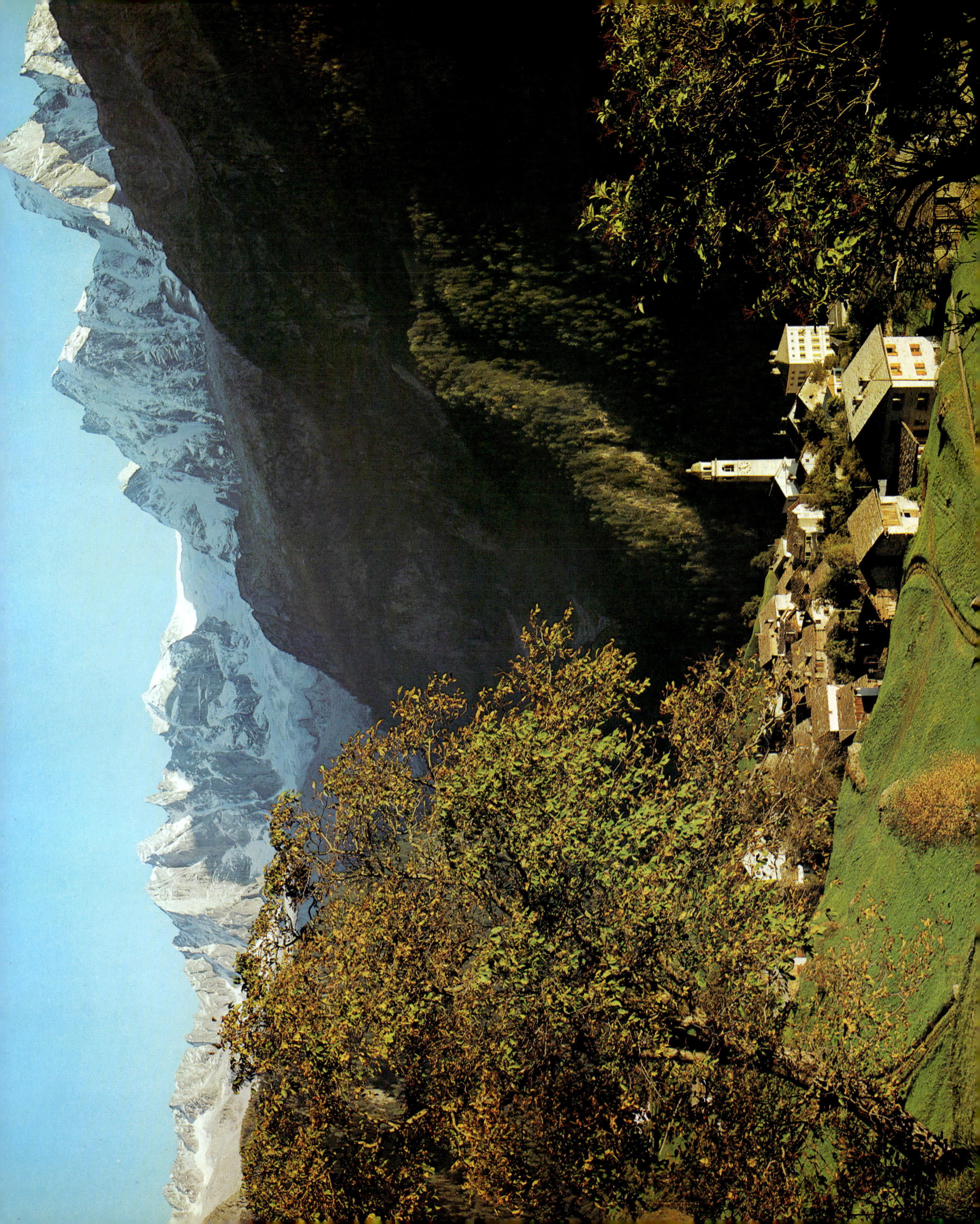

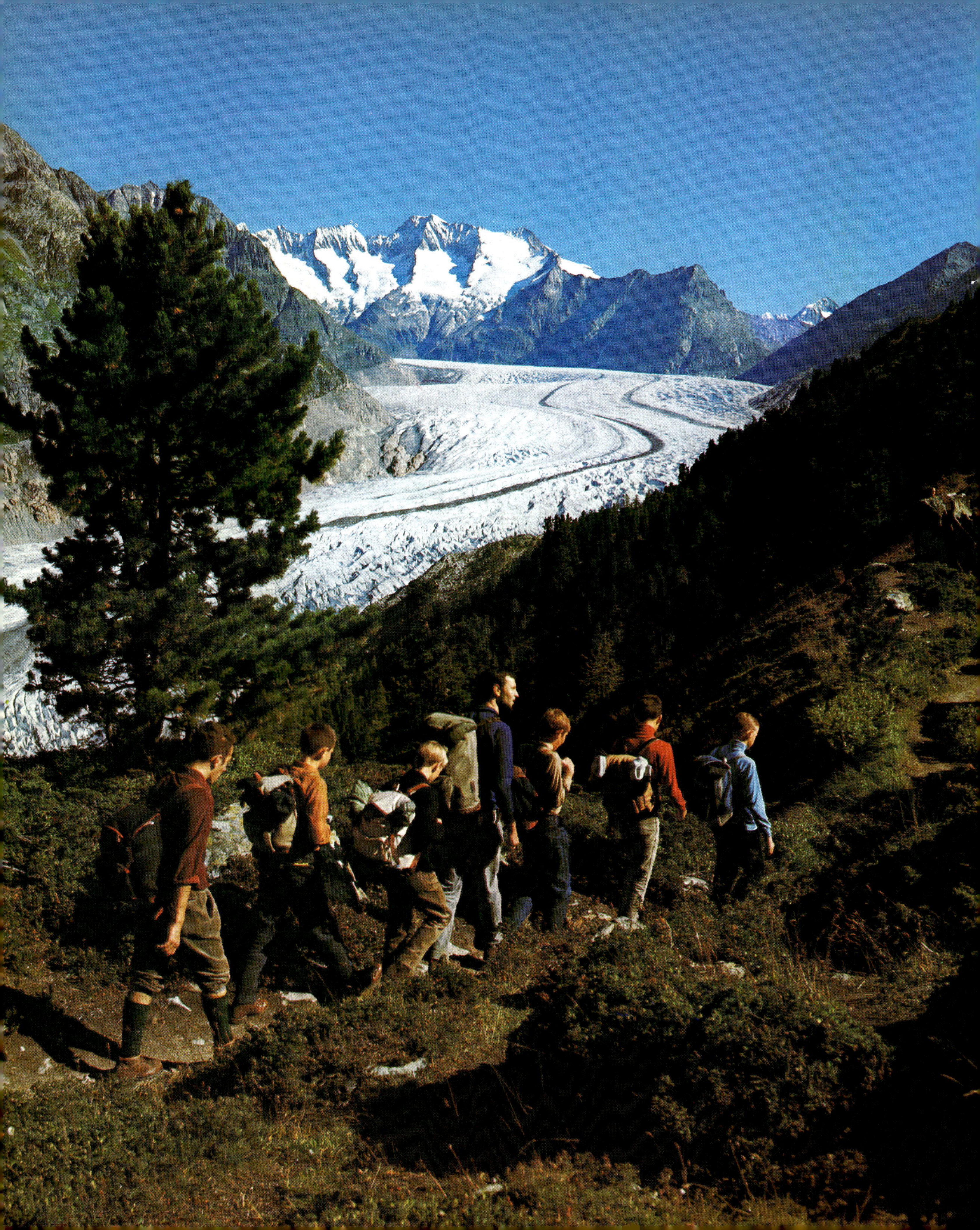

The Great Aletsch Glacier (Bernese Alps)

The Aletsch Glacier, seventeen miles long and covering an area of one hundred square miles, is the longest and largest in the Alps. The peaks fringing it rise to more than 13,000 feet, and the lowest point of the glacier's tongue falls to about 5,000.

It is fed by the southern snow and ice faces of the Jungfrau and the Mönch, and one of the best vantage-points from which the ordinary tourist can view its superb curve past the ›Concordiaplatz‹ towards the depth of the Rhône Valley, is Jungfraujoch (11,340 feet), the top station of the Jungfrau Railway in the saddle between the two great peaks (see plate 66). For the expert glacier walker, the ascent of the glacier from the Eggishorn Hotel (7,195 feet), three hours above Fiesch in the upper Rhône Valley, past the little Märjelen See, with miniature icebergs floating on its almost black surface, to the Joch, breaking the journey at one of the huts overlooking the sublimely beautiful cruciform junction of four glaciers at Concordia, is a long but highly rewarding tour, occupying eight or nine hours.

For those who prefer a long ramble, like the young people in the photograph, there are a number of fine paths from the Rhône Valley villages, leading up to and along the true (eastern) left bank of the Aletsch, through the so-called Aletschwald. The background of the photograph shows a small sector of the high peaks containing the glacier: from left to right, they are the Kamm (11,697 feet), Fiescher Gabelhorn (11,717 feet), the almost level summit ridge of the Schönbuhlhorn (11,678 feet), the Schönbuhljoch separating it from the twin-peaked Gross Wannehorn (12,812 feet), the broad white Wannehornsattel and the Klein Wannehorn to its right.

The dark rock mass in the centre is the 9,626-foot Eggishorn, easily reached in two hours by path from the Eggishorn Hotel, whose view of the glacier, the Bernese Alps to the north, the Valais Alps to the south and extending as far as Mont Blanc, eighty miles away to the west, is one of the finest and most famous in the Alps.

The Klausen Pass (Glarus)

The 6,390-foot Klausen Pass, whose thirty miles connect Altdorf in Canton Schwyz, just beyond the southern tip of Lake Lucerne, with Linthal in Glarus, provides the essential link between historic Central and Eastern Switzerland, Liechtenstein, the Arlberg and Austria. There are references to it as far back as the end of the twelfth century AD, and the present motor road, which took seven years to build, was completed in 1899. The stiff hairpin windings on its southern side were, up to the Second World War, the scene of annual international motor races, producing amazing average speeds of over fifty m.p.h.

The road leads mostly through beautiful and pleasant scenery, though there are some fine mountain tracts on the way. To the north of the road rise the precipitous walls of the Jägerstöcke (seen in the picture), while to the south there are splendid near views of the savage peaks and glaciers of the Tödi group, among them the Grosse Ruchen (10,290 feet), the Claridenstock (10,730 feet), the Gries Glacier, the dominating Scheerhorn (10,815 feet), the Kammlistock (10,625 feet) and the rather lower Windgällen.

For those who are not speeding over the Klausen Pass in a car, bound helter-skelter for some distant objective, there are numerous quiet and deserted path-walks traversing this lovely landscape, and plenty of huts and refuges are to be found in the mountains to either side of the road.

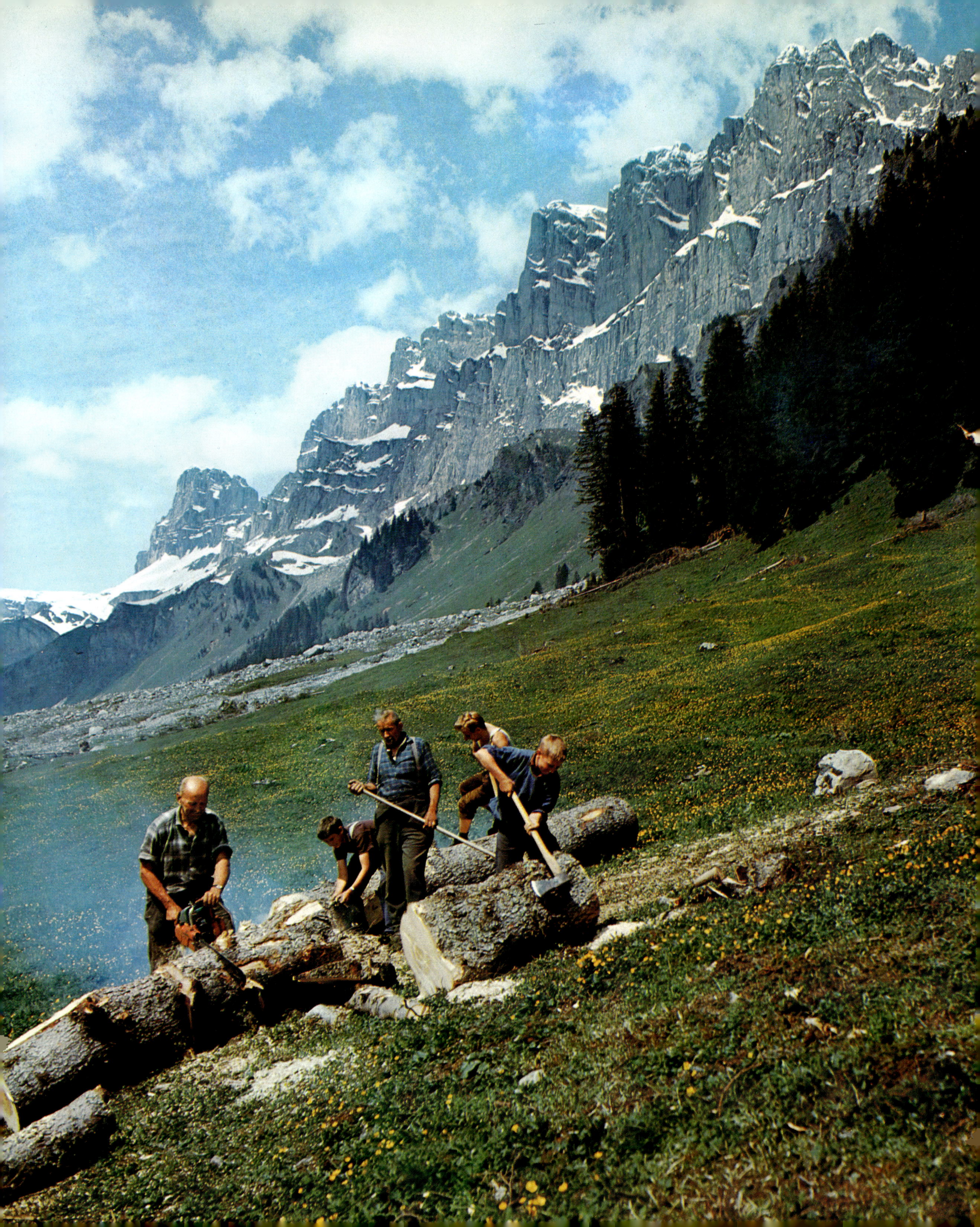

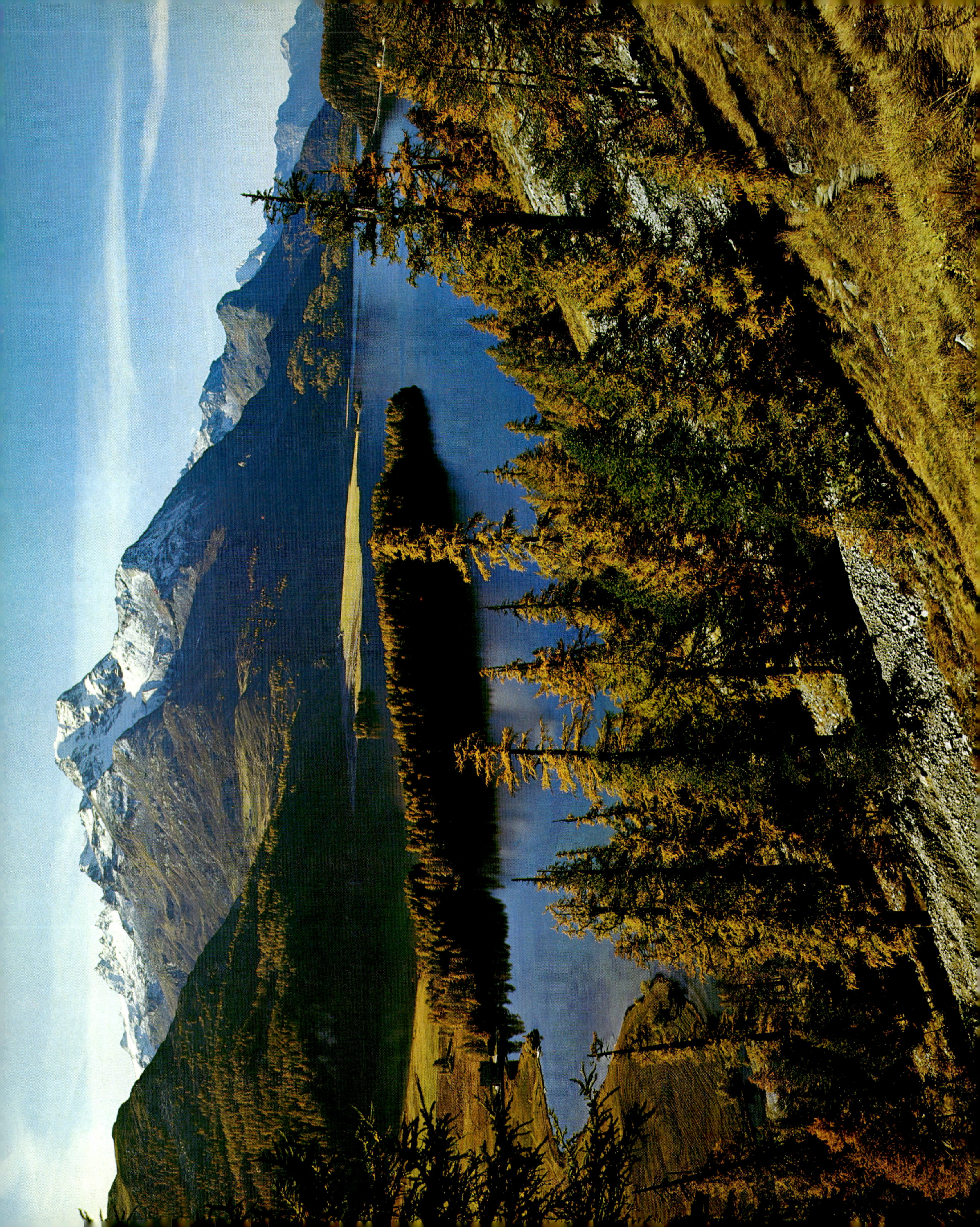

The Lake of Sils (Upper Engadine, Grisons)

This lovely photograph shows the deep, unruffled blue of the Lake of Sils in the Upper Engadine, enhanced by the autumnal flame of the pine forests and the first powdering of the winter snows on the peaks overlooking this loveliest of valleys.

The lake lies at an altitude of 5,940 feet, to the left of the main Engadine highway running almost level from St Moritz to Maloja, then suddenly diving over a gap in the precipitous rim of the Alpine watershed, on its way to the Bregaglia and on into Italy to the north of Lake Como. The Engadine landscape is rich in contrasts, varying from idyllic valley-corners overlooking a chain of five jewels of lakes, to the glaciated peaks of the Bernina Group's western ridges. The region is beloved of holiday-makers from all over the world both in summer and winter. One of its great admirers was Frederic Nietsche, who wrote his *Zarathustra* in this his favourite setting between 1881 and 1888.

The wooded peninsula of Chasté, on which stand the ruins of an ancient castle and a memorial to Nietsche, juts far out into the lake from the left of the picture, with the tiny islet of Isola, the ›Liebesinselchen‹ (›little love of an island‹), just above its far tip. Dominating the whole scene, rises the trapeze-shaped, snowy summit of Piz la Margna (10,353 feet), a mountain ascended without any great difficulty in four hours from the valley, and a marvellous view-point.

The opening of the sunlit valley of Fedoz is seen at the left base of the peak, which is snowless in summer; in the Val Fedoz ramblers will find the delights of lovely and deserted paths. Rising behind it are the towers of Piz Fedoz (10,643 feet) which, with its continuation to Piz La Margna constitutes the most westerly spur of the Bernina Group.

The blue peaks in the extreme background to the right rise from behind the Bregaglia Valley. Just to the left of the highest foreground pine the north-east face of Piz Badile (see plate 79) is outlined against the sky. The southern windings of the Maloja Pass start just beyond the far end of the lake.

Steinbock in the Swiss National Park

The Swiss have not only their achievements in the sphere of foreign tourism to be proud of; they have also been pioneers in the field of nature conservation, for as long ago as 1909 they founded a huge National Park in the Lower Engadine, which has grown till today it embraces an area of over one hundred square miles.

The Park lies to the south of the Engadine villages of Schulz and Zernez, and to the north and west of the Ofen Pass (7,070 feet), whose unexciting though picturesque road runs through the middle of it. The highest mountains in the area are Piz Quattervals (10,369 feet) and Piz Nair (9,868 feet), not to be confused with the one above St Moritz, to the east.

The numerous rambles in the National Park are unusually interesting – though it should be noted that there is a strict ban on leaving any of the paths – for, quite apart from the variety of rock to be found here (granite, gneiss, limestone, dolomite and slate) every kind of Swiss conifer is to be met with here, including the Arve and the mountain pine peculiar to the Grisons which they call the Bergfohre.

In addition, of course, every species of wild creature is represented from the rock-mouse to the steinbock, a colony of which was introduced four decades ago. It is often possible to approach quite close to them, for these splendid animals have long since ceased to be as wild and shy as they still are, for instance, in the Caucasus; and one is left in no doubt that their numbers are on the increase.

In this picture, it looks almost as if the inquisitive steinbock family had posed specially for the photographer.

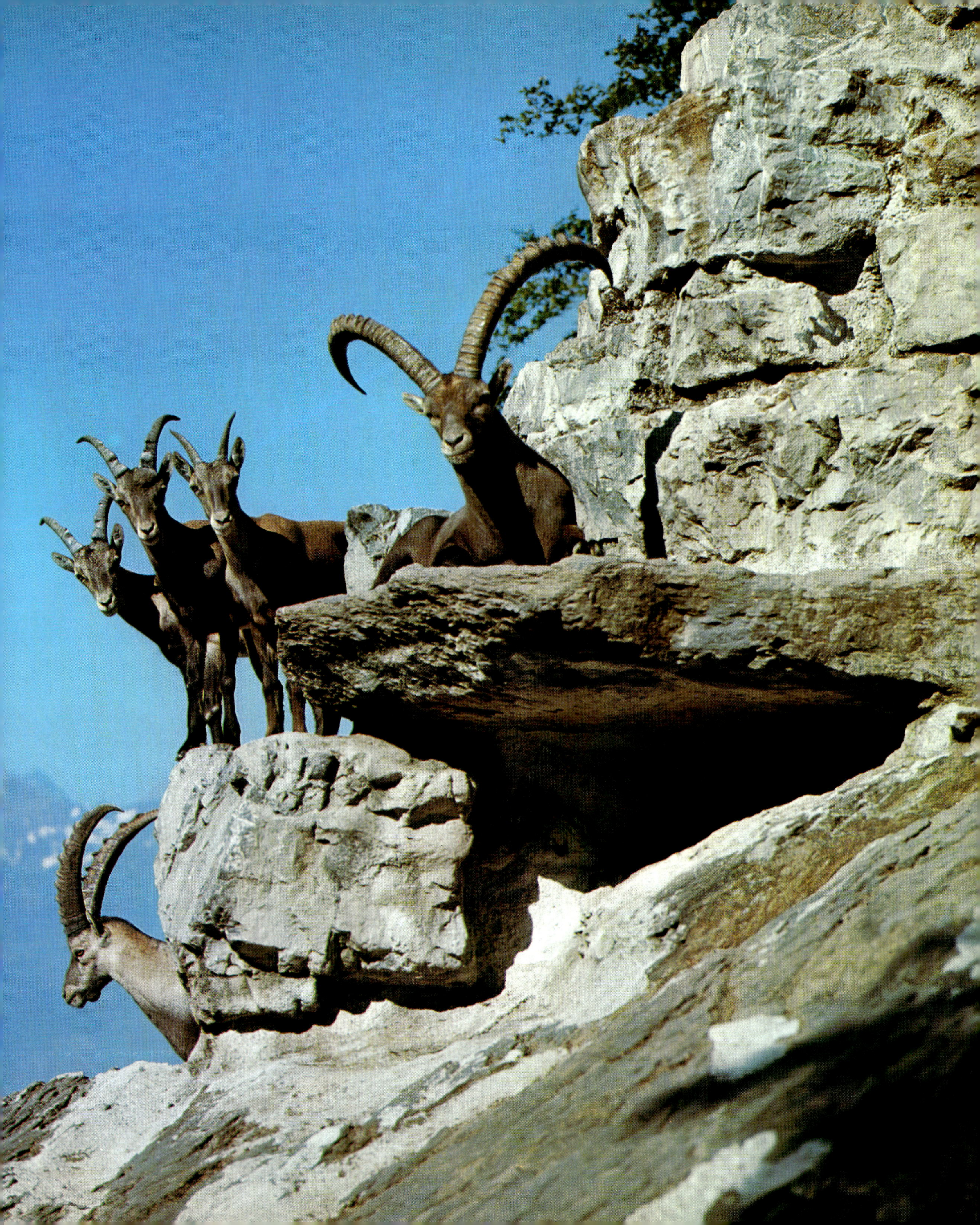

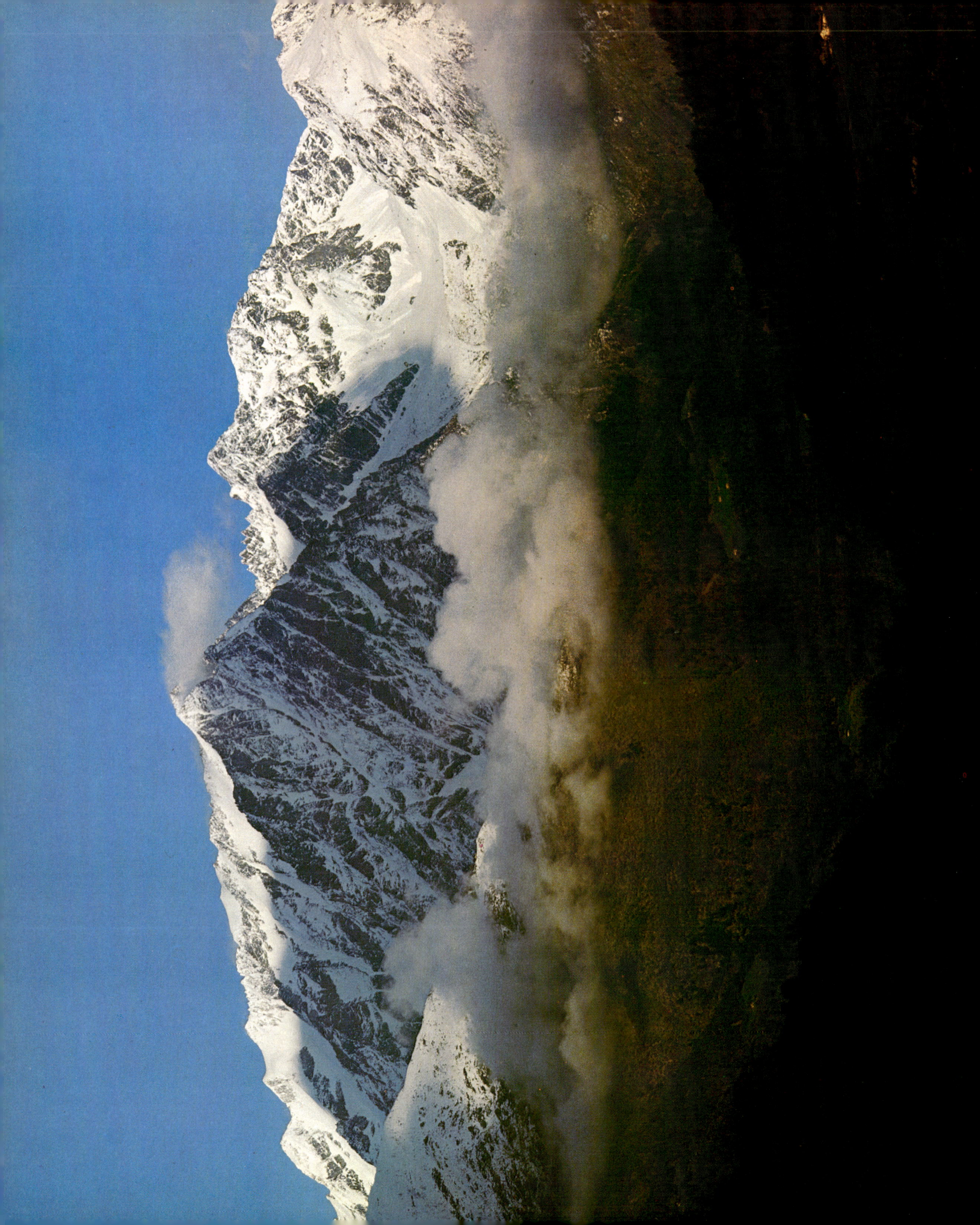

The Adamello

The Adamello range, rising southwards of the Ortler group, belongs to the southern sector of the Eastern Alps and consists of two distinct groups, the Presanella Massif (see also next plate), to the south of the beautiful 6,180-foot Tonale Pass, in which rises the highest peak in the whole Adamello complex, the Cima Presanella itself (11,690 feet).

The group consists of steep, heavily crevassed glaciers contained by slabby, sharp-crested ridges; massive boulders lie in the rifts at their feet and there are several small lakes embedded in the north-eastern part of the range. The separate groups of the Adamello and the Presanella are divided from one another by the deep Val di Genova, the Passo Lago Scuro and the Val Narcane.

The photograph shows the Adamello Massif (11,640 feet) from the west, near the small town and important road junction of Edolo, where the Tonale and Aprica passes meet, at a distance of ten miles.

The eastern side of the range, towards Pinzolo and the lovely resort of Madonna di Campiglio (4,970 feet) on the road to the 5,580-foot Carlomagno Pass, is much gentler and more accessible; and the summit of the Adamello can be reached from the Mandron Hut (8,010 feet) above Pinzolo, at the foot of the pass, and thence through Bedole in the Val Genova to the refuge. The climb then takes four or five hours and demands nothing more than some experience in glacier mountaineering.

The Presanella

The Presanella Massif (11,690 feet), seen in this magnificent picture from the north-west, at a point above Ponte di Legno, at the western foot of the Tonale Pass, belongs to the Adamello-Presanella complex (see previous plate 84). This range of the South-eastern Alps presents an unusual feature, for here one can still walk and climb for days on end without meeting crowds of others.

The actual massif of the Presanella is starker, more imposing and demands a greater degree of climbing skill and experience than its neighbours, the Adamello. Its main summit can, however, be reached by even the average mountaineer, without much difficulty, by its north-eastern approach, starting from the Denza Hut (Rifugio Stavel, 8,210 feet) above Fucine, at the eastern end of the Tonale Pass; or from the Presanella Hut (7,230 feet) above Pinzolo on the opposite, south-eastern side (plate 84 again). A climb of some four hours brings one to a marvellous summit panorama of the great Ortler peaks to the north and, to the east, the yellow spires and precipices of the Brenta Dolomites, in whose huts the goings-on are a great deal more loud and lively than in the relatively deserted ones of the Adamello-Presanella area.

It need hardly be added that this very beautiful mountain region holds a wealth of attractions for the walker and rambler for whom glacier and rock have no appeal.

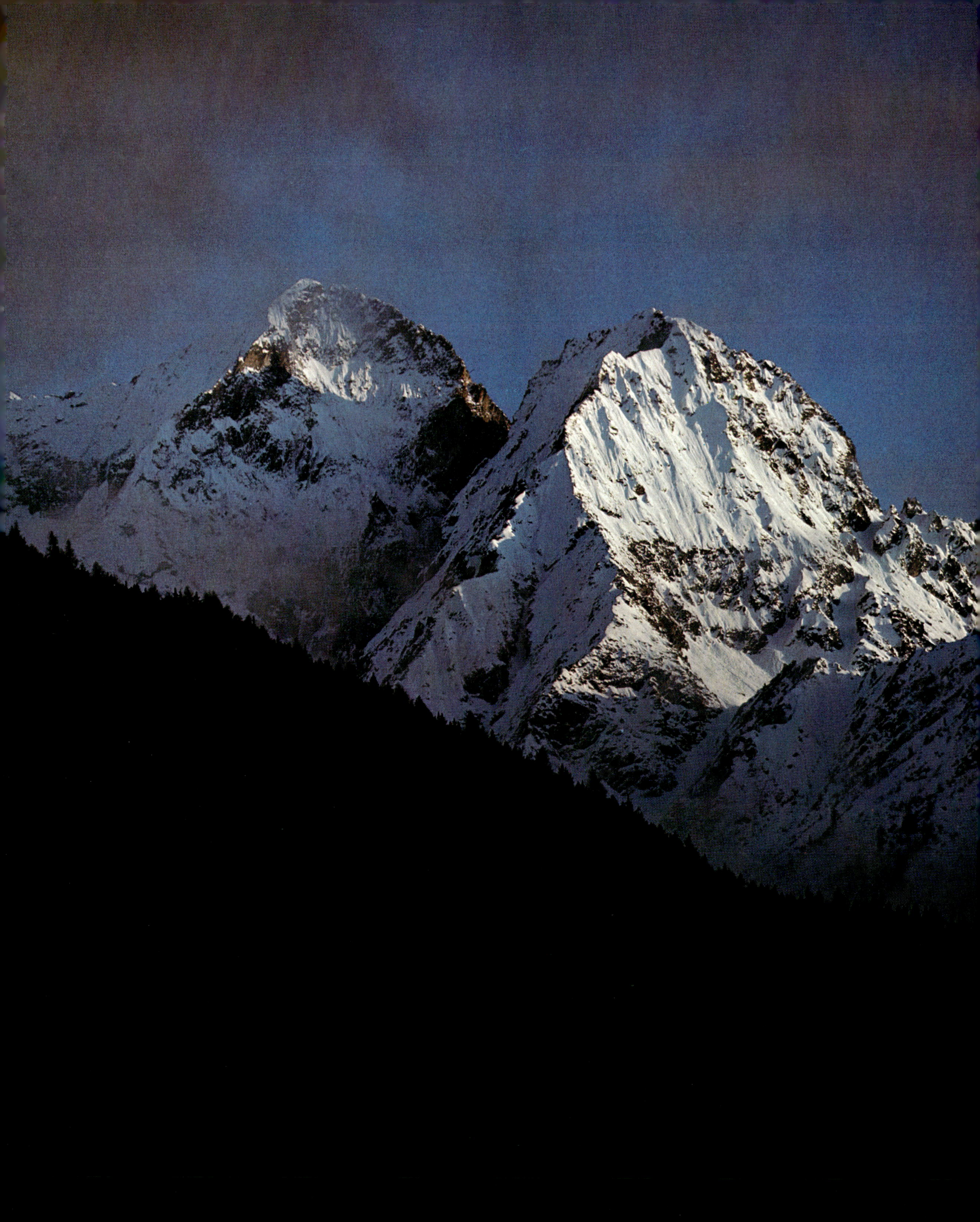

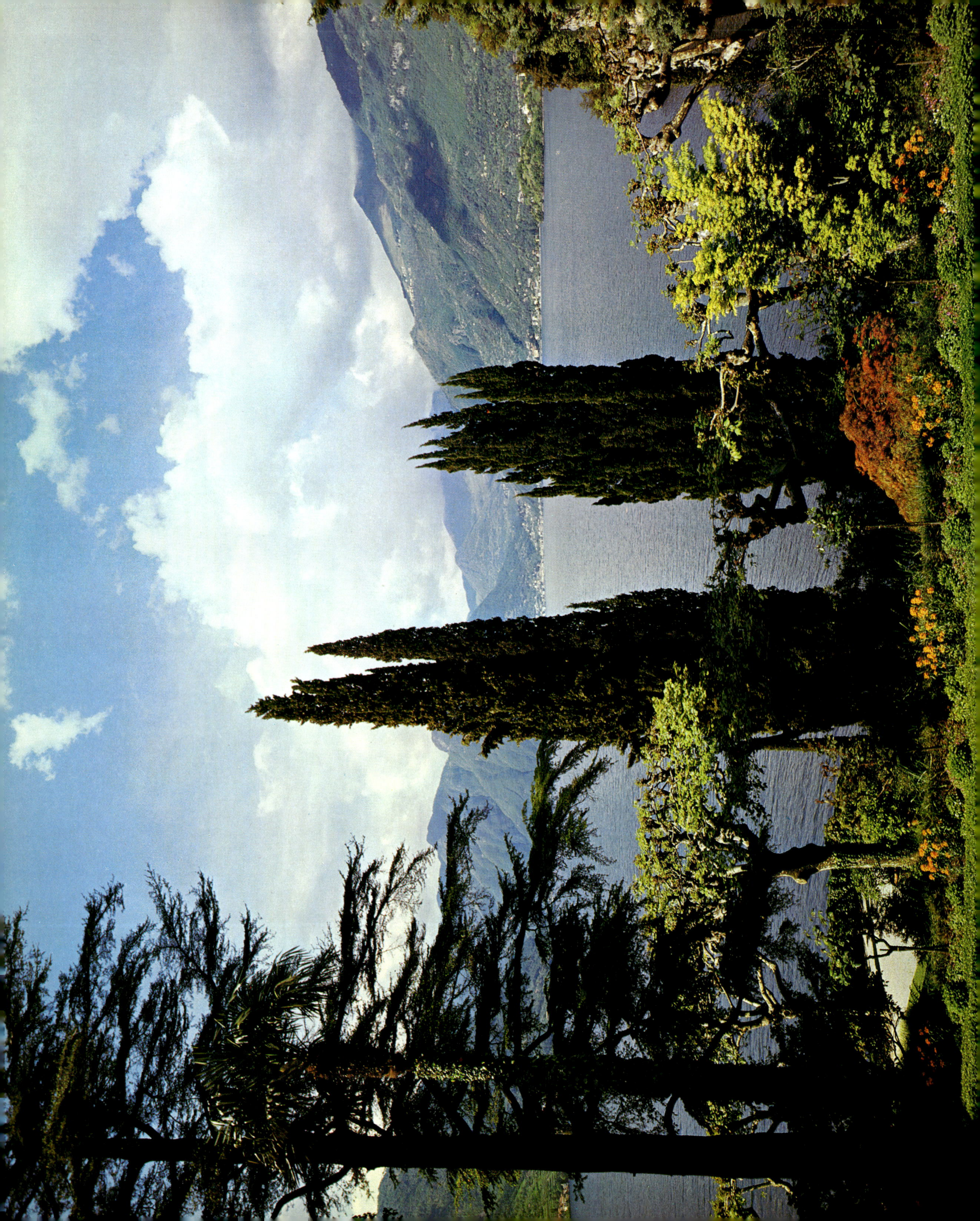

The Lake of Como

The ›Lacus Larius‹ was already famous for its beauty in Pliny's time, and poets of every nation from Virgil onwards have sung its praises. Here the warmth and lush fertility of the South meet the cool breath blowing down from the mountains, for the western spurs of the Bregaglia ranges extend almost to the northern tip of the lake.

There are also quite respectable mountains along the lake's eastern shore; these include the Grigne Group, where the Lecco district has nurtured many a famous Italian mountaineer.

However, one must not expect to encounter along the shores of this lovely lake, thirty-one miles long and in places three miles wide, the weather-beaten faces of high-mountain addicts; for the crowds which throng the resorts fringing the waters of this international holiday playground come there for rest and relaxation, for excursions by car and coach, for bathing and water-skiing, and such visitors usually prefer to contemplate mountains from below, while they sunbathe in their deck-chairs or on the rafts out in the lake.

For the more active there are, however, innumerable opportunities for combining delightful walks with the joys of lazing in the sun and swimming in the lake's blue waters.

The Lake of Lugano and Monte San Salvatore

This strangely-shaped and extremely beautiful lake, whose north-eastern and south-western arms water Italian shores, is known to the Italians as Lago Cerisio. It lies a little to the west of Lake Como and its arms push northwards deep into the Swiss Canton of Ticino, whose atmosphere and language are nonetheless wholly Italian.

The Lake of Lugano lies at an altitude of 900 feet above sea-level and with its area of thirty square miles is a typical Alpine lake, even if the high peaks of the main Alpine chain cannot be seen from it. It is Switzerland's seventh largest lake and ranks fourth in size among the lakes of Northern Italy. It is luxuriantly vegetated; olive and chestnut trees cluster round its picturesque villages, and the sharp, dark outlines of the cypresses provide an unusual touch in the bright colour of one lovely picture after another.

To the south of Lugano – in summer a vastly overcrowded place, almost a tourist city – a peninsula juts out into the lake from the north and from it, sheer above the deep trench of the lake, rises the 2,893-foot rounded mass of Monte San Salvatore. Its structure is of white Triassic Dolomite and harbours an unusually rich and varied flora. It takes two and a half hours to walk up to the top by path from Lugano, but there is a funicular railway which makes the journey in a quarter of an hour. Whichever way is chosen, no visitor to Lugano should fail to visit this outstanding view-point with its lovely panorama across the many-armed lake and, away over the Ticino foothills and valleys, to the snow-capped peaks of the Gotthard Group in the main Alpine chain to the north.

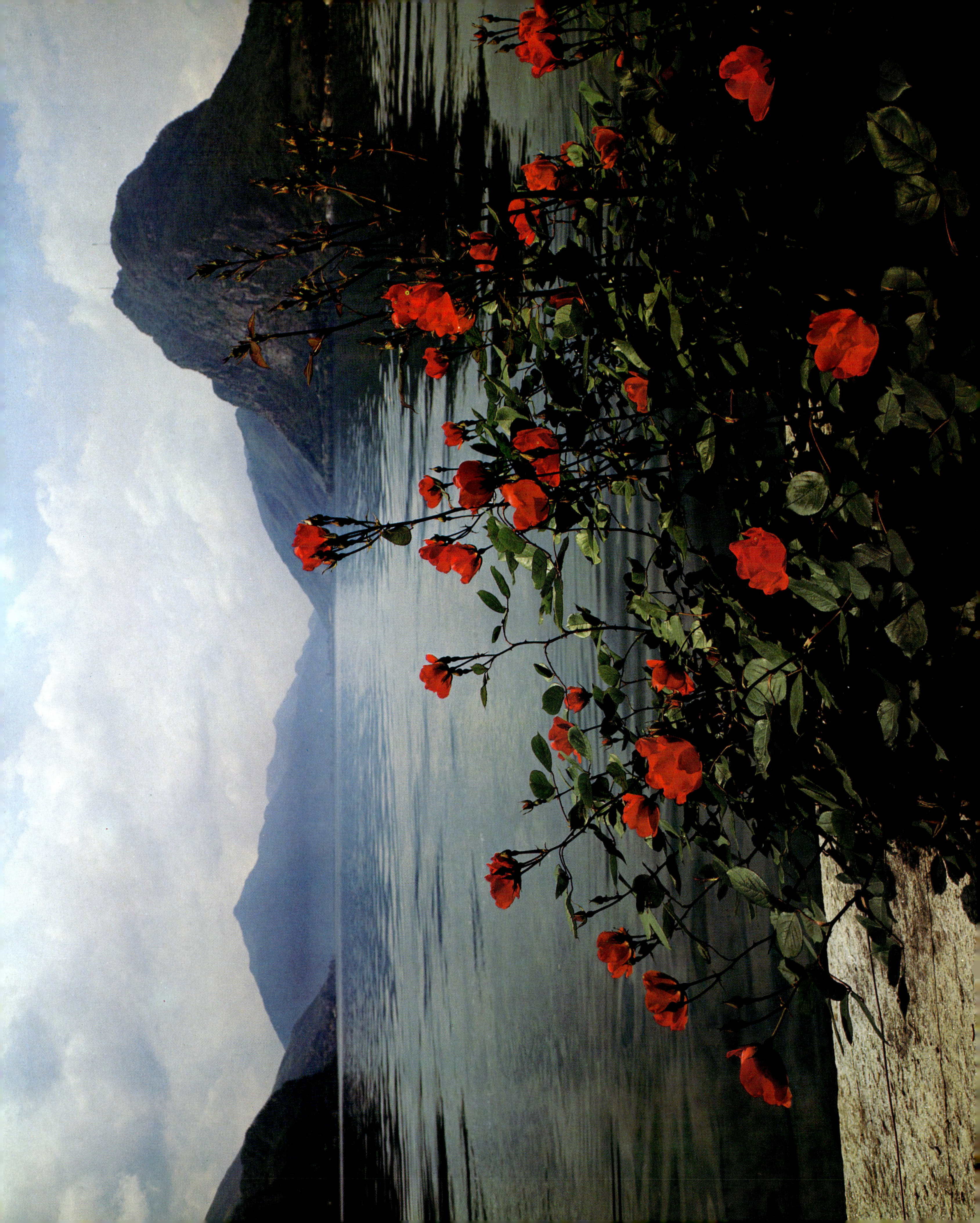

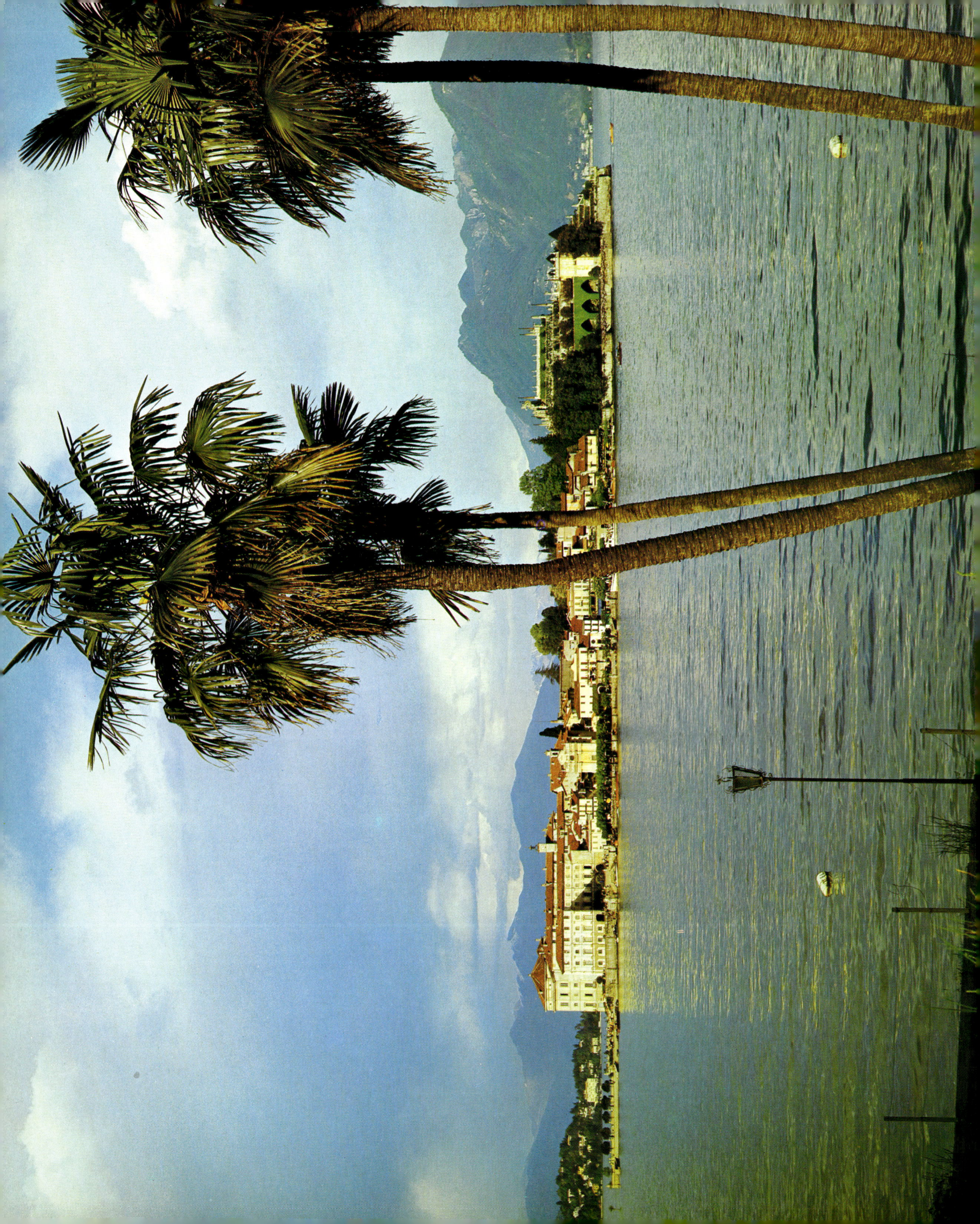

Isola Bella, Lago Maggiore

Lago Maggiore, known to the Romans as to us today for its verbena-fringed shores and named by them Lacus Verbanus, is thirty-eight miles long and varies in width from a mile to nearly ten; its area is nearly 130 square miles, most of which lies on Italian ground, for only the northern fifth of the lake around Locarno belongs to Switzerland.

The mountains which contain it rise steeply from its shores, clad in raiment of gorgeous hues; here the lighter tones of vines and chestnut trees mingle with the darker colours of cypresses, myrtles and cedars. All around the rim of the lake gaily-coloured towns and villages nestle amid the luxuriant foliage.

While the spring storms are still raging in the high regions of the Alps, Lago Maggiore offers all the delights of a bathing holiday and of delightful rambles on the paths which honeycomb the lovely hillsides overlooking the lake basin. It is even possible to combine the ›Crazy Threesome‹ of walking, skiing and swimming from the resorts which ring the west shore; for Macugnaga (4,350 feet) at the foot of Monte Rosa's stupendous east face is not much more than an hour's journey by car from the lake, and there it is possible to enjoy the delights of the great winter sport well into the summer.

The photograph shows the lovely island of Isola Bella, perhaps the best-known of the trio of the Borromean Islands facing Stresa at the bottom of the lake's northern arm: Isola Bella, Pescatore and Madre. The beautiful palace is the summer residence of the Borromean Counts and is surrounded by a typical Italian park and ornamental garden, open to visitors who care to make the short crossing by lake steamer or motorboat.

The Castle of Chillon and the Dents du Midi

The crescent-shaped Lake of Geneva's expanse of 360 square miles is easily the most impressive of Switzerland's lakes. Forty-five miles long and in places nearly ten wide, with a maximum depth of 1,000 feet, it is more of an inland sea than a lake, and the storms blowing down from the mountains with great suddenness can swiftly whip its surface into ›white horses‹ and pound its shores with sizeable breakers.

It is fed mainly by the Rhône, which flows into it at Villeneuve after its long passage from the glacier at Gletsch, through the broad, smiling sub-Alpine valley to which it gives its name, and out again at Geneva on its way to the distant Mediterranean.

The beauties of this lovely tract of mountain-girt water have made it world-famous. On its southern (French) shore rise the sparsely-inhabited ridges and gorges of the Savoy mountains, knee-deep in dark forests and dense chestnut groves, with here and there a ruined castle and some ancient, deserted village. On the narrow strip of plain at their feet lie the populous and popular resorts of Evian, Thonon and a number of smaller ones.

The Swiss shore, to the north, is a long, lovely necklace of picturesque cities, towns and villages, the thriving centres of a vast tourist industry, separated by parks and vineyards, hills and heights, on whose sunny terraces stand castles and villas. Here, in forty miles of supreme loveliness, stand Geneva itself, Nyon, Rolle, Morges, the great city of Lausanne, Ouchy, Vevey and Montreux, from the first three of which there are superb views of Mont Blanc, the 15,781-foot Monarch of the Alps, lifting its white domes and towers, forty miles away, above the green of valley openings in the foothills and on clear, still days reflecting them, even at that distance, in the calm blue waters of the lake.

The photograph, taken a little south-east of Montreux, shows the castle of Chillon, one of the lake's outstanding historic show-pieces. Built on a rock reef in the lake, this water-girt castle was originally, in 1150 AD, the seat of the Dukes of Savoy, and its dungeons, which are open to visitors, have housed many a famous prisoner. Bonnivard, the last of them, imprisoned in 1530, was the subject of Byron's poem, ›The Prisoner of Chillon‹, which he wrote at Ouchy in 1817, and as a result of which the poet's name was later chiselled into one of the pillars.

Less than twenty miles from the eastern end of the lake, the imposing snowy wall of the Dents du Midi (10,695 feet) is seen rising in the right-hand background of the picture.

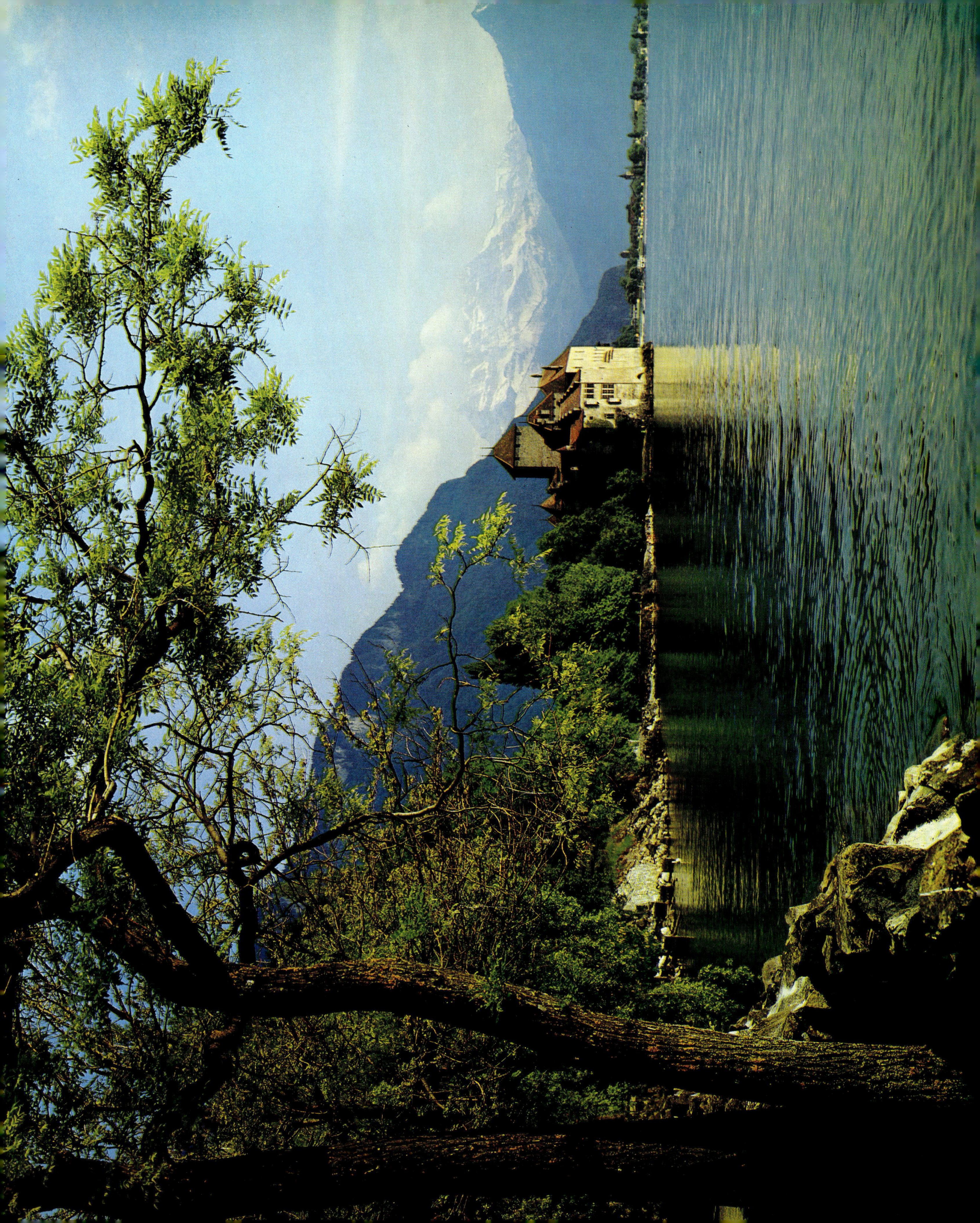

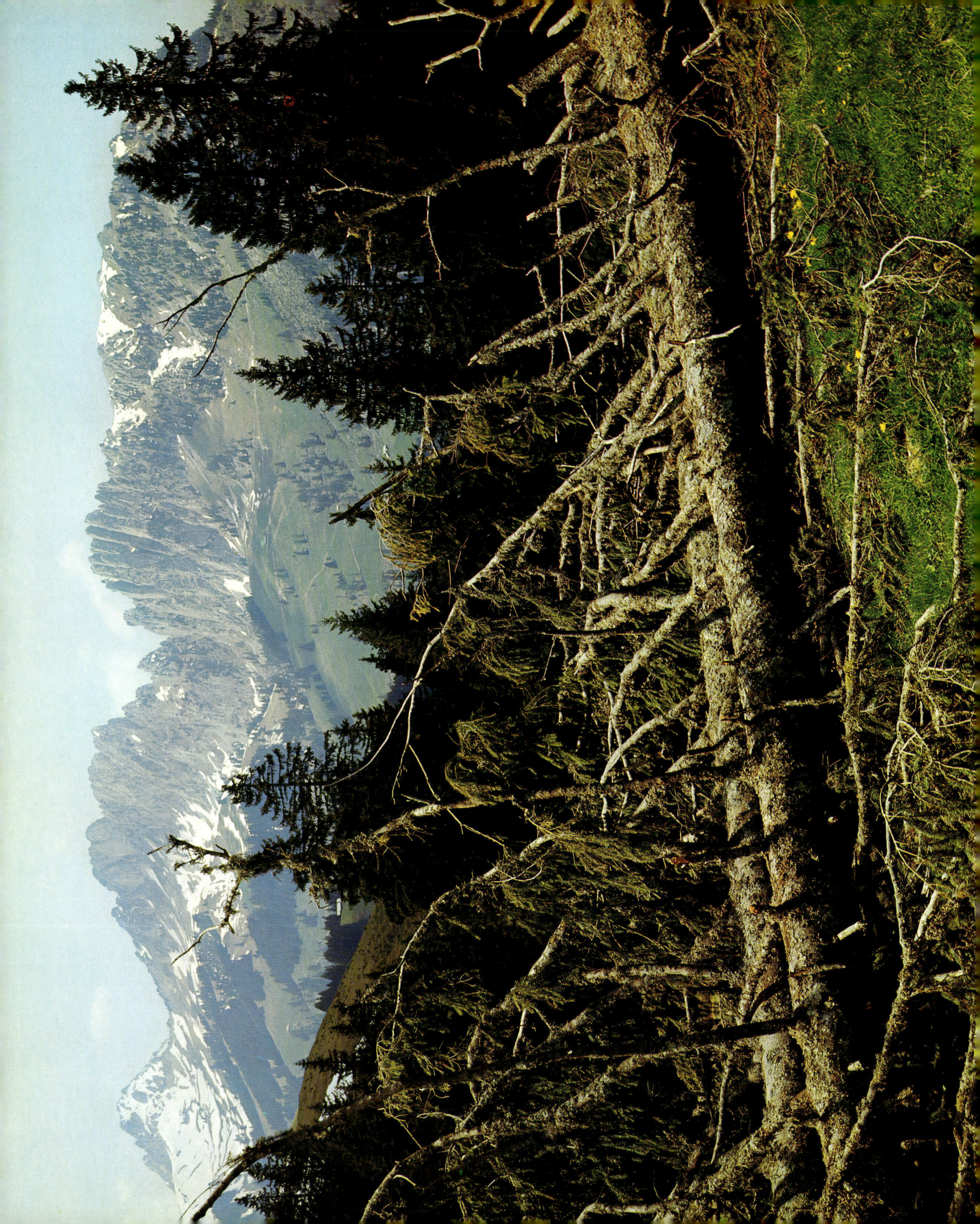

The Gastlosen, near the Jaun Pass (Fribourg Alps)

The modest Jaun Pass (4,941 feet) is a well-engineered motor road running between Bulle in the Fribourg area at its western end and the Simmental lying to the east and falling away northwards to Spiez on the Lake of Thun. It thus provides the shortest link between the north shore of the Lake of Geneva and the famous mountain resorts of the Bernese Oberland.

To the south of the village of Jaun, but still on the western side of the pass, the traveller's attention is riveted by the strange shapes of the rocky Gastlosen chain and its summits.

Gastlos means ›unvisited‹ and this may have been true of the region in the past, but it is not so today, for nowadays numerous walkers, ramblers and even climbers – for these comparatively low peaks, which do not much exceed the 7,000-foot level, can be used as a practice ground long before the summer season starts among their loftier rivals – visit this charming region. Paths criss-cross the meadows and woods, and the rock climber can choose routes of every degree of difficulty among the peaks.

Our picture shows, on the left, the broad mass of the 7,002-foot Wandfluh and on the right the shattered towers of the slightly lower Sattelspitzen. There is a great similarity between the scenery in this area and that of the foothills of the Bavarian Alps.

Mont Blanc, the giant between France and Italy

The scene in this picture illustrating the terrifyingly inhuman chaos of Mont Blanc's north face can, surprisingly, be observed in its full impressiveness by young and old alike; for the astonishing view-point from which it was taken was the 12,608-foot Aiguille du Midi, which can be reached in the gondola of a cable-car, without the slightest effort, from Chamonix.

The only thing you need consider seriously is whether your heart and circulatory system are fit to stand being whirled up to a height differential of 9,000 feet in twenty minutes; not a few who gave no thought to the question beforehand have found themselves completed knocked out at the end of that fantastic and exciting journey to the highest ropeway station in the Alps. In any case it is essential, for a trip into those icy altitudes, to be warmly clad and shod; and if you are protected against the cold, and the lack of oxygen in the thin air at 12,000 feet does not affect you too much, the close-up views of a dozen mighty peaks besides the overpowering sight of Mont Blanc itself, and the huge circular panorama north and westwards over the lower ranges of Savoy, eastwards away to the giants of the Valais and southwards to the Graians, provide a spectacle unrivalled in its magnificence and sublimity.

In the photograph, below to the left lies the relatively gentle snow basin of the Vallée Blanche, one of the snowfields nourishing the huge ice-river of the Mer de Glace. Above the basin rises the north-western ice slope of the Mont Blanc du Tacul (13,927 feet), whose summit fills the top left of the picture. Up to it runs the route of the complete traverse of the Mont Blanc massif, a long and magnificent undertaking. The second crest in that tour is the imposing pyramid of Mont Maudit (14,650 feet, right centre) and, far behind it, the final objective, the snowy dome of Mont Blanc itself (15,781 feet), the highest mountain in Europe. This super-traverse, high on Europe's roof-tree, requires ten to fourteen hours of normal climbing; it can, however, also be done on ski but, it hardly needs stressing, only by the truly expert.

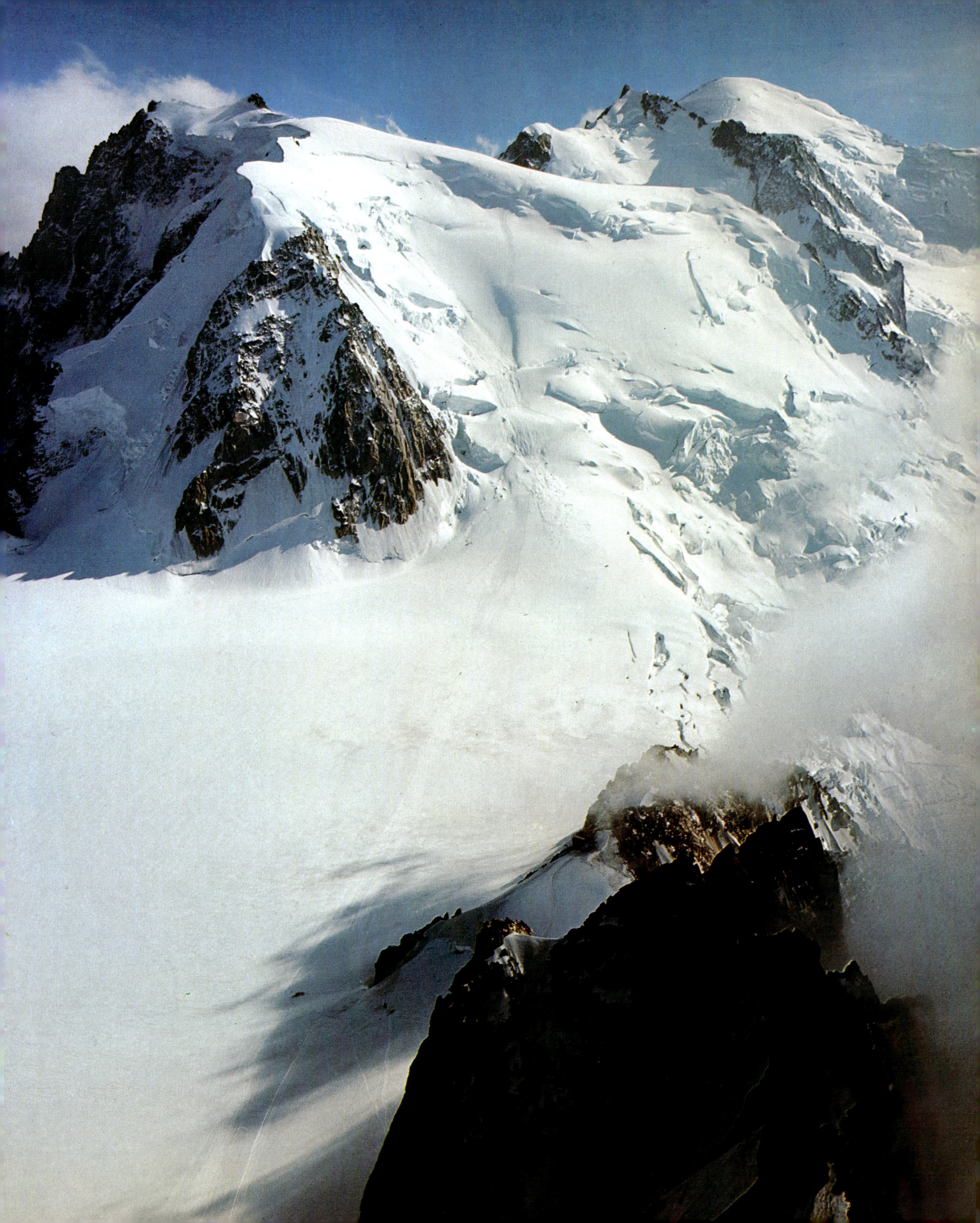

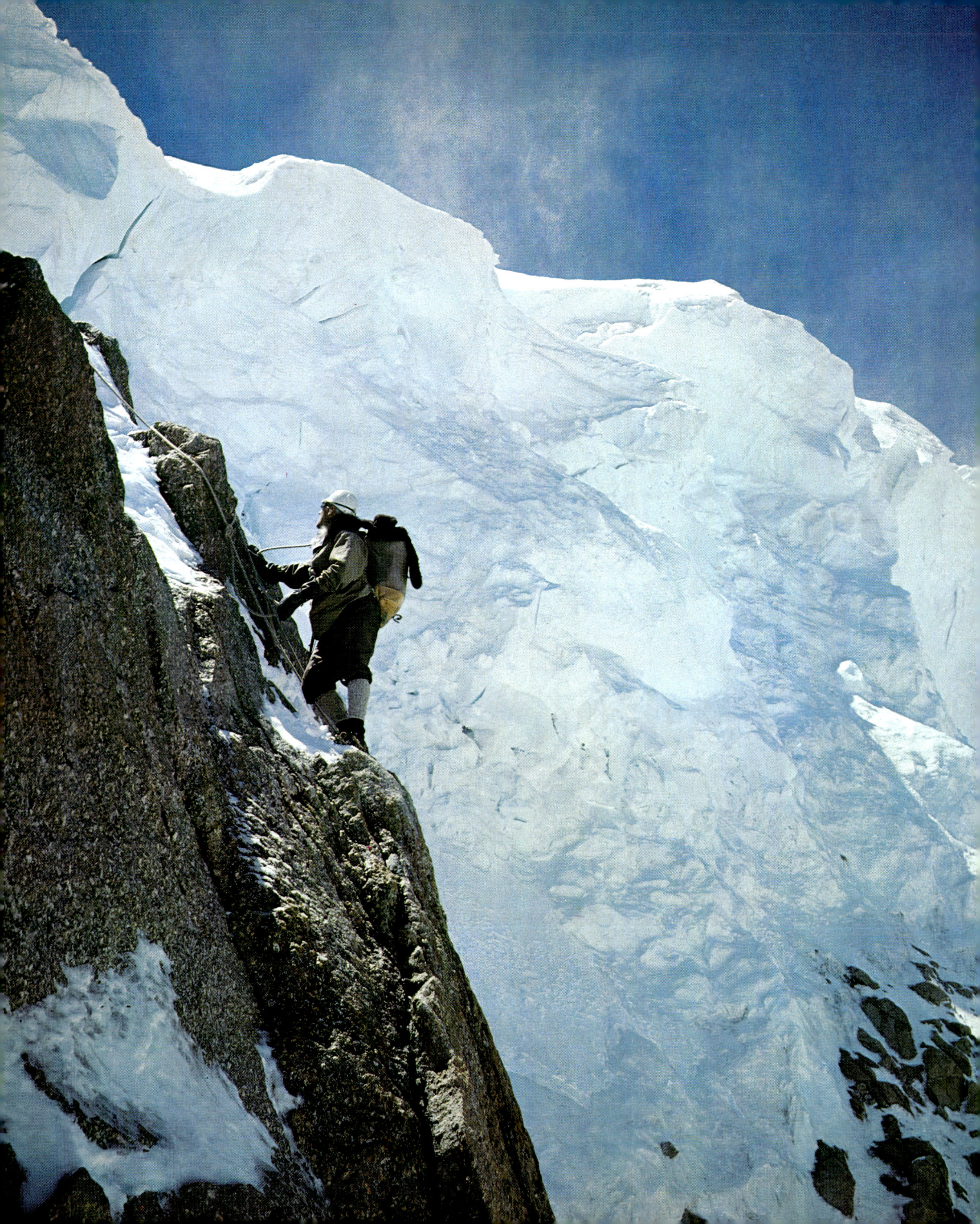

On the Brenva face of Mont Blanc

The eastern (Italian) face of Mont Blanc (see previous plate 91) falls away in the Brenva face, a mighty wall almost three miles broad and nowhere less than 3,000 feet high, to the Brenva glacier on Italian ground. Although it was first climbed as long ago as 1865, the ascent of this face still ranks among the greatest of ice climbs in the Western Alps.

The photograph was not taken on the Brenva Arête, by which the first ascent was made, but on a pitch of the far more difficult Route Major, which was first mastered by F. S. Smythe and T. Graham Brown, climbing together guideless. This route presents difficult rock pitches as well as long, steep work in its ice, and those who climb it are also exposed to the external hazards of falling stones and ice, as is well illustrated by the great ice masses seen ready to collapse, in the background of the picture.

The photograph, which shows the last man of a rope of two or three, was taken by Roland Röbl, while he was following up in another party. The climber has secured a rope-sling, to which the leader above him, out of the picture, is attached, around a firm bollard of rock; so that if the man on in front should by any mischance ›come off‹, they will be held by the rope, which should at least prevent their both being dragged down into the abyss below.

Satellites of Mont Blanc: Tour Ronde and Grand Capucin

The mountains in this picture are familiar to all those glacier ski-runners who make the fabulously lovely run down from the Aiguille du Midi through the Vallée Blanche and down, by the Glacier du Géant and the Mer de Glace, to Montanvert. On the left is the ice-plastered north face of the Tour Ronde (12,440 feet), whose summit can be easily climbed by average mountaineers up its east arête, and provides a magnificent view of Mont Blanc's Brenva face (see previous plate 92); on the right is the tremendous granite pillar of the Grand Capucin, whose east face, 1,700 feet high, the top half of which is seen in profile on the right of the picture, consists of vertical slabs and overhangs of yellow granite. This is a supremely difficult climb, open only to ›Extreme‹ climbers of the Sixth Grade.

Both mountains can be admired in comfort by tourists who take the ropeway to the Aiguille du Midi (see plate 91) and then onwards by the three-mile long cable-car extension to the Pointe Hellbronner above Courmayeur (11,255 feet); thus traversing the whole wonderful world of Mont Blanc's eastern (Italian) side in perfect safety, an experience which has no parallel anywhere else in the Alps. They will, however, not be able to enjoy the marvellous close-up view of the two peaks shown in the photograph, for it was taken during an ascent of the north-east face of Mont Blanc du Tacul (13,927 feet), their near neighbour.

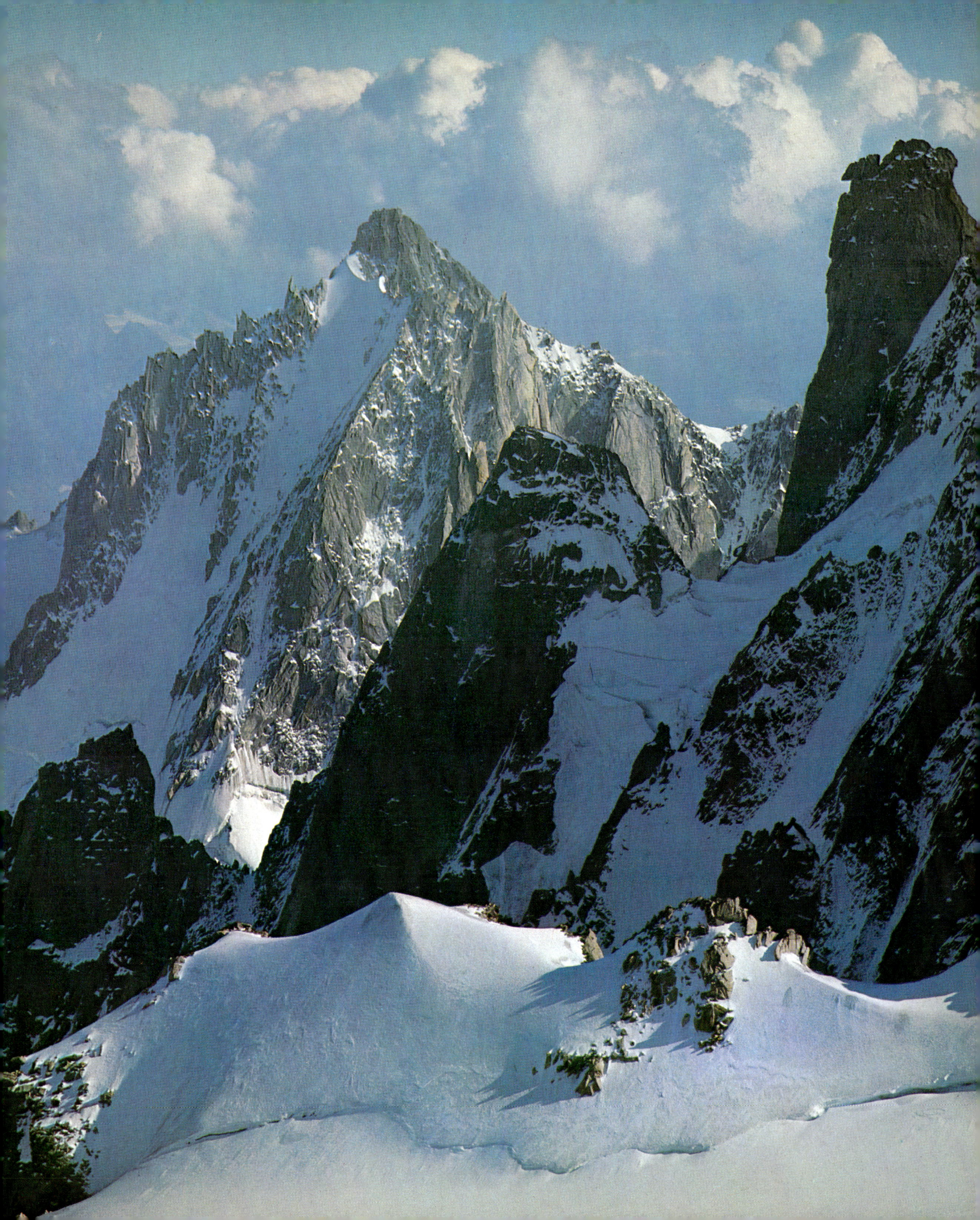

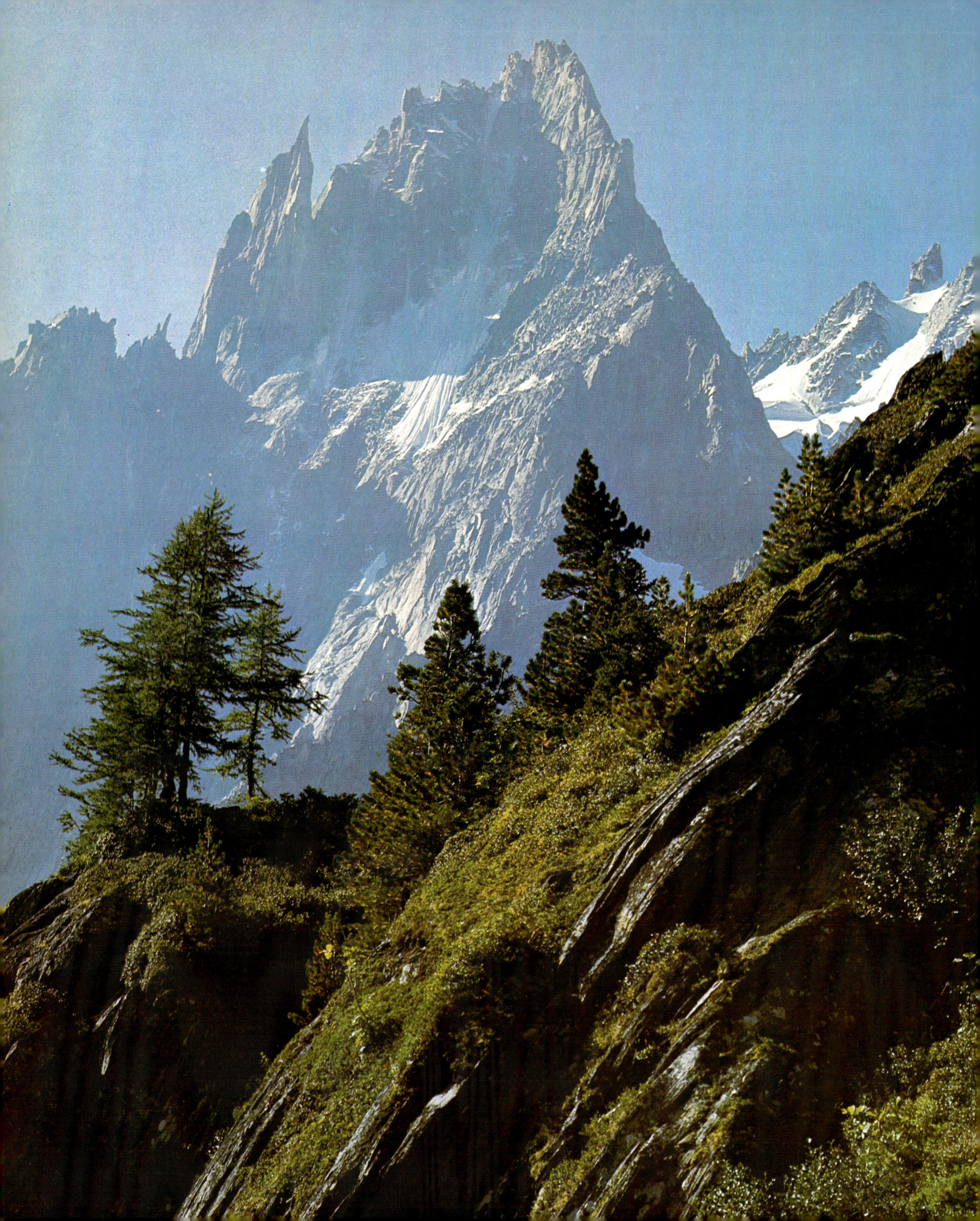

The north face of the Grand Charmoz

The 11,302-foot Aiguille des Grand Charmoz is the northern cornerstone of the three-mile-long comb of the Chamonix Aiguilles, that chain of rock needles which have for so long thrilled tourists and climbers alike for their savagery and challenge. From the peak's north-east (left-hand) ridge there thrusts a slender and truly horrific-looking needle of considerable stature, which bears the proud name of Aiguille de la République (10,833 feet) and whose extreme tip can only be reached by lassoing it with the rope. It was first climbed by H. E. Beaujard in 1904.

The north face of the Grands Charmoz, nearly 3,000 feet high, with its breastplate of ice falling towards the Mer de Glace, presents a fearsome spectacle. A highly dramatic first ascent was achieved in 1931 by the German climbers Willi Welzenbach and Willi Merkl. 1961 brought tragedy when Roland Löbl, the son of the photographer whose work is collected in this volume, himself a fine Alpine photographer and one of Germany's most promising young climbers, lost his life on that sombre wall.

The summit of the peak is barely two miles in a direct line from the teeming international tourist centre of the Montanvert (6,267 feet). Easily accessible by rack-and-pinion railway from Chamonix, this Alpine ›grandstand‹ is one of the finest half-way view-points in the whole Mont Blanc area, or indeed in the Alps. The photograph was taken only a few minutes above the upper terminal of the railway and shows only a minute sector of the tremendous Montanvert panorama, which one can enjoy and admire for hours on end from the terrace and surroundings of the hotel.

The Drus and Aiguille Verte (Mont Blanc Group)

It is the great mass of the Aiguille Verte (13,520 feet), which, with its subsidiary courtiers, the Grand Dru (12,320 feet) and Petit Dru (12,247 feet), dominate the huge Mer de Glace ice-stream descending from Mont Blanc to where its tongue penetrates well below the tree-line into the deep Chamonix corridor, the Valley of the Arve.

The peak's south-western precipices, measuring some 7,000 feet, present the eye with a crazy chaos of hanging glaciers, granite buttresses, arêtes and ridges; yet the climber – and none but a practised mountaineer should set foot in this wilderness of rock and ice – recognizes an ordered system in this wild disarray, sees lines of approach, routes by which it can be surmounted, and even finds a hut at his disposal.

The photograph shows the view from the summit of the Grands Charmoz (see previous plate 94), the Verte's lower but no less savage neighbour, across the basin of the Mer de Glace. To the left rise the twin summits of the Drus from which, deeply shadowed, fantastically smooth precipices plunge to the depths. At the foot of the Verte is the steep Charpoua glacier, on whose central rock island stands the Charpoua Hut (9,324 feet), the ascent to which is in itself a mountaineering expedition. In the background, to the right, the sunlit summit of the Droites (13,120 feet) soars above the Jardin ridge of the Verte, deep in shadow, which provides one of the favourite ridge climbs in the Alps.

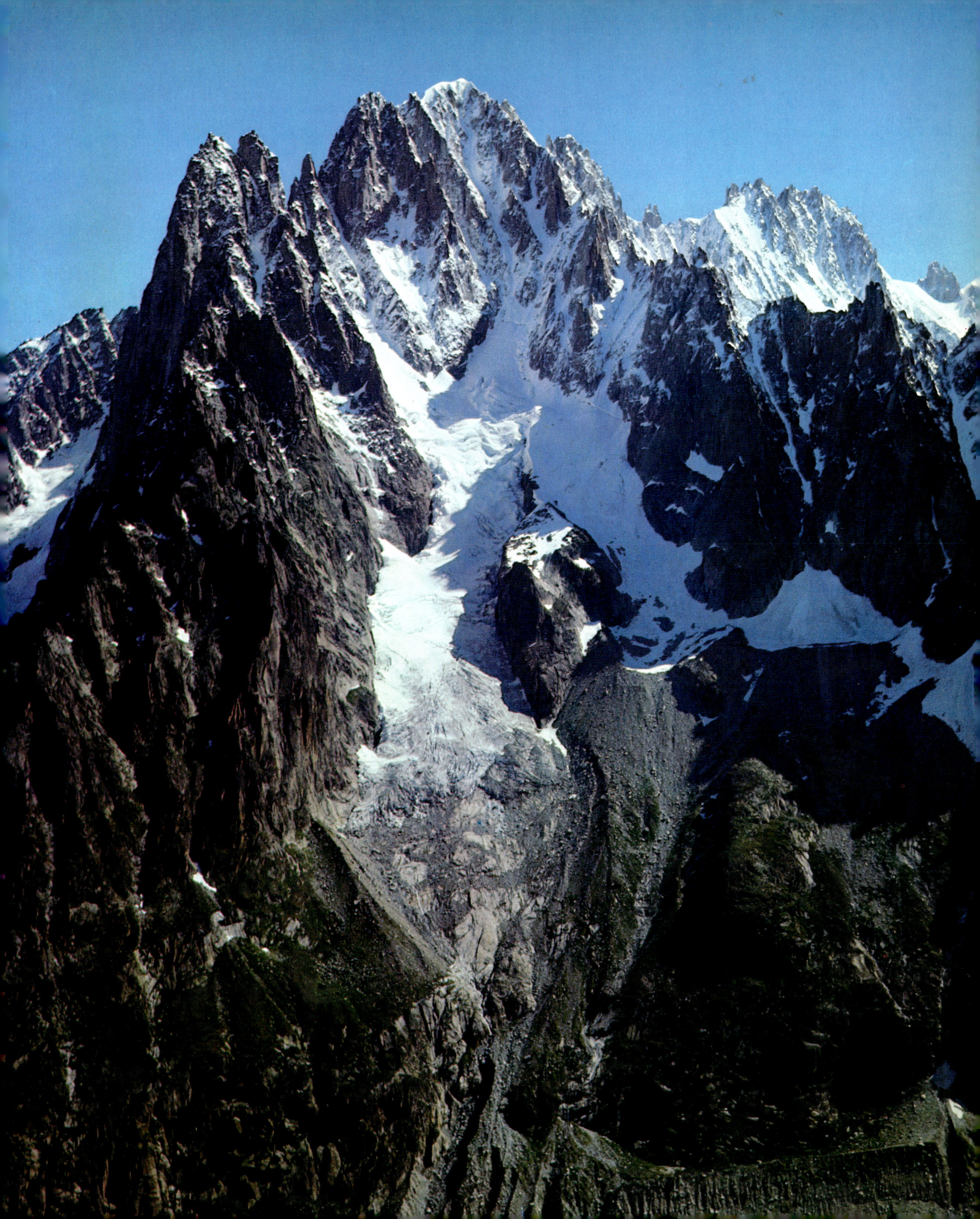

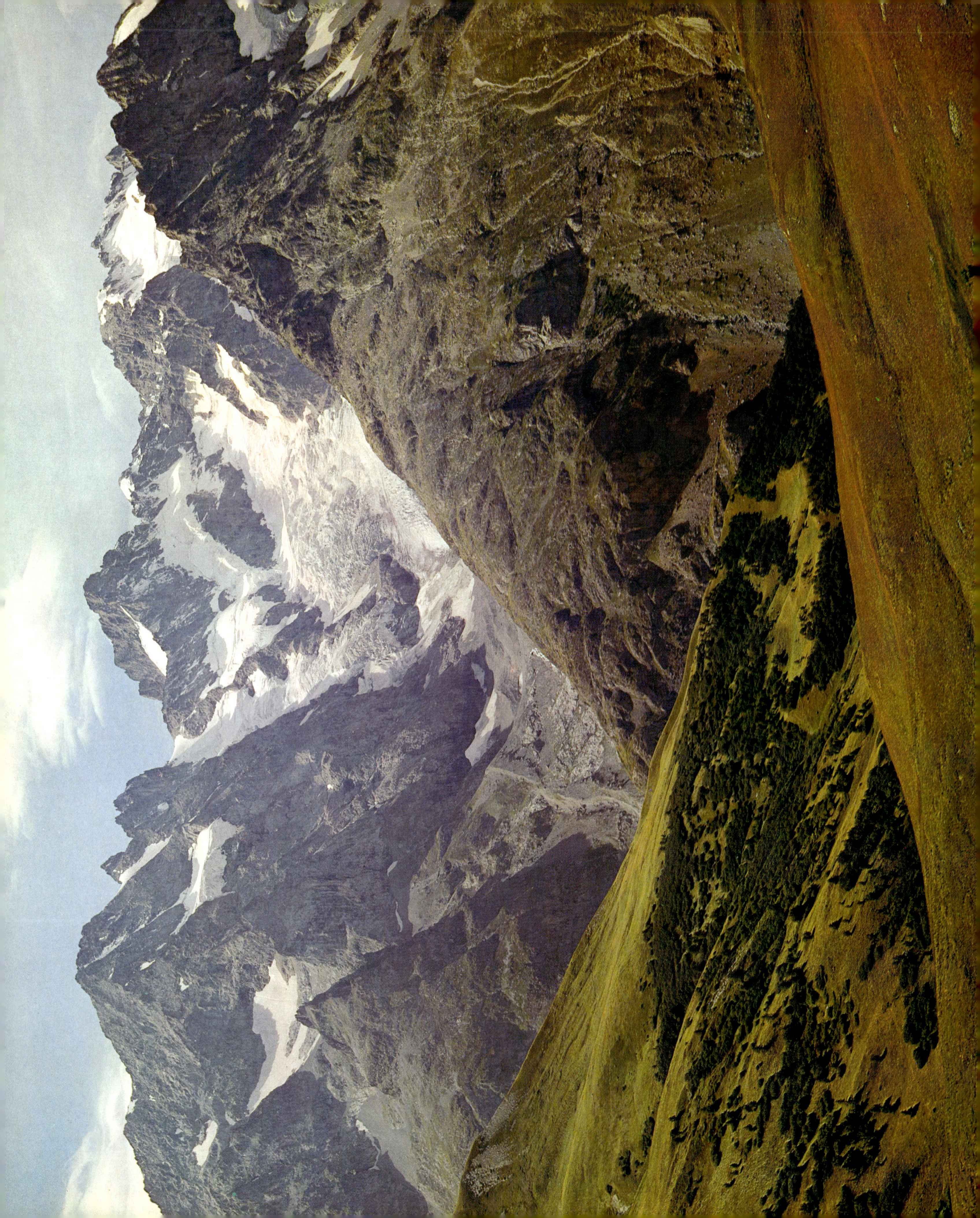

The Pic Gaspard and the Meije (Dauphiné)

The scene pictured in this photograph should be closely related to the next plate (97) and its descriptive text, for the peaks shown here virtually constitute an eastward prolongation of the Meije's long summit ridge.

The picture was taken about six miles to the east of La Grave, a little short of the Col du Lautaret (6,790 feet), that magnificent mountain pass carving its way through the glorious scenery of the Dauphiné massif of the French Alps on its way from Bourg d'Oisans to Briançon. It shows the enormous and rugged amphitheatre lying at the eastern base of the Meije massif. On the left is the rocky trapeze of the Pointe Nerot, separated from the sharp Pointe des Pichettes (11,595 feet) by the little notch of the Col des Pichettes, beyond which rise the dark rocks of the Pointe Piaget, to whose right lies the deep, snowy saddle of the Col Claire (11,180 feet) with the narrow glacier d'Armande flowing down from it. To its right again rises the great rocky knob of the Pic Gaspard (12,730 feet) dominating the broad icefall of the Lautaret glacier. Immediately to the right of the Pic Gaspard is the deep indentation of the Brèche Pavé-Gaspard, with the rounded snowy crown of the Pavé (12,570 feet) beyond it, joined to the main massif of the Meije by its rocky right-hand ridge. In the long-drawn-out comb sweeping away to the right of the picture, it is possible to distinguish the snow dome of the Meije Orientale, the Brèche Joseph Turc, the Pic Centrale and the Grand Pic, the main summit of the Meije (13,034 feet) looking like a tiny rock pyramid.

The long dark ridge and rock comb in the foreground is the Crête de la Palun (11,329 feet), which rises from the depths of the valley of the Romanche, whose waters flow down the western slope of the Col du Lautaret to the Oisans and on to join those of the Isère near Grenoble.

The Meije

The mountains of the Dauphiné, rising to the east of the Winter Olympic city of Grenoble, constitute one of the largest, most savage and scenically most wonderful groups in the Alps. The great peaks of the High Dauphiné embrace an area of some 400 square miles and reach their culminating point in the Barre des Écrins (13,642 feet) at the eastern end of the main range.

The Meije, though some 400 feet lower (see previous plate 96), is one of the most impressive and beautiful mountains forms in the Dauphiné and, some think, anywhere in the Alps. The photographs shows it from the north, close to the hamlet of La Grave (5,000 feet) on the Lautaret road in the narrow Romanche Valley, from which 8,000 feet of the great peak's precipices tower more steeply overhead than those of the Matterhorn above Zermatt. The view is still better from the paths behind the village; but the best is the prospect over the whole snowy massif from the tiny hamlet and chapel of Le Chazelet, high up the slope and now reached by a well-engineered motor road leaving the main Lautaret highway a little beyond La Grave.

High in the left of the picture, the long continuous ridge of the several summits and saddles, already enumerated in the description facing plate 96, sweeps up to the sharp head of the main summit, the Grand Pic (13,034 feet), above whose steeply-falling frontal ridge the even sharper spire of the Pic du Glacier Carré just shows. From it the ridge sweeps down to the deep gateway of the Brèche de la Meije (10,827 feet), which enables mountaineers to cross the range to the tiny climbing centre of La Bérarde, in the Véneon Valley to the south (see plate 99), after an ascent of six hours from La Grave. To the right of the Brèche stretches the long massif of the Râteau (12,317 feet).

While these northern precipices of the Meije are savagely riven, its southern face consists of a single sheer rock wall, a mile broad and 2,700 feet high, providing extremely difficult climbing. A no less magnificent, but far less difficult, climb is the long traverse of the whole summit crest of the Meije massif from west to east.

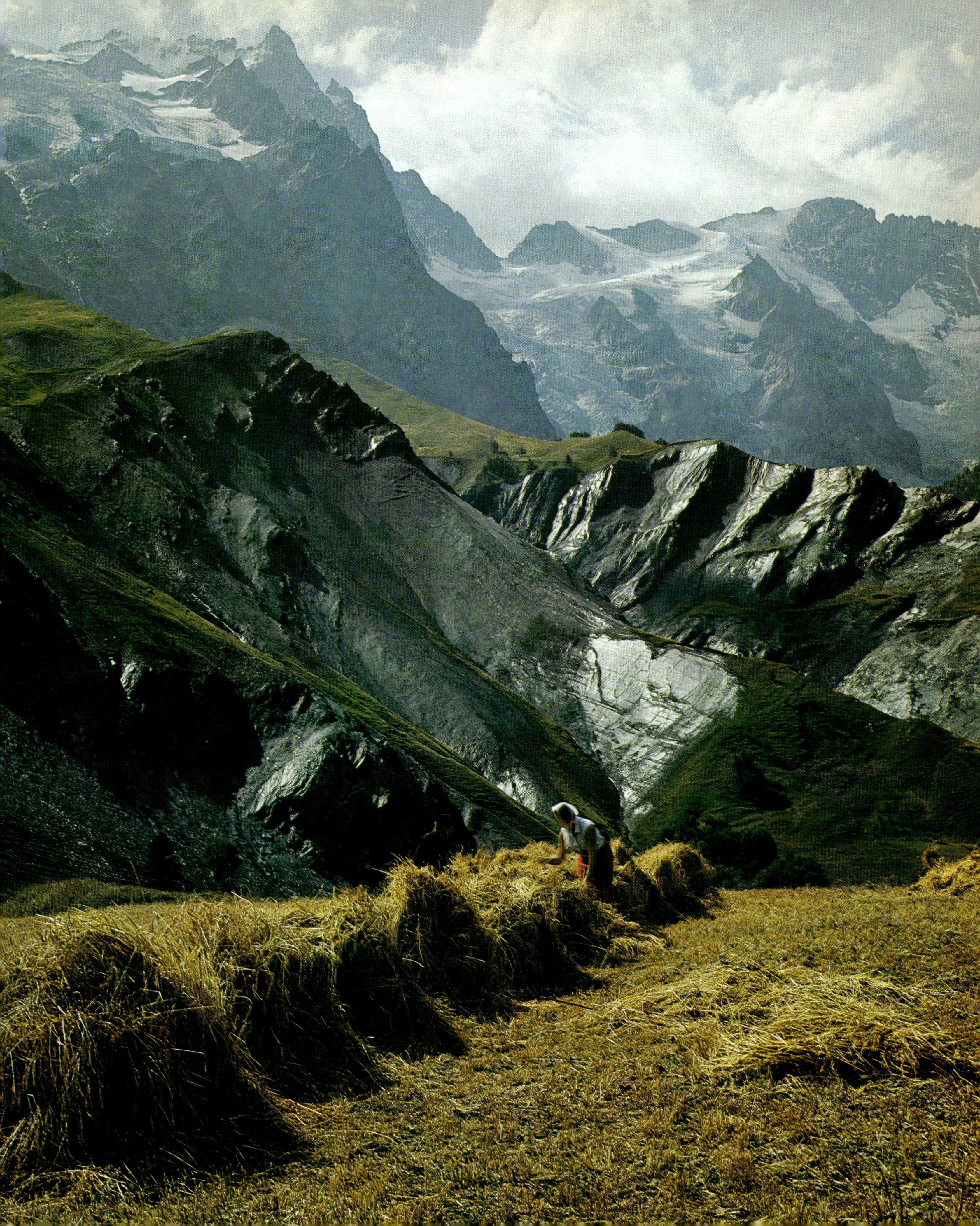

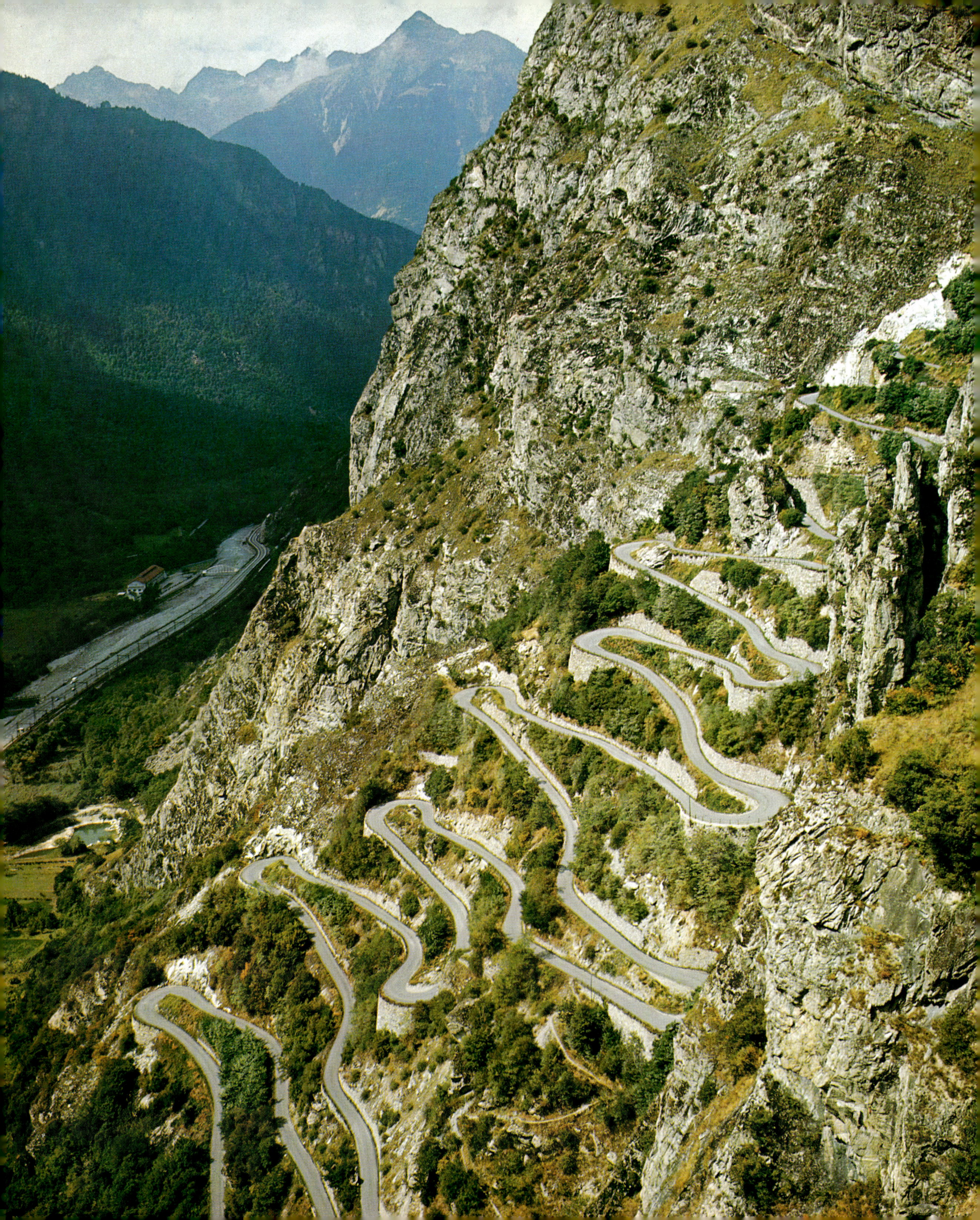

A hairpin problem in the Maurienne

The Valley of the Arc, curving eastwards from the main Isère Valley at Aiguebelle and providing the splendidly-fast approach road to the Mont Cenis Pass (6,834 feet) – in spite of its height, one of the easiest passages of the backbone of the Alps into Italy, by way of Susa and Turin – is known as the Maurienne.

To the north of it lie the peaks and glaciers of the fine Vanoise Group (Grande Casse 12,665 feet) in the Tarentaise, separating the lovely valleys of Pralognan and Val d'Isère; to the south, somewhat more remote, rise the higher and far more spectacular summits of the Dauphiné (see plates 96 and 97). The Maurienne is, however, far too deep a rift between its high containing walls for either group to be seen from its green floor.

The hardy and experienced mountain motorist in search of scenic glories will find, between St Jean and St Michel de Maurienne on the main highway, a not very broad and extremely curvaceous side road, climbing the southern face of the valley in innumerable hairpin turns, splendidly built out from the mountainside, as this remarkable photograph shows.

It leads to the little hamlet of Montricher and beyond it to Albanne, at an altitude of 5,250 feet. As you swing up the turns, the valley falls away impressively below and the prospect northwards to the Vanoise peaks opens up more and more splendidly. At the top of the road at Albanne, a magnificent view southwards to the fantastic summits of the high Dauphiné peaks is added to the splendours of the scene.

This is a digression well worth making for its glorious views, but it should only be undertaken by drivers with considerable Alpine experience and confidence, for this is no drive for the timid, the giddy or the accident prone, and an error of judgment could well prove disastrous.

The Barre des Écrins (Dauphiné)

To the south of the Meije, in the great complex of the rugged Dauphiné Alps, the narrow Véneon Valley leads by an equally narrow road, equipped with innumerable turning-out places for passing (›garages‹), to the tiny hamlet of La Bérarde (5,700 feet), which has been a climbing centre, and little else, for a century.

It lies not far short of the foot of the mighty Barre des Écrins (13,462 feet), the highest peak and the only ›Four-thousander‹ in the Haut Dauphiné. The mountain is a typical example of a peak with two completely different faces; its southern and western side (shown in the picture) consists of massive rock precipices, suitable only for first-class climbers, while on the north it presents an unbroken sweep of snow and ice.

The photograph, taken near La Bérarde with the Véneon in the foreground, shows the two main summits of the peak in the centre. At the left-hand edge of the picture is the Roche Faurio (12,190 feet), whose opposite face is a favourite skiing-ground; its right-hand ridge falls to the 11,205-foot Col des Écrins and then sweeps up in the fine north ridge to the Dôme de Neige des Écrins (13,058 feet), to whose right again the north-west ridge leads to the Pic Lory (13,462 feet), the highest summit in the massif.

The 3,300-foot north-west face of the Dôme de Neige, half obscured in the photograph by the rocky peaks in front of it, was first climbed in 1913 by the Viennese Guido Meyer and the famous Dolomite guide Angelo Dibona. The ascent of the face (Grade IV, ›Very Difficult‹) is still considered one of the great Alpine rock climbs.

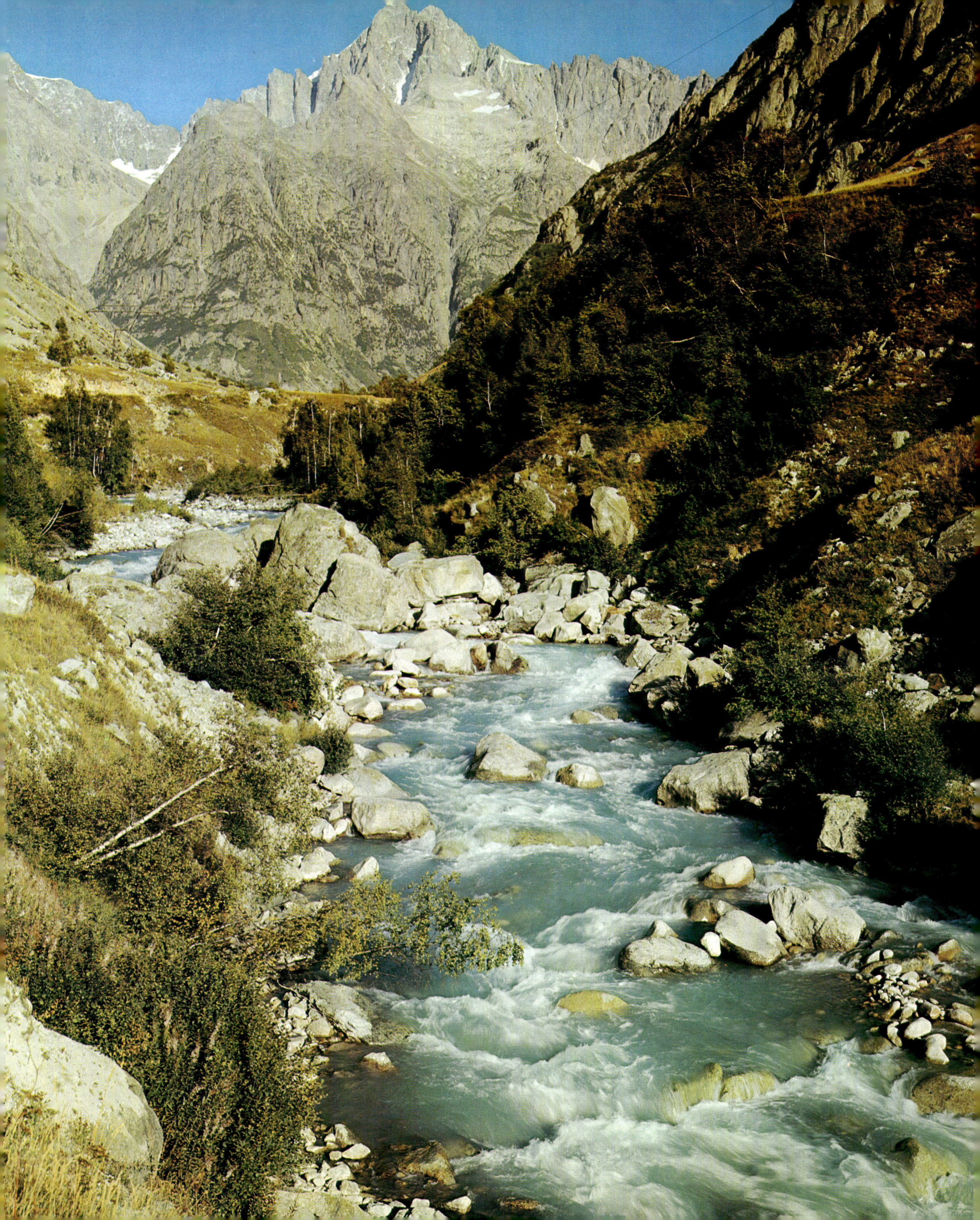

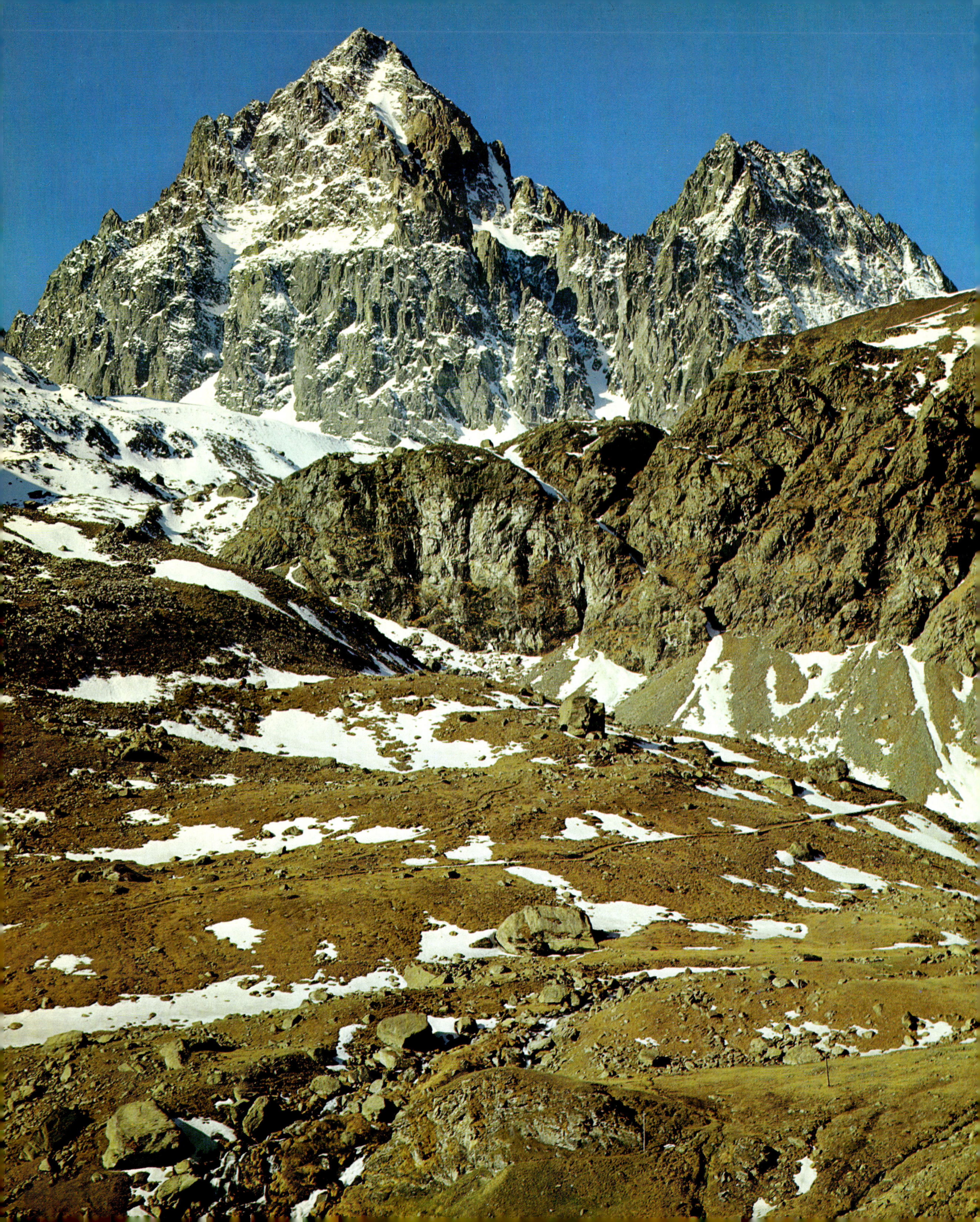

Monte Viso and the source of the Po

A little more than forty miles as the crow flies to the north-west of Turin, the shapely pyramid of Monte Viso (12,614 feet) dominates the western plain of the Po. It is as though the mountain, at whose foot the river starts as a tiny streamlet, were anxious to watch the growth of the headwaters till they swell into a great river.

Monte Viso is an important landmark in the history of Italian mountaineering, for two years after the first ascent by a party consisting of two English climbers, J. W. Mathews and F. W. Jacomb, with the two French guides Michel and J. B. Croz in 1861, the Italians Quintino Sella, Giovanni Baracco and Counts Giacinto and Paolo di St Robert achieved the first Italian climb on 12 August 1863.

The picture shows the Viso from the east, with the slender trapeze of the 10,997-foot Visolotto to its right. It is well worth while for any mountain lover to break his journey through the sunny plains of the south and enjoy a couple of days in the Viso region, whose two huts are accessible from Crissolo in the valley below with relative ease. The Rifugio Quintino Sella is reached by an excellent motor road as far as the little inn at the Pian del Re, from where it is three hours by path to the hut.

The normal route up the south face is only Grade II (›Moderate‹) and takes from four to five hours, though it is sometimes difficult to pick up the right line. The walks in the neighbourhood of the Viso massif are also full of delights.

The icy satellites of the Gran Paradiso

No more appropriate name could have been chosen for the southern ranges and glaciers of the Graian Alps, lying to the south of Italy's Aosta Valley, than the Gran Paradiso Group; for since 1925 this region has been Italy's *Parco Nazionale*, the national park or ›paradise‹, which has remained relatively unspoiled ever since. Besides a bewitching wealth of plants and flowers, stretching far up into the glacier regions, it boasts a populous, carefully-protected steinbock colony.

Here there are many lovely peaks, offering plentiful opportunities for the average mountaineer, the showpiece being the 13,324-foot Gran Paradiso itself, the highest peak in the Graian Alps and their only ›Four-thousander‹. The fairly easy glacier ascent from the Rifugio Vittorio Emanuele does not take much more than three hours.

The photograph shows only a couple of the Gran Paradiso's satellites, rising to the south-west of the main ridge of the range. The left-hand peak is the glaciated Ciaforon (11,946 feet), whose north face, directly facing the viewer, can be dangerous on account of its hanging glacier.

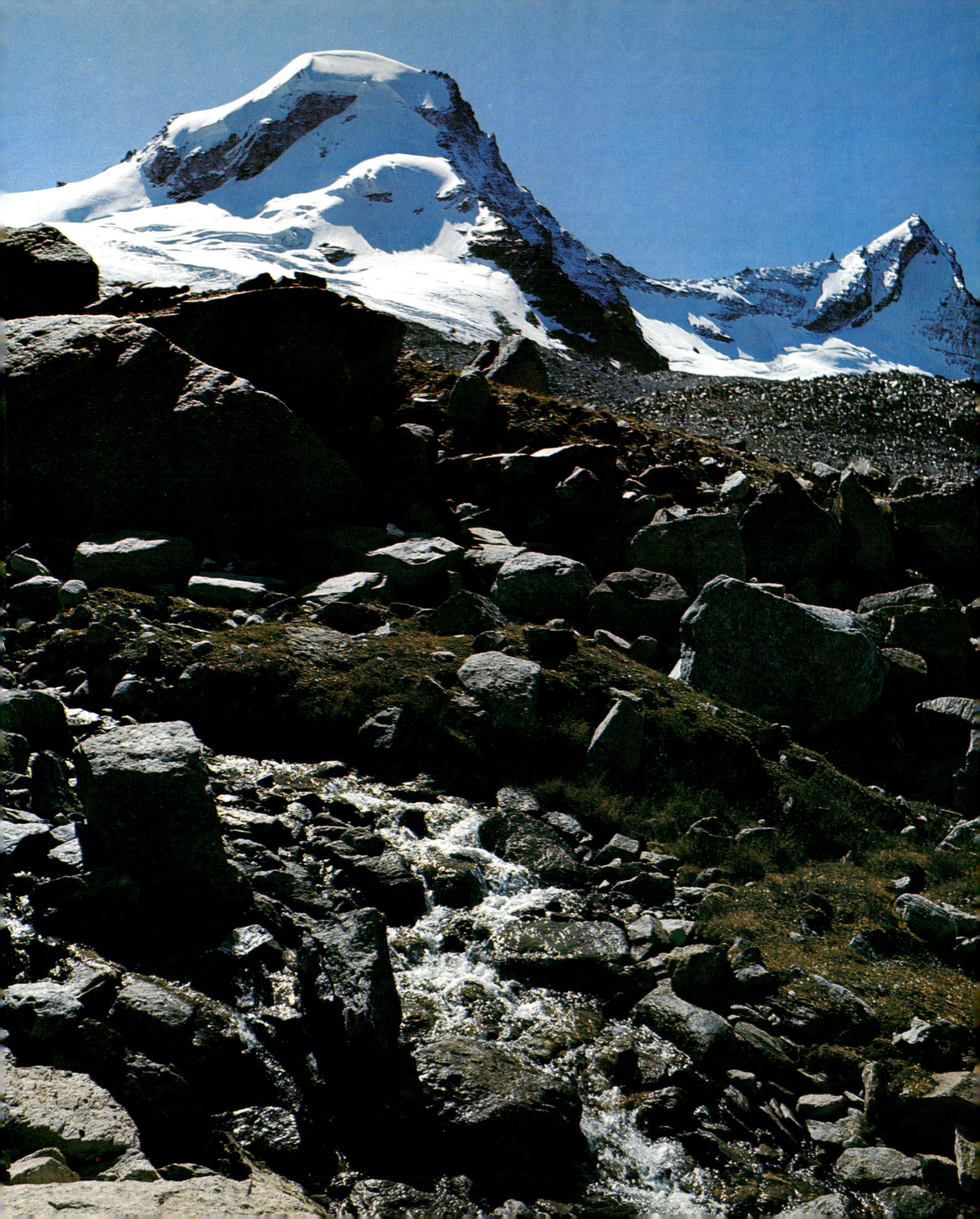

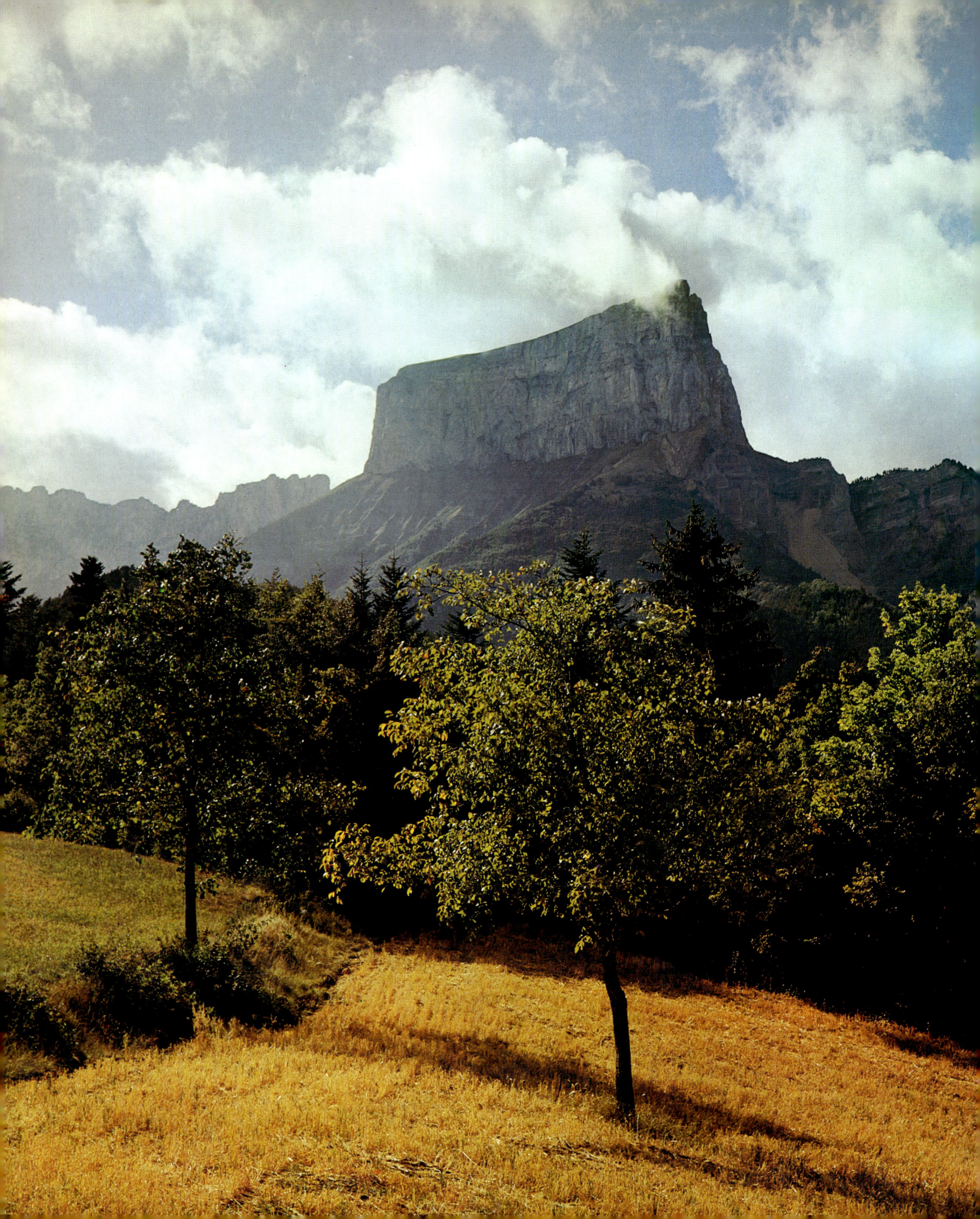

Mont Aiguille, in the Vercors

The Mont Aiguille (6,880 feet) rises in the Vercors district to the south of Grenoble, close to the highroad linking that city with Provence and the Riviera, by way of the Col de la Croix Haute, Serres and Sisteron. This isolated mountain, which has no parallel in the whole of the Alps, holds a unique place in the history of mountaineering; for it was climbed in 1492, on the orders of Charles VIII of France, by a hireling guide Antoine de Ville, accompanied by a chamberlain, Julien de Beaupré and seven others, a feat not repeated till 1834 when a local peasant made his way to the top. Not only was this the first serious rock climb to be recorded, but the use of ropes, ladders and iron stakes marked the birth of the artificial climbing methods and aids universally employed today. To their astonishment, the daring climbers found at the top of those vertical cliffs a flat, grassy plateau large enough to pasture a flock of sheep.

Ives Levy, the King's envoy, sent to the scene to confirm the contents of the despatch written by de Ville on the top of the mountain to announce the success of the attempt, stated on his return to the court: ›The very aspect of this mountain is enough to set all who behold it in a state of terror.‹

Today's route to the top is the same as that by which the intrepid pioneers mastered those terrifying cliffs nearly 500 years ago, but it has had its teeth drawn; for it has been amply safeguarded with fixed steel cables and iron hand-grips, though even now it is still classified as Grade II (›Moderately Difficult‹).

The Organ Pipes near Dié (Dauphiné)

The extraordinary rock formation shown in this photograph is to be seen near the little town of Dié in the Department of Drôme to the south-west of Grenoble, and so is still part of the mountain scenery of the Dauphiné.

The rock cliffs, nearly 700 feet high, have been moulded by erosion into what looks like a huge church organ. Individual towers, which appear to be on the point of falling at any moment, are very similar to the famous earth pyramids near Bozen (Bolzano); but here at Dié the difference is that the rock is much more stable and compact.

This riven barrier of rock, if you come upon it unexpectedly and when it is brightly lit, really does look for all the world like a gigantic organ, far beyond the competence of any human hand to have constructed.

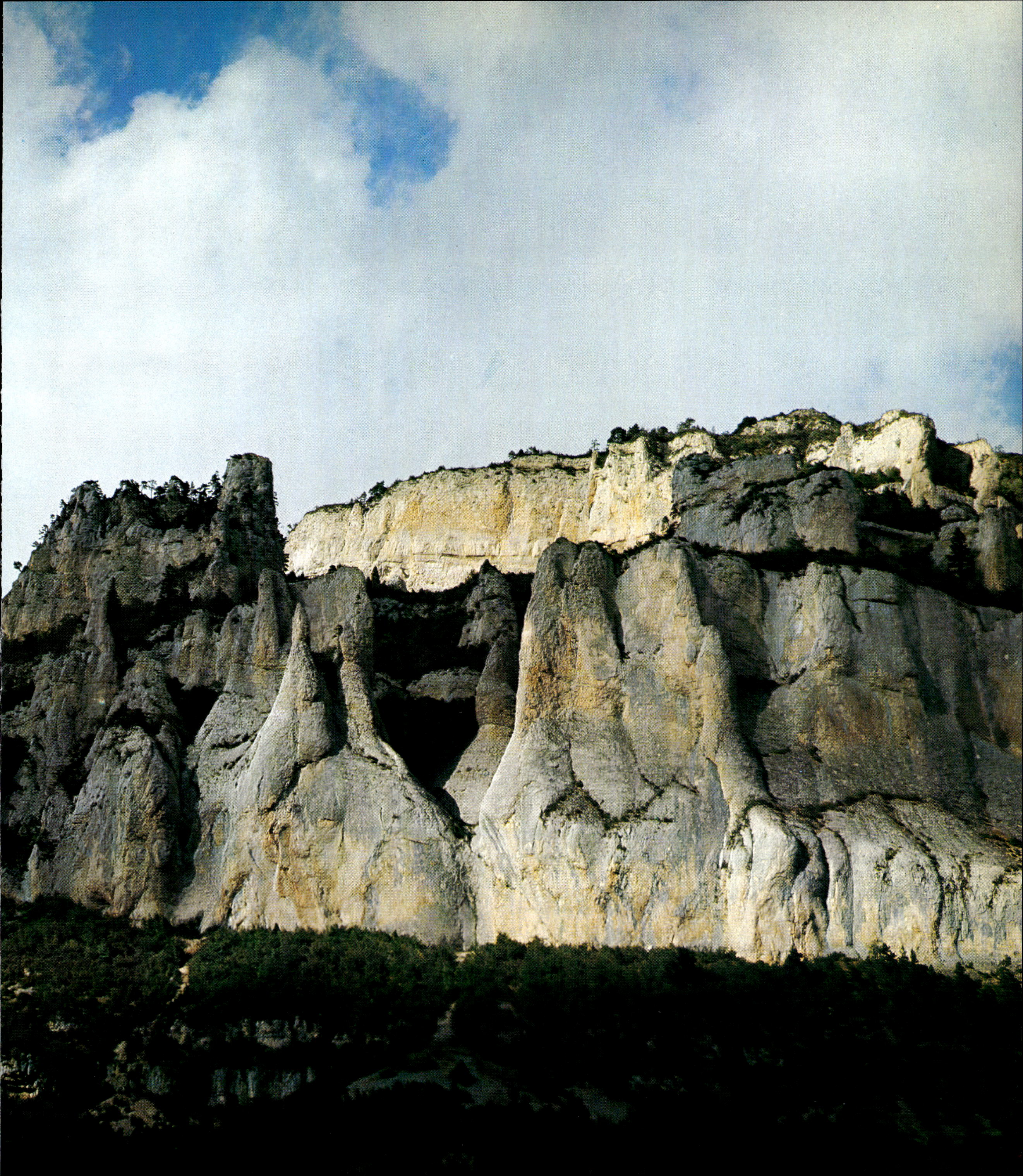

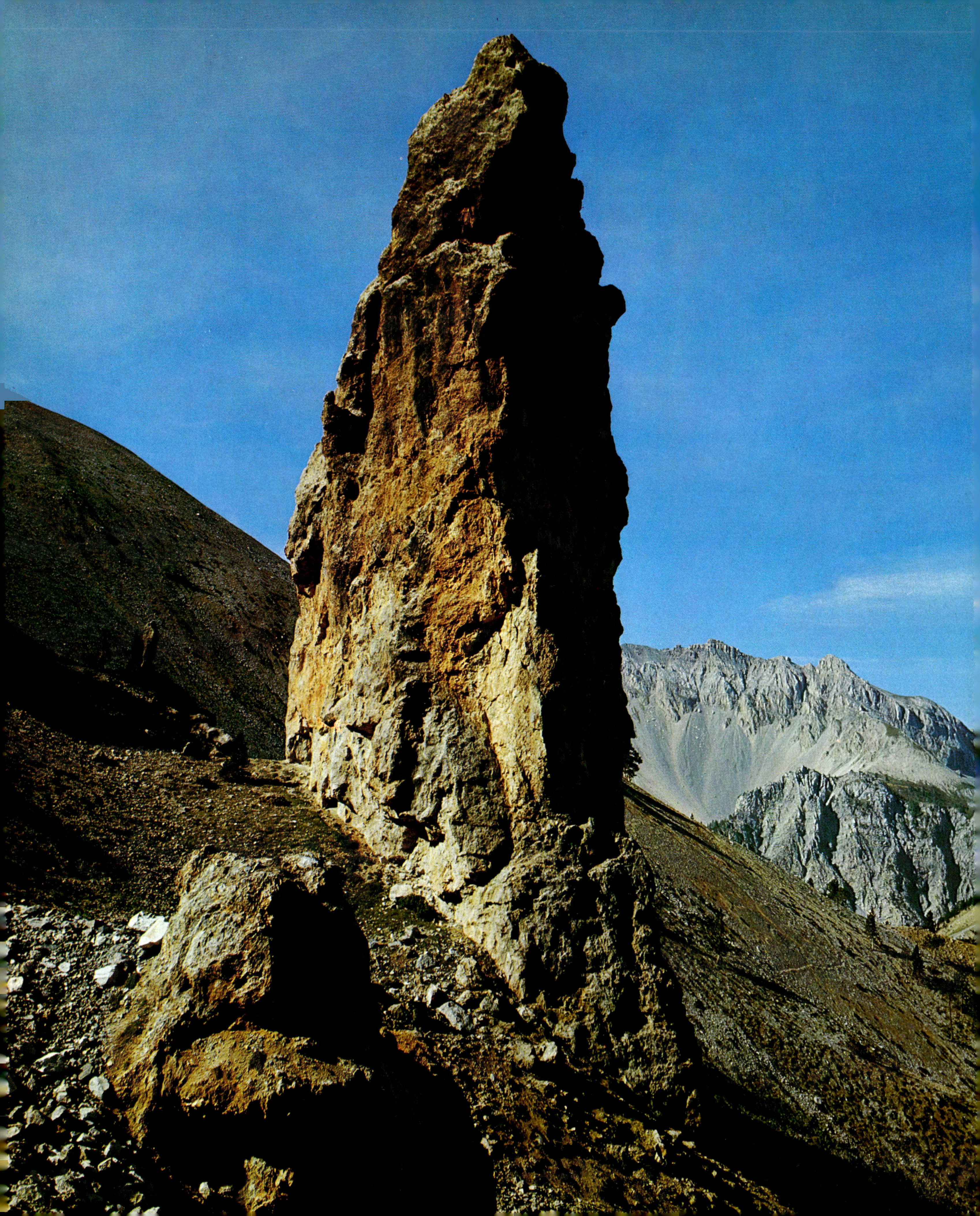

A stony desert: the Col d'Iseran (Savoy Alps)

On his way from Grenoble to Aosta, the motorist with a suitable car and an appetite for hairpin turns comes, after 125 miles of driving on mountain roads, to the summit of a great French strategic highway, the Col d'Iseran, in the Vanoise district of Savoy.

This pass, 9,088 feet high, disputes with the far less easy Col de Restefond the honours of being the loftiest motorable road in Europe. As a matter of interest, it is only 650 feet lower than Germany's highest mountain, the Zugspitze (plate 33).

The vegetation hereabouts is sparse, though still considerably richer than that found at equivalent altitudes in the Eastern Alps, the tree-level reaching a level of from 5,250 to 5,900 feet. Here and there an isolated pinnacle or hump of rock lifts from the bouldery floor, and only a few minutes from the road utter solitude is the order of the day.

Only six miles to the west of the Iseran, the famous ›Footpath from the Lake of Geneva to the Mediterranean‹ crosses the Col de la Leisse (9,110 feet), in the heart of the Vanoise area, set in similar stark scenery which, if a little depressing, still possesses a magic of its own.

The ten-mile long north-western side of the Col d'Iseran road sweeps down nearly 7,000 feet to Val d'Isère, the fashionable and world-famous winter sports resort so tragically devastated by the avalanche disaster of the winter of 1969–70.

The Col de la Cayolle (Alpes Maritimes)

The mountain tract of the Maritime Alps between Barcelonette (3,470 feet), that pleasant provincial capital set in a bowl surrounded by high mountain walls, and the beaches and bathing beauties and bright lights of the Côte d'Azur, is rocky and rugged, but its structures and outlines already hint clearly that the great chain of the High Alps is soon to lose itself in the waves of the Mediterranean.

The Col de la Cayolle (7,630 feet), to the south-east of Barcelonette, gives one the opportunity of enjoying this distinctive scenery. The twenty-mile long road, a narrow one, only permitting passing at the widenings knows as ›garages‹, climbs, with fine views of the cliffs of the 10,017-foot Mont Pelet on the right, to the secluded pass and so provides one of several mountain links with Nice. It then winds down through savagely wild scenery, into the valley of the Var (great care being required on this southern descent) and, after forty miles in all, which call for a measure of experience in this kind of motoring, the road descends to Guillaumes, a favourite summer resort lying at 2,687 feet.

From here to Nice, is another sixty-five miles, the first part of which, to Puget-Théniers (1,325 feet) in the open main valley, runs through the Gorges de Daluis, one of the most remarkable ravines in the Maritime Alps. For nearly two miles the road clings hazardously above the torrent far below in a narrow chasm, crossing tributary streams by dizzy bridges, and threading through a succession of tunnels. The vivid red and yellow rocks, seen against the green of trees and the blue Provençal sky, provide a beautiful and colourful contrast all the seven miles to Daluis.

The rest of the way from Puget-Théniers to Nice offers pleasant and easy motoring along the valley highway.

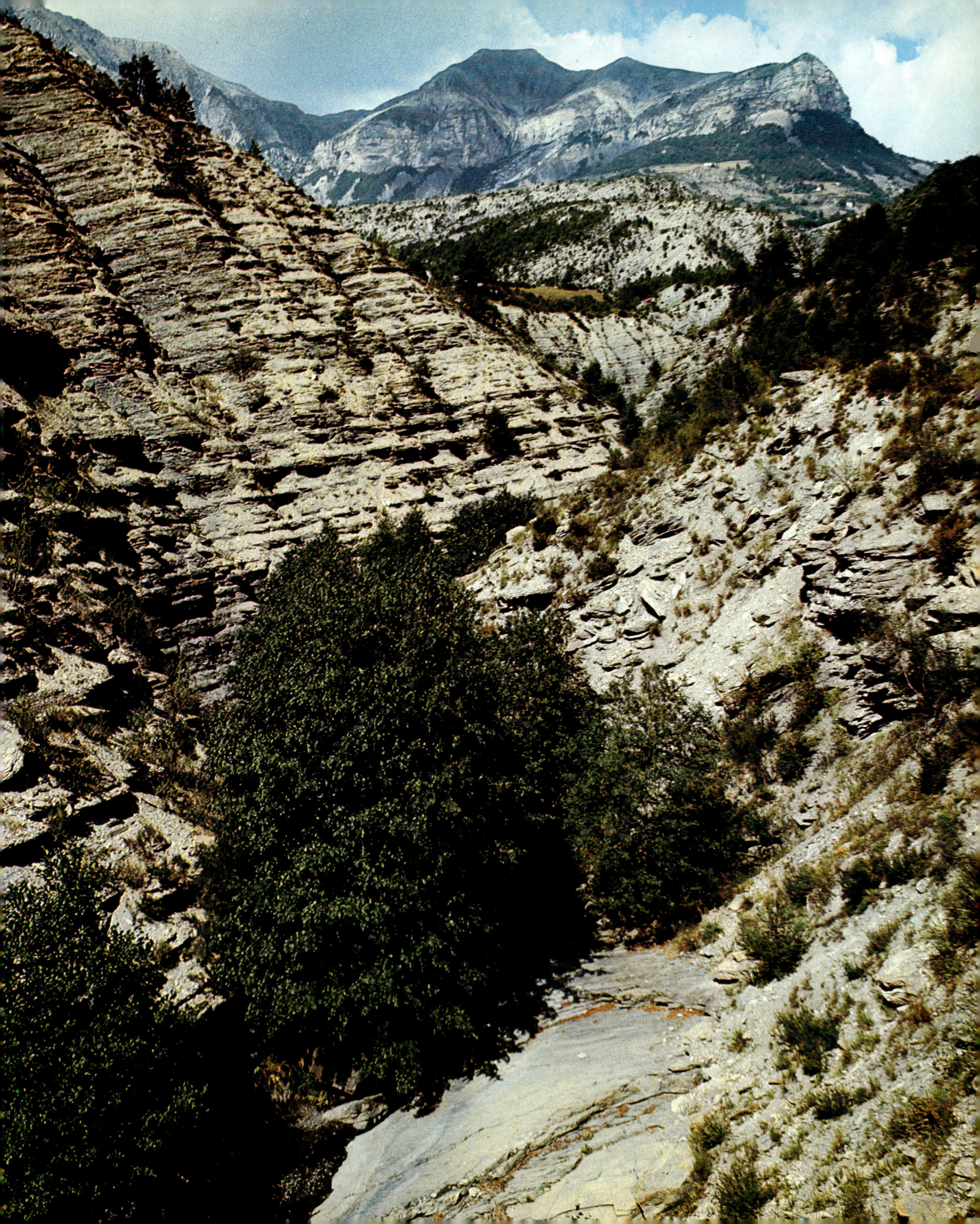

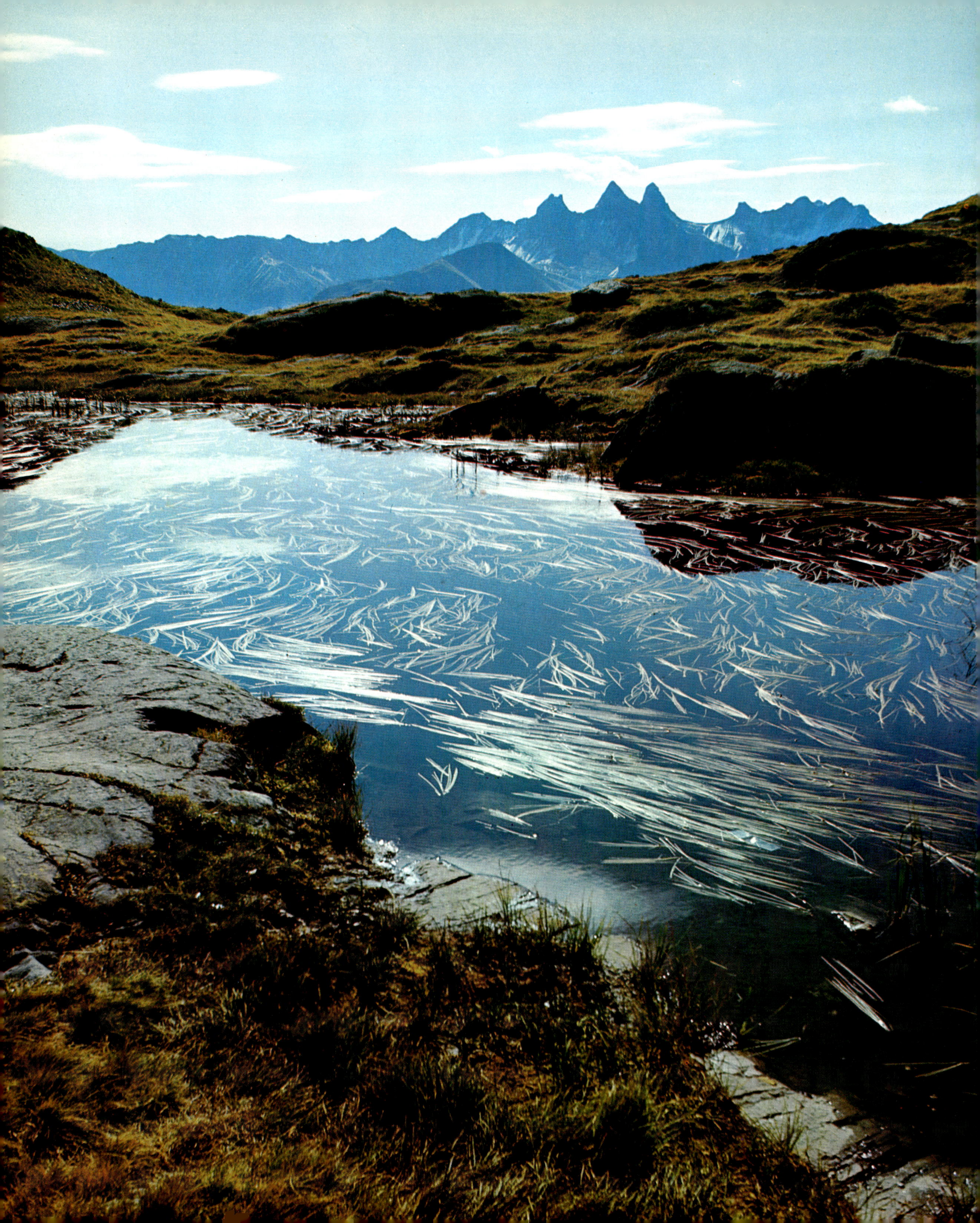

The Col de la Croix de Fer and the Aiguilles d'Arves

The Col de la Croix de Fer (6,780 feet) is a little-known minor pass at the northern edge of the Haut Dauphiné, providing a link between the Valley of the Romanche and the Valley of the Arc in the Maurienne.

It runs from Rochetaillée, just short of Bourg d'Oisans, on the Lautaret road (see plates 96 and 97), north-eastwards to St Jean de Maurienne in the Arc Valley (plate 98). The road is thirty-five miles long, very narrow, and often in a condition only just acceptable for even a secondary pass; but the traveller looking for views of quite unusual quality should steel himself to make this somewhat strenuous détour to the Col de la Croix de Fer, for the scenery he will find there will compensate him for all his toil and tribulations.

At the top of the pass it is necessary to leave the car and walk for fully five minutes, for the observation point from which the panorama unfolds in its full splendour lies a little to the south on a little pyramid. Far to the south rises the vast glaciated massif of the Meije. Farther round still, as shown in the photograph, rise the three imposing spires of the Aiguilles d'Arves, the highest of which, the Aiguille Centrale (11,512 feet), is the least difficult to climb, for the other two, the slightly lower Meridionale and Septentrionale, are both ascents of some severity. At their feet, on the slope facing the viewer, stands the Refuge de Rieu Blanc, all around which there are splendid rambles for the walker and fine climbing for the mountaineer, though the routes in the group are comparatively rarely visited by other than French climbers.

The area can also be approached by its opposite, south-eastern flank from the Col du Galibier (8,399 feet), the splendid pass linking the summit of the Col du Lautaret with the Maurienne, or from due south at La Grave on the Lautaret road itself (plate 97).

The Gorges du Verdon, Alpes Maritimes

A little way before the great curve of the Alps finally sweeps to its rest near Nice, on the shores of the Mediterranean, nature has provided yet another incomparable example of her handicraft for us to marvel at. This takes the form of the Gorges of the Verdon, at some points over 2,000 feet deep, sometimes known as the Verdon Canyons, for not altogether without reason they have been compared with the Grand Canyon of Colorado.

The Verdon rises near Barcelonette (see plate 105) about sixty miles to the north-west of Nice and, after carving its way through its fantastic gorges, flows into the Durance, which in its turn debouches into the Rhône near Avignon.

There is nothing comparable to the Verdon Gorges anywhere in Europe, and the fact that they are to be found in the Alps is merely another reminder how infinitely varied is the Alpine scene.

The marvels of these gorges can be enjoyed by the hiker from a perfectly safe path; the motorist can speed through them along a superbly comfortable and scenically wonderful road; while for the mountain-torrent canoeist their waters offer a hair-raising challenge and adventure.

The gorges were discovered and thoroughly explored for the first time by the geologist and pioneer of pot-holing, E. A. Martel; the walker's path which penetrates them bears his name.

Every visitor to the South of France should make sure of visiting the Verdon Gorges, even if his main objective is a sun- and sea-bathing holiday. They can best be approached by Castellane to their east, Moustiers-Sainte Marie to the north or Draguignan to the south.

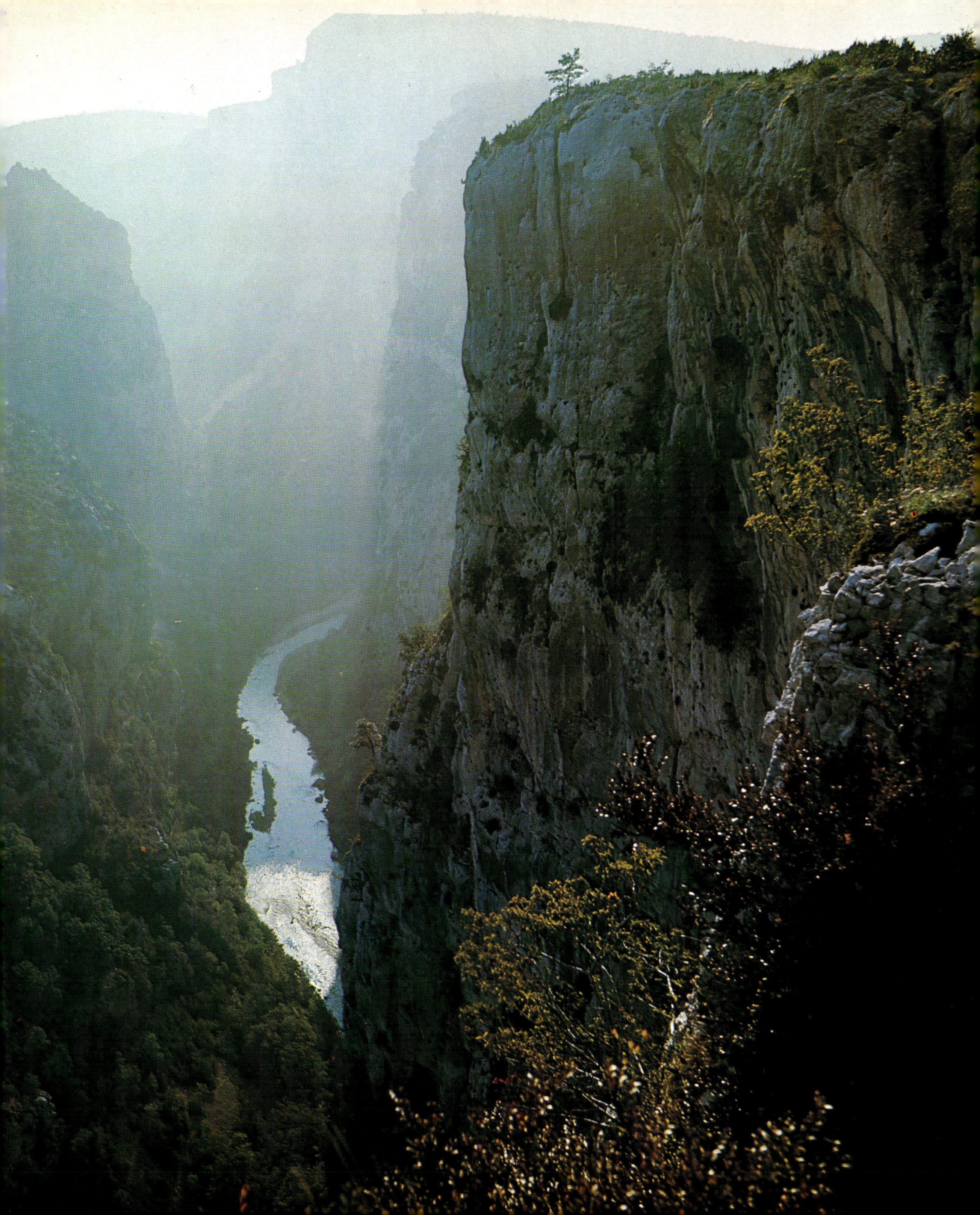

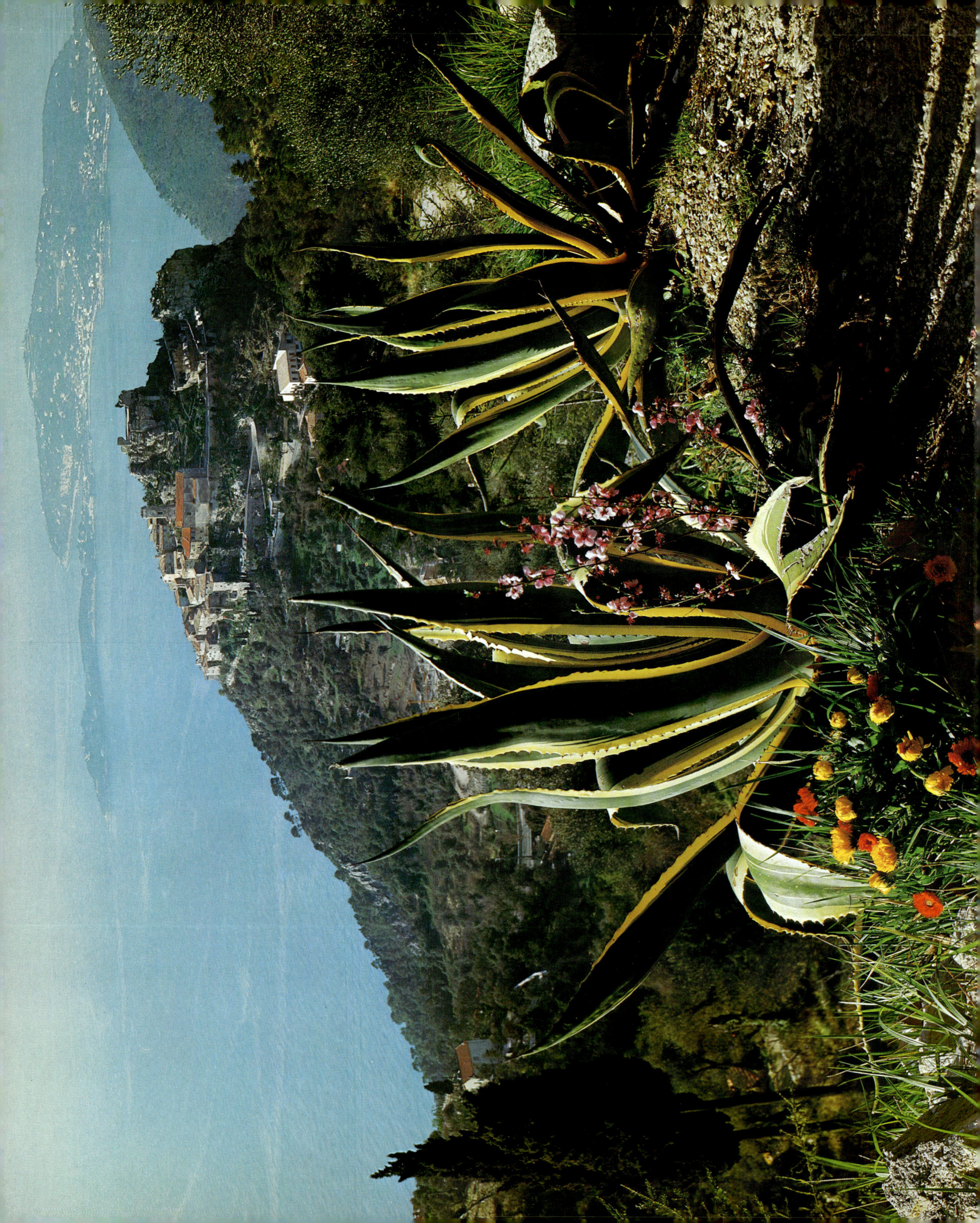

The Côte d'Azur, the Mediterranean rim of the Alps

The true lover of the Alps will surely, at some time or other, experience a desire to see for himself where the vast 400-mile long sweep of his beloved mountains comes to its final rest.

It is easy enough for a Viennese or a citizen of Munich or of Berne or Geneva to get to know the Eastern and Western Alps, for the mountain tracts lie virtually on their doorsteps, or at least within easy reach by car. For the Central European mountaineer, who prefers quiet mountain paths to the strident glitter of the glamorous strip at the southern termination of the Alps, the Côte d'Azur, that goldmine stretching from St Tropez to Monte Carlo and Menton, is a more difficult proposition. He should, however, if only once, have seen and learned to know the lovely coastline between Nice and Menton, where the southernmost spurs of the Alps literally plunge into the blue waters of the Mediterranean. For it is essential to have savoured the atmosphere of this bewitching land, so rich in contrasts, where in days gone by rich *rentiers* spent their lazy, luxurious winters and today all the well-off holiday idlers of the world congregate in summer.

Here too the Alps have their beauties, for the narrow coastal strip is protected from the cold northerly winds by the last of the mountains, and so enjoys a wonderful climate.

The photograph shows the little village of Eze, on a rocky spur 1,300 feet above the sea – a picturesque huddle of narrow alleyways, ancient houses and the ruins of a castle while, behind, the blue Golfe de Saint-Hospice stretches away to Cap Ferrat, hidden by which, only a mile or two farther on, lies Nice.